POWER UP

The smart woman's guide to unleashing her potential

Antoinette Dale Henderson

www.get-known.co.uk

PRAISE FOR 'POWER UP'

"There are many challenges that women face which can make it harder for them to fulfil their potential. This book provides a valuable toolkit for women to find the inner strength to create their own success and will make a massive difference to anyone who reads it."

Sally Keane, Head of Sales UK LinkedIn Marketing Solutions

"I've worked with Antoinette for over a year and it's made such a big impact on my personal development. Working with her has given me the confidence to stand up for what I think and say 'no' when needed. I know her new book will make a powerful difference to women at all stages of their career."

Andrea Plasschaert, Senior Manager, Global Communications, PwC

"A very inspiring book – the debate about women and power is long overdue a makeover and this is it!"

Lisa Conway Hughes, Female IFA, Financial Advisor, Chartered Financial Planner, Westminster Wealth LLP

"A timely and valuable new book that brings a fresh perspective to personal development. Using the tools and exercises will help you to unleash your power and be the driving force for your success."

Anna Parfitt, Head of HR, Oliver Bonas

"It's so refreshing to read a book that empowers intelligent women with well researched information and practical tips. Antoinette has clearly taken great care to reference a variety of contributors, including some in neuroscience, that are all relevant and enlightening. A thoroughly enjoyable read."

Dr Lynda Shaw CPsychol, Specialist in the Science of Embracing Change

"Antoinette's words will leave you feeling inspired to lead your life fearlessly... A must-read book, today more than ever!"

Lynn Tabarra, Curator at TEDx Covent Garden Women

"Antoinette captures the important challenges that women face in fulfilling multiple roles at the same time as a mother, friend and boss and how this affects career progression and confidence. A practical and inspirational guide to connecting with the power that drives you."

Jo Lyall, Country Manager, Freeda Media UK

"Antoinette has enabled me to see how I can use my attributes to gain what I want, at work and in my whole life, without changing what I value in myself. It is refreshing that her approach deals with real life situations which are easily relatable and accessible."

Penny Creswell, Head of HR, BW

"Despite the recent momentum towards Gender Parity, women still face an uphill struggle to reach their potential. Power Up is exactly the type of resource that can help them to achieve their goals. It's easy to digest, practical and beautifully presented with achievable steps that any woman can take to command respect in the workplace."

Gillian Jones Williams, Managing Director, Emerge

"This book is for any woman who has experienced sensations of niggling self-doubt, being powerless or has aspirations to ignite her purpose and further realise her potential, a rallying cry to realise that you're in no way broken or ineffective, you just need to harness what is already there."

Zara Bryson, Strategy Director, Publicis Media

"Antoinette's hit the zeitgeist because more and more women across the globe are stepping up, speaking up and finding their voices. Even if you think you've unleashed your potential, read this book and think again. You'll come away brimming with fresh ideas, ready to rise to new challenges, with an energy your peers will find contagious."

Annie Brooks & Hela Wozniak-Kay, Co-Founders, Sister Snog

"We need more women leaders in the world right now and anything we can do to inspire each other to reach the heights we deserve is to be supported, encouraged and celebrated."

Sue Knight, NLP Master Trainer and author of NLP at Work

"Power Up causes the reader to hold a mirror up and confront the fears that may be holding us back, paving the way to find our own unique power potential. I will be sharing it with colleagues, teams and friends; passing on the practical lessons learned, and the encouragement to 'power up' in the moments that matter most."

Natasha Gorman HR Consultant, HMRC

"A beautifully written book to help you turn up your inner power to maximise your impact and potential."

Lucy Cutter UK Activation Director, Kinetic Worldwide

"*Antoinette has a wealth of experience in her field. She speaks from the heart but also from a place of knowledge. This is an easy to read, easy to follow guide which will help you think bigger and sharper. Whoever reads this will certainly 'power up.'*"

Faye Watts, Strategic Business Adviser and Coach, Partner at FUSE Accountants LLP

"*Although this book is aimed at women, it is really a handbook about how everyone, however they identify, can power up to benefit their organisation as a whole.*"

Reetu Kansal, Senior Business Change and International Partnerships, University of London and Chair, Chartered Management Institute (CMI) Future Leaders

"*For every woman who has struggled to speak up and get her voice heard, who's been plagued by self-doubt or whose imposter syndrome even leads her to self-sabotage, this book is a life-saver. Antoinette has coached hundreds of people to find their voice, and with this book she'll pass on her unique wisdom to many more.*"

Marina Gask, editor, copywriter and co-founder of audreyonline.co.uk

"*Wow. Power Up will definitely contribute to breaking down the barriers that exist for young women, internally and externally. With the nuggets in this book, they will be equipped to unashamedly stand in their power and push forward with their career, education and so much more.*"

Marsha Powell, Director, BelEve UK

"*Once again, Antoinette's advice is well researched, beautifully observed and above all, incredibly human.*"

Sarah Matthew, Founder of The Vibrant Company

"In Antoinette's powerful new book, she rightly points out the phenomenal importance of having a great support network, absolutely critical for the *new* wave of female entrepreneurs who are reinventing what it means to multi-task. Take a moment to absorb Antoinette's advice - you will not regret investing in the book or the time!"

Michelle Ovens, Director of Peak B, Ltd

"Power Up offers a whole range of practical tips, advice and insights to allow women to find their potential. Written in an accessible style, Antoinette offers guidance on finding that inner strength, using others to support you on the journey and how to access help when you need it. Exercises and self reflection are critical and I would recommend this book to any woman who wishes to find her inner power."

Sandra Elliott, Director of Communications, University of London

To Zoë, for your wisdom, strength and beauty,

to Mia, for your majestic brilliance

and to Steve, for your love, support

and encouragement, every step of the way

CONTENTS

MY RELATIONSHIP TO POWER

To understand what power is, and how it feels, you have to know what it is to be powerless.

My earliest experience of powerlessness was my first day at primary school in the UK. Although I was born in London and spent my early years in Sussex, my parents had only spoken to me in French up until then. I was used to the gentle confines of the home environment, and the food that my Mum grew up with in her native Switzerland. The English language, culture and diet were foreign to me.

On that first day, I suddenly felt like I was on a totally different planet. Everything was big, loud and scary: I had no reference points and no map. That first lunchtime I struggled through the weird-looking food, but when they put a bowl of viscous white matter with a blob of jam in front of me, I felt instantly repulsed. Was I seriously supposed to eat it? Cautiously putting a spoonful in my mouth, I was seized with panic, but unable to ask or do anything else, I spat it out into my cup, earning a huge telling off from a livid teacher. That day was a rude awakening. Struck dumb in a foreign land, I felt utterly powerless to defend myself or justify my actions. And that theme of not having a voice has been so significant to me that I've made it my life's work to help people get theirs heard.

Since that day, I've been a dedicated observer of how power can develop, how it can be used for good, but also how it can be misused. Firstly, during my corporate leadership career, where I witnessed organisations and their people thrive on the basis of a powerful idea, and crumble through misguided leadership. Latterly, through my Gravitas Programme, in which I've worked with thousands of hugely talented managers, leaders and business owners who, for various reasons, have underestimated their value and compromised their power as a result. I've also coached people accused of being 'too much' on how to rein in their exuberance and ground their power for greater impact.

Although I've observed that tapping into your power can be a challenge for everyone, it's clear to me that, for now at least, there are specific factors that make it more difficult for women to be assertive as they navigate through life. These factors, combined with ingrained conditioning about how we 'should' behave, stop many of us from comfortably standing in our power. In my 25 plus years of working with women, I've witnessed power squashed before it's even had a chance to emerge; power that's been lost through a myriad of identity changes; power that's lain dormant in those who haven't yet found inspiration in what they do. In seeking to express their power, I've heard women's voices talked over, silenced, patronised and bullied. Each time this happens, the impact of that first day at school wells up in me, and I'm drawn to defend. All of this has struck me as a crying waste and an appalling shame.

The fact that you're reading this book indicates that you may be wondering what would be different if you could power up, at will. I'm imagining that, as a self-aware woman, there are times when you've felt powerful and times when you've felt powerless. You may be reassured that this isn't just the case for some, it's the case for all of us, whatever our gender.

In researching this book, I've gained an ever-deeper understanding of the full spectrum of power, and it's made me think: what would it be like if women had the ability to conjure up this force in all its forms, whenever they wanted? What would be different for them? And what would be different in the world?

As you make your way through this book, you'll see that there are many shades of power, from a quietly compelling magnetism to an emotionally charged, high-octane strength and everything in between. Which is just as well: imagine if we were all tuned to maximum power all the time, striding around like Wonder Woman on steroids. It would be too much! Power should be available to all of us, equally. We all have the right to express ourselves freely and get what we deserve. The paradox of power is that unless we're power-hungry egomaniacs, we only want it when it's absent or taken away.

This book is for smart women at all stages of their lives and careers. I've written it with the greatest respect, in the knowledge that we all have the most unimaginable power within us, waiting to be released, but that sometimes life brings hurdles and other times we get in our own way.

This isn't about fixing something that's broken, it's about unleashing what's already there. Often the most powerful catalyst for change is when I look into women's eyes and tell them: "You *can* do this." It's incredible how, sometimes within an instant, that energy can be identified and channelled. It starts with a decision to change; the rest will undoubtedly follow. Through stepping out of your comfort zone, having the courage to try something new and choosing to think in a different way, you will move beyond the status quo to achieve what you want.

15

My aim is that this book will contribute to the diversity and inclusion conversation and make a difference. I'm saddened when debates become an 'us and them' where one group can only become powerful at the expense of another. This isn't about winning power back, it's about how we can all learn to co-exist in a diverse world. This is about how we can all Power Up together.

I wish you every success as you make your way through this book, reflect on your own inner power and apply the exercises to all areas of your life.

A lot has changed for me since that first day at school. I have found my voice and have helped countless women to find theirs. I know you will too.

Antoinette Dale Henderson

INTRODUCTION

I n this book, we'll explore why power is such a valuable energy, and at what points in our lives and careers we particularly need to harness it. We'll examine why using our power can be challenging for all women, irrespective of life-stage, and what we can do to smash through our own glass ceiling and fully embrace power in its many forms. Throughout these chapters, I'll share my research into truly powerful women, from thought leaders to politicians, academics to social media influencers, social scientists to psychologists, successful business professionals to performers. I'll share experiences and challenges from my own life, as well as those faced by my clients. I will also share the practical tools and techniques I've developed to help them overcome obstacles and have their voice heard.

These insights are encapsulated in the Power Up Model©, a results-proven, practical resource which I've designed to help you assess your progress and Power Up day-to-day, so that you can perform at your best and fulfil your potential in all aspects of your life.

The guidance, techniques and tools will be relevant to you whether you're at the start of your career, in your first management position, an experienced leader or running your own business. You'll learn how to develop your personal power through a range of exercises and self-reflection aids, which will make an immediate difference in your professional and personal life. I've also created a downloadable workbook which you can access via the Power Up website: (**www.womenpowerupbook.com**). This includes all the exercises in each chapter for you to complete in one place to aid your learning.

My aim is that this book and the accompanying workbook will become a trusted resource that you'll refer to regularly as you progress through your life, as well as a guide to support you when navigating change. Some of the chapters you'll find particularly valuable when facing specific challenges; for example, handling a difficult relationship, staying resilient during personal difficulties, knowing how to ask for what you deserve and increasing your visibility in a competitive environment.

My goal is that you'll find *Power Up* so valuable you'll pass on its guidance to others, so that they can be more powerful too. Not everything you'll read in these pages will be easy to take on board. Some of the women's stories that I'll share with you have sickened me to the core. The need to Power Up has been born out of a feeling of powerlessness. But knowing what it is you don't want can be a galvanising force, unleashing a strength and energy to power forwards towards what you do, enabling you to achieve your goals and accelerate your potential. So let us begin.

Power and you

What is your relationship to power? Do you ever feel like you haven't been able to reach your full potential at work, whether at the start of your career, as a manager, running your own business or sitting on the board? Have you ever felt held back by wobbly confidence, an inability to articulate your thoughts when it counts, a need to please and be liked? How about outside of work? Have there been times when someone has taken advantage of you or maybe just not given you the respect you deserve? If you would dearly love to shine and approach each situation with self-assurance, to find your inner power, this book is for you. Welcome.

In over 25 years of working in global organisations, I've had the privilege to meet thousands of incredible women. And what's struck me is how hard many of them have found it to command respect and have their voice heard, irrespective of seniority. I wonder whether you might relate to some of my clients' stories here...

There was Dee, who blushed head-to-toe every time she had to stand up and speak in front of people, caused by being made to feel that she wasn't worth listening to from an early age. And Ally, who despite her First in English and huge ambition, was frequently in tears because a bullying boss had left her confidence shattered. And Nadia, whose opinions always came out as a self-deprecating joke, and who often found herself being talked over in the boardroom.

There was unassuming Jade, who was mortified that she could never stand up for herself when other people took credit for her great work. Marcia, who would sit quietly and go along with what was being said in meetings even when she profoundly disagreed. And the way Lola's skin crawled every time her manager made a sexual innuendo while placing his hand on the small of her back. These are just a small sample of the many stories I have heard of women struggling to feel truly empowered.

It's not only at work that women find themselves boxed in by society's narrow definition of how they should be. Only this morning, I was shocked that a car salesman directed all his patter to my husband, oblivious to the fact that fifty per cent of the buying decision would be mine. Last week, I witnessed a bright and articulate daughter being mansplained by her well-meaning father and a waiter automatically handing the menu to the only man on a table of women.

And yet we keep hearing that this is a great time to be a woman. Since some time in 2017, post #MeToo, post-Weinstein and the ensuing avalanche of public declarations, the world has changed and women are finding their voice. We're harnessing our power, challenging disparity and sexism in its many forms and forging ahead in professions that were previously dominated by the male sex. Whether or not you call yourself a feminist, it's hard not to be cheered by women speaking openly about their challenges and gradually bringing about change in significant areas like sexual harassment and gender parity.

But sadly, change is not happening as fast as you might think. Across the UK – and the world – women still struggle to gain leadership roles in most industries. A report published in July 2019 revealed that, despite government-backed initiatives, 14 companies in the FTSE 350 still have no women or just one on the board[1]. This is undoubtedly one of the causes of the UK's glaring gender pay gap. In 2018, the European Commission published a report which showed that women are underrepresented in decision-making positions in politics, and they still earn on average 16% less in business than men across the European Union[2]. So in this, and many other ways, true equality is still a far-off goal on a dim and distant horizon.

Of course, there are many well-documented reasons for this, and we aren't going to explore them all here because, for the purposes of this book, our focus is on power. Not the kind of power that you get when you are appointed to a lofty position that involves hiring and firing, like a CEO or COO, but the kind of power that comes from within and enables you to operate at your best.

Power: Why do we need it?

If you think back over your life, when have you felt at your most powerful, if at all? For some, it's when they've fought hard to accomplish a challenging task, or summoned inner reserves to have their voice heard, whether that's standing up to a bully, asking someone to give up their seat on the bus or delivering a presentation to a large audience. For others, feeling powerful comes from being in a group, maybe when they are out with friends or working as a team. Some feel at their most powerful when they feel physically fit and mentally agile. For others, the idea of being powerful feels entirely alien, a quality harnessed by stronger beings.

There are many reasons why exercising your full range of powers could be highly beneficial. There will be times when we find it easy to get our own way. But there are also times where we feel powerless to act, tongue-tied, gagged or held back by some invisible force. And there are other times when we're triggered and experience an uncontrollable upsurge of power, flipping our lid and doing or saying something that we later regret or capitulate to the avalanche of emotion through an explosion of tears. Sound familiar?

As the old saying goes, 'If you always do what you've always done, you'll always get what you always got; if you want something different, you need to do something different'. In this way, the most influential people are those with the flexibility to choose their response to the different situations and people they come into contact with and as a result, become powerful in a variety of ways.

This book is about how you can harness your power, rather than having it engulf you. How you can become attuned to its presence, and gain confidence from the knowledge that you can access it whenever you need it to make the most of opportunities life has to offer.

What is powering up?

Power is a very personal force – we all want it for different reasons and express it in different ways.

Powering up is about connecting with the force that drives you – that steely determination that propels you forward, that energy that's sparked whenever you're inspired or provoked. It's about building your inner confidence, developing an unshakeable belief in your right to fulfil your potential, and having a certainty that you can do whatever you choose to. Powering up is also about knowing how to communicate assertively, speaking your truth and staying strong in the face of adversity.

I want you to know that you can access more power than you thought possible. It's not about 'Faking it til you make it'. It's not about 'Putting your big girl pants on', 'Growing a pair' or 'Manning up', which are all expressions I loathe. It's about finding your voice and knowing how to express it – whether that's through a compelling whisper or an earth-shattering cry. Becoming the most impactful, influential and successful version of you.

As you make your way through these chapters, you'll see that my take on power is quite different from what you may have read in leadership manuals or personal development books; it's way more than power poses and driftwood quotes. It's power at work and power at home. It's power throughout your whole life.

My message is that although life isn't always easy, if you make friends with yourself, tap into the power of humanity and lead yourself by the hand through the challenges that come your way, you will get there.

By the end of this book, you will know how to access your inner power reserves and feel confident using them. You'll have the secrets to powering up, so that you'll never be walked over, talked over or passed over again.

PART ONE

POWER AND YOU

INTRODUCTION TO PART ONE

In this section, we'll start by answering the question 'What is Power?' and explore how it's evolving to meet the demands of an increasingly diverse and inclusive society. We'll look at how women have powered up throughout history and why tapping into our inner power is so important for us now. We'll also examine the qualities that powerful women share, qualities you can emulate to fulfil your potential.

Studying power in this way will help you to broaden out your understanding of power and what you can do to tap into the full power spectrum of it, from the softer kind, traditionally associated with women, to the harder kind, which we need for assertiveness and handling challenging situations.

Developing a wider appreciation of power will help you to expand your own power repertoire, giving you greater flexibility in your communication style and more control over your emotions. It will also enable you to step back and objectively assess how different people use power, making it easier for you to engage with those who use it positively and avoid those who use it negatively to overpower.

As part of this section, we'll examine how female power can be compromised, from career roadblocks which threaten to derail us to times when we unconsciously give away our power, whether that's trying too hard to please or hiding our light. Thinking about the different ways you might react to challenges in your career and life and learning from them is a great way to ensure that when curveballs do come your way, you'll make the more empowered choices.

We'll then explore the Power Up Model©, a unique tool that I've designed to encapsulate the six sources of power which together give you inner confidence and the ability to express yourself powerfully to the outside world. This model will become your guide as you make your way through the chapters of this book. Completing it will help you to assess your strengths and identify what you need to do to increase your power, and referring back to it will help you to track your progress.

Learning how to access your full range of power is a game-changer which will bring you greater freedom and permission to be whoever you want to be. Once you've read this book and completed the exercises, you will have a solid understanding of your unique personal power and a wealth of tips and techniques that you can use to fulfil your potential at work and in the rest of your life.

By the end of this section, you'll be ready to deep dive into the six sources of power that will propel you forward to your goals.

Let's go!

Chapter 1

WHAT IS POWER?

===

"The day the power of love overrules the love of power, the world will know peace."

—MAHATMA GANDHI

As we begin our Power Up mission, let's start by examining what power is in its many forms, how it's been used throughout history and look at the key studies into traditional power. Once we've understood how power has been defined up until now, we'll move on to focus on how I believe power could evolve in the future, when everyone breaks through the barriers that hold them back and expresses themselves freely. As we begin to reflect on how women can power up, we'll explore the various qualities that powerful women share, qualities you can emulate to fulfil your potential. We'll then discover the importance of emotional versatility and the difference between passive, aggressive and assertive communication and how these link to how your power could be expressed.

WHAT TYPES OF POWER EXIST?

Many people have a narrow definition of power and believe that either you have it or you don't. In fact, power has a variety of forms, with both positive and negative connotations. Like Kali, the Hindu goddess who symbolises motherly love on the one hand and death on the other, power has many faces, some fair, some foul and it pays to recognise them all if you want to power up.

The word power comes from the Latin word 'potere', which means "to be able". Since then, the term has evolved beyond meaning simply 'being able' to the ability to exert force. "The powers that be" are those who hold authority, and "the power behind the throne" refers to the people who exert influence without being formally in charge.

Power [noun]

1. The ability to influence or control what people do or think.

2. Political control of a country or government.

3. Energy obtained from oil, coal, the sun etc., used for operating equipment and machines.

4. Physical force or strength.

5. The ability of a machine or vehicle to operate quickly and effectively.

6. A person who exerts influence on someone powerful without having a formal status.

7. Someone with no official position in an organisation but who secretly controls it.

Linked to the word power is the related term 'empower', which represents the taking up of arms, or the permission to take action in response to a cause.

Power can be about strength, but also resistance to a particular force. It can be used to protect, but also to overcome.

WOMEN AND POWER HISTORICALLY

Throughout time, power has been misused to keep certain groups in a subordinate position. Key moments in history have felt like a 'fightback', contributing to the sense of power being one-dimensional: a battle with a winner and loser.

For women, the concept of power can be highly charged and emotive. For centuries, if we came into contact with it, we were usually the victim. At certain points in history, women had enough of being on the receiving end and so rose up in response.

"

POWER CAN BE
ABOUT STRENGTH,
BUT ALSO
RESISTANCE TO A
PARTICULAR FORCE.
IT CAN BE USED TO
PROTECT, BUT ALSO
TO OVERCOME.

■ The women's rights movement signalled a tipping point in the 1880s, where visionaries like Emmeline Pankhurst led the suffragette movement, which helped to secure for women the right to vote.

■ Seventy-five years later, Rosa Parks stood up for black and female rights when she rejected a bus driver's order to relinquish her seat in the "colored section" to a white passenger, after the whites-only section was full, and went down in history as being "the first lady of civil rights" and "the mother of the freedom movement"[3].

■ In the sixties and seventies, the women's liberation movement sought equal rights and greater personal freedom, touching on every aspect of a woman's experience, including work, family and sexuality. This was represented through various dramatic acts, including a protest against a Miss America beauty pageant where a group of women threw mops, lipsticks, bras and high heels into a 'Freedom Trash Can', giving birth to the term 'bra-burning feminists'.

■ More recently, we've seen another upsurge of female power, with the #TimesUp and #MeToo movements galvanising women across the world to call time on predatory behaviour and sexist views. This has triggered a cultural debate and an overhaul into how we relate to one another, as well as what is acceptable and what is not.

STUDIES INTO POWER

Over the years, there have been various studies into power that have broadened out the perception of power from being a one-dimensional concept where one force overcomes another. Examining how the different forms of power have been categorised as a valuable route to increasing your understanding of the variety of ways it could be expressed and considering how you could use them all to power up.

One of the most famous studies was conducted by social psychologists John R. P. French and Bertram Raven in 1959[4]. They divided power into seven separate, distinct forms – *coercive*, *reward*, *legitimate*, *referent*, *expert* and *informational* – all of which can be used both positively and negatively.

Becoming familiar with all seven power forms is useful because it helps you to appreciate there is not just one type of power, but a plethora of ways you could be powerful, should you need to be. Being able to step back and objectively assess how different people use power also makes it easier for you to engage with those who use it positively and avoid those who use it negatively to overpower.

I'll explain each one below. As you read through them, consider which ones you've used or been on the receiving end of and how you might broaden out your power repertoire for greater impact.

- **Coercive** – this power exists when one person can punish others for noncompliance. Although no one likes the sound of this, it is valid and necessary – imagine if speeding violations carried no penalty or drink driving didn't result in a ban. However, history is full of examples of tyrannical leaders who exerted authority through sheer force and brutality when coercive power went to their heads.

■ **Reward** – this power exists where one person can compensate another for compliance. Bonus structures are a good example of this, where a boss has the power to reward results through recognition, money or promotion.

■ **Legitimate** – this power exists where one person has the formal right to make demands, and expects others to be compliant and obedient. People in all positions of authority are examples of this, such as a chief of police or military commander.

■ **Referent** – this power exists where one person has earnt the right to others' respect. This could be due to their worthiness or achievements. Mahatma Gandhi was an example of this, as is Oprah Winfrey. You might also give referent power to a Paralympic athlete because you're so impressed with their prowess and triumph over adversity.

■ **Expert** – this power exists where one person's high levels of skill and knowledge commands others' respect. David Attenborough or Dame Judy Dench are both examples of this.

■ **Informational** – this power exists where one person controls the information that others need to accomplish something and was added by Raven six years after the initial study. Subject matter experts have this power because there's no one else in the organisation who knows what they do or can do it; you will have this power if you have access to data that your team need to complete a report.

Thinking about power in all these different ways helps us to understand how valuable it can be when used wisely and how destructive it is when abused. For example, French and Raven's 'legitimate' power is positive when a manager uses it to brief their team on safety standards, but negative when they use it to force them to work late or join in a teambuilding activity against their will.

In my leadership courses, I talk about the difference between manipulation and influence, which use similar techniques for different motivations. Any type of power can be used for good and for evil: it's all about the intent behind it. For example, one salesperson could 'influence' you to make a purchase by helping you to understand which product you want to choose; another will 'manipulate' you into buying something you don't want.

Following on from French and Raven's study into power, Joseph Nye, the political commentator and author of various books on power, coined the terms "soft power" and "hard power" in the late 1980s to describe how a country might persuade other countries to do what it wants. Using his definition, hard power involves commanding or ordering and soft power lies in the ability to attract and persuade[5].

When I began researching this book, it was Nye's distinction that got me thinking about how the hard and soft extremes

MY AIM IN THIS BOOK IS TO CREATE A NEW POWER PARADIGM WHICH IS NO LONGER ABOUT ONE-DIMENSIONAL WIN/LOSE POWER.

of power could be expressed through our behaviour and communication style, as well as how using each of them affects our personal impact and influence, and what would be different if we were able to embody the full range. Imagine how liberating it would be if you could summon up power in its varied forms at will whenever you needed to!

Emotional intelligence or EQ (which stands for Emotion Quotient) is an example of an often underestimated soft power. A term made famous by Daniel Goleman in his 1995 book *Emotional Intelligence*, it describes the ability to be aware of, control and express your emotions, and to handle relationships wisely and empathetically. It is often branded a typically female trait. Developing emotional intelligence gives you the power to read situations and people and know how to select the most appropriate response. When practised regularly, it can help you to love your enemy, as referred to in the Gandhi quote at the start of this chapter, or at least try to understand what's behind their behaviour so that you can find a way to get along with them better. Given that most people are not aware of EQ and simply react blindly to what happens 'to them', I believe this is a superpower which holds the key to accessing the most positive manifestations of power so that everyone wins. So if your boss speaks to you in a patronising way, do you let it happen or do you use your EQ to work out why they're treating you like that and how you can best respond?

My aim in this book is to create a new power paradigm which is no longer about one-dimensional win/lose power, which expands beyond the seven sources of power, as defined by French and Raven, and explores the whole spectrum of power, from hard to soft and everything in between.

In encouraging women to access their full power potential, my aim is that we'll move beyond the lazy and inaccurate stereotypes, where male power equals force and logic and female power equals feelings and intuition, so that we can all access the full range. This is not a battle, it's not about winning over but winning through opening up our eyes to the whole range of power at our disposal.

WHAT QUALITIES DO POWERFUL WOMEN SHARE?

In researching this book, I examined the characteristics that women with power share, characteristics which you can emulate if you are looking to develop your personal power. I found that there is no 'one size fits all', that power encapsulates a multifaceted array of qualities and that, in describing it, people tend to value the qualities that they see, or would like to see, in themselves.

As part of the process, I interviewed and observed women who exemplify power in its varied forms. To qualify as being 'powerful', they had to have achieved a level of success in their professional and personal lives – earning positions of authority in the workplace or community. My definition of success was not confined to material wealth, but authority and respect in their field. Throughout this research, I've met women who feel just as comfortable exercising hard power – being directive, even summoning and channelling anger when required – as they do exercising soft power – for example, choosing to remain quiet to give others space to share their points of view.

Through my research, I found that at a fundamental level, women who access their full range of power possess the following qualities, all of which are explored in more detail in the chapters of this book. They are:

- Driven, purposeful and clear about what they'd like to achieve, radiating an inner confidence in their ability to accomplish their goals.

- Aware of their natural strengths, as well as their weaknesses, and how they can compromise their power, dedicating time and effort to reflect on the opportunities and threats they face.

- Conscious of their values and beliefs and how to stay true to them through the various roles they play in all aspects of their life.

- Clear on their boundaries and areas of flex – where they are prepared to compromise and the lines they will not cross.

- Willing to draw on all sources of power, unafraid of using hard power when necessary, choosing when to lead from the front and when to join the ranks and lead from the back, with and through people.

- Comfortable 'standing in their power', with a strong posture, bold movements, a clear voice and direct message.

- Able to manage their own emotional state and regulate their moods, minimise negative self-talk, handle

nerves and remain cool-headed while all about them
are losing theirs.

■ Adept at conserving energy, knowing when to move
   from the fast to the slow lane, when to Power Up
   and power down and how to choose patience over
   impatience.

■ Aware of their magnetic power of attraction and able
   to 'switch it on' at will to get what they want.

■ Highly attuned to other people and prepared to work
   with them, knowing when to compromise and when
   to stand their ground.

■ Willing to sacrifice being liked for being respected
   and prepared not to make friends and remain somewhat apart if necessary, whilst at the same time
   appreciating that relationships are the foundation
   for their success.

These qualities are encapsulated in the Power Up Model©,
which represents three internal power sources that reflect
your inner wisdom, knowledge and strength and three external power sources, which determine how you present yourself and relate to the outside world. They form the basis of
this book and are explored in detail in parts two and three.

PURPOSE: THE POWER THAT PROPELS YOU FORWARD

In addition to possessing strong foundations, my research revealed that although power is expressed in many different ways, one thing that powerful women have in common is they have spent time exploring who they are and their unique purpose and direction in life.

Power on its own is merely a force; what's relevant is the impact it creates. Truly powerful people are the ones who are clear about the outcome they'd like to achieve and then consciously plan their approach to achieve that outcome.

This is not ego-led, as it's not about doing things entirely for their own fame and/or benefit. Instead, the main driving force of powerful women is wanting to make a difference in relation to something they truly believe in. And this drives everything, giving them seemingly unlimited reserves of power. Watch someone deliver a talk on the charity they've supported, the book they've written or the new system they've designed with the aim of changing the world (or their part of it). The strength of their belief and resolve can be incredibly powerful. And when people are totally clear on what they are doing and why, they can transcend a lot of the roadblocks and negativity that get put in their way.

We can take power from knowing that our mission really matters. If you really care about something, if it has genuine meaning for you, it will propel you forward and give you the impetus to make it happen.

Purpose

⊕

Power

⊟

Unlimited
Potential

EXERCISE 1:
TUNING INTO
YOUR POWER

The questions below have been designed to help you increase your awareness of your purpose, as well as your identity, values and beliefs. All these are sources of your power. Take some time out to think about your answers, noting down your responses somewhere so you can come back to them.

These are not questions we usually reflect on and so the answers may not come quickly or easily. Allow the questions to percolate over time and remember, self-awareness is an ongoing process.

Purpose

1. As you think about your life to date and your aspirations for the future, what forces have propelled you forward and why?

2. What moves you to take action; what are the causes that inspire you and why?

3. Why have you chosen to live the life you lead? What difference do you want to make and how would you like to be remembered?

Role and Identity

1. How do you define your role at work and in life?

2. How is the way you lead your life an expression of who you are?

3. When have you been at your most powerful and in what way?

Values and Beliefs

1. What values do you represent and stand for?

2. What are the principles that steer you and the values you hold dear?

3. What beliefs do you hold to be true: how might they be supporting you or holding you back?

Goals

Moving from the general to the specific, consider the life you're leading, events you've lived through and events coming up and think about what you want out of those situations.

Consider your hopes, dreams, goals and objectives and what outcomes you want to attain. Getting super clear on what you want and expressing it isn't selfish, it's self-ful. Value yourself and your rights, but make sure you consider the world around you too, so that this doesn't tip over into arrogance or self-righteousness.

1   Knowing that 'what gets measured gets done', what goals are you aiming to achieve over the next six, twelve months, eighteen months?

2.   How about in five years' time, or ten years, where would you like to be then? What would you like to be doing? Who would you like to be?

3.   If you visualise yourself fully standing 'in your power', what will people see, hear and feel in your presence and what goals will you have accomplished to get there?

Boundaries

Now think about your boundary lines. These are usually directly linked to your values and represent those areas of your life where you're not prepared to compromise. For example, my number one value is respect and so I have very clear boundaries which dictate what I consider to be acceptable and unacceptable behaviour. I know this because I have an extreme reaction when I believe someone is being disrespectful, either to another person or the environment. And I will harness the powerful reaction that I experience when I witness this to call it out, assertively; for example, pointing out when someone's deliberately dropped litter or insisting that someone be allowed to finish their sentence if they've been interrupted.

"Simply put, a boundary is a limit or space between you and the other person; a clear place where you begin and the other person ends. Think of it as a fence in your backyard. You are the gatekeeper and get to decide who you let in and who you keep out, who you let into the whole back yard, or who you let just inside the gate."

–'BOUNDARIES DEFINED', MARTHA CHILDERS

To help you identify your boundaries, complete the table below by listing in the first column the values or behaviours that are significant to you. Then write down what is 'OK' in relation to that, i.e. within your boundary, and in the final column what is 'not OK', i.e. outside your boundary. I've provided a couple of examples below to get you thinking.

Value/behaviour	OK	Not OK
Respect	People expressing their opinion, even if I disagree with them	People singling out an individual or group for criticism; discrimination of any kind
Interrupting	If you have a valid point of view which isn't being heard	Repeatedly cutting in or talking over someone to the extent that they're not being heard

Areas of flex

Also, consider those areas of your life where you're prepared to be flexible. The most obvious example of this for me at the moment is my teenage daughters' bedrooms! Although I do expect them to be respectful of the family environment, I also respect their right to arrange their own space how they want (even though I can't stand mess) and simply look the other way when I'm passing their door!

IMAGINE WHAT IT WOULD BE LIKE IF YOU COULD RECOGNISE RESENTMENT TOWARDS SOMEONE AND KNOW HOW TO TURN THAT EMOTION INTO ADMIRATION.

Emotional Versatility

Linked to their ability to draw on power in its many forms, powerful women have honed their ability to manage their own emotional state and developed what I call emotional versatility: the ability to access and channel the whole spectrum of emotions, including the less palatable ones, from empathy to anger, elation to envy, passion to indifference. This is no mean feat, but incredibly empowering when accomplished. People are often embarrassed or frightened in the face of extreme emotion and I'm sure you've experienced times when your feelings have got the better of you, resulting in behaviour you later regret.

Imagine what it would be like if you could recognise resentment towards someone brewing within you and know how to turn that emotion into admiration by thinking about them in a more compassionate way.

Watching a toddler explode with fury as a result of their inability to be understood is akin to having an upsurge of powerful feelings but not knowing what to do with them. Having access to your full range of emotions is linked to your emotional vocabulary. In the same way, as you can't imagine the flavour of a pineapple unless you've tasted one, it follows that it's impossible to fully experience an emotion unless you can label it. Pinpointing a feeling of contempt as opposed to generalised anger is the first step to moving beyond it.

EXERCISE 2:
EMOTIONAL VERSATILITY

The first step to developing your emotional versatility is recognising the full range of emotions at your disposal.

1. Over the course of a day, keep a diary of all the emotions you're experiencing, which emotions make you feel powerful and which compromise your power.

2. Notice when you're experiencing negative emotions, take care to label them, and note down their impact.

3. As this is happening, think about which emotions would be more positive and think about how you can change your own thought process to a more empowering one. We will explore how to manage your emotions in more depth in the Resilience chapter.

The Power Continuum

As well as understanding the forces that drive you, mastering your power enables you to control your behaviour, even when you're feeling under threat. The expression of power – or lack of it – can be measured on a continuum, with passivity at one end and aggression at the other, with every shade in between, including self-deprecation, passive aggression and coercion, with assertiveness, the final segment of the Power Up Model© in the middle. Power is a display of emotion, expressed or suppressed and linked to our response to threat with:

- **'Fight'** expressed as aggression: acting out, shouting, becoming physically threatening

- **'Flight'** experienced as passivity: doing or saying nothing, physically moving away

- **'Freeze'** or **'Falling asleep'** seen as disengagement: going quiet, shutting down

- Passive aggression, a potent mix of all three: an iron fist in a velvet glove, expressed as rolling eyes, a dramatic sigh or muttered "whatever", belying a simmering anger underneath.

How these behaviours come across is open to the interpretation of others. What we see as a perfectly reasonable display of strength may be interpreted as threatening behaviour; on the other hand, our desire to involve everyone in a decision can be experienced as wishy-washy leadership.

FLIGHT

Passivity

Humility

Self-deprecation

ASSERTIVENESS

Passive aggression

Arrogance

Aggression

FIGHT

Unlike men, who have traditionally been conditioned to release an upsurge of emotion in a physical way, channelling that energy into an act of defiance or decisiveness, women will often remain in the safety zone, where they can't cause offence or rattle anyone's cage, suppressing any emotions that could be perceived as ugly or unfeminine.

It's in that safety zone that we find the highly powerful, but undervalued qualities of persuasive, diplomacy and emotional intelligence that are so often associated with women: asking rather than telling, collaborating rather than steamrolling. But it's also here that we find the feelings of being tongue-tied, the 'what ifs' and the limiting beliefs that prevent us from moving forward hold us in place as firmly as a clamped car.

Anger suppressed has to find a way out somehow, however much we try to hide it. This is why passive-aggression, so often a female trait, often backfires, leaving us feeling frustrated and misunderstood and others walking on eggshells, suspecting something's wrong but not really understanding what or why.

If you look at the expression of power, the whole range serves us at some point. Persuasiveness has its place, as does kindness and compassion. Both sexes are more effective and useful in the workplace if they exercise 'softer' skills when they're called for. But neither end of the spectrum is ideal. Power is vital for growth and innovation to occur, so it can be a force for good. But too hard and uncompromising is overbearing, while too soft is a pushover. It's in the middle that we find assertiveness, the kind of power that is the most effective of all.

EXERCISE 3:

WHERE ARE YOU ON THE POWER CONTINUUM?

Take a look at the Power Continuum above. Of course, we'd all like to operate from a place of assertiveness all the time – and this book will help to achieve this. However, there will be times when we find ourselves drawn to other places on the line. The more we know where we tend to go when under pressure, the more we can keep ourselves in check, decide which position will serve us best and therefore continue to act from a place of power.

1   Start by identifying which circumstances trigger you and make you feel under threat in some way; for example, a loud, dominating colleague or noisy neighbour who swears at you when you ask them to turn the volume down.

2. Consider your natural response to threat and how this comes across in your behaviour. Are you more likely to swear back at that noisy neighbour, scuttle off or shut down?

3. Identify which places on the Power Continuum are your 'go-tos' that compromise your power.

4. Think about what you need to be thinking and feeling to remain in a powerful state. For example, reminding yourself that you have a right to peace and quiet and speaking to other neighbours about mounting a formal complaint should the noise continue.

5. Notice how you express yourself assertively. If you currently do so – what do you say and do, and how does this compare with when you express yourself in a passive, aggressive or passive-aggressive way. If you don't think you currently express yourself assertively, think about how you would if you did. We will cover this in greater depth in the Assertiveness chapter.

IN SUMMARY

★ Many people have a narrow definition of power and believe that either you have it, or you don't. In fact, power has many different forms, all of which can be used positively and negatively.

★ Understanding the different types of power that exist enables you to broaden out your power repertoire, giving you greater flexibility in your communication style and greater control over your emotions.

★ The expression of power – or lack of it – can be measured on a continuum, with passivity at one end, aggression at the other, and assertiveness in the middle.

★ Powerful women have learnt how to access both their soft power – e.g. emotional intelligence and influencing skills – and hard power – e.g. being directive and exerting force where required.

★ Powerful women are clear about their purpose, role, identity, values and beliefs and have spent time defining their goals, boundaries and areas where they are prepared to flex.

★ Powerful women have honed their ability to manage their own emotional state and developed 'emotional versatility': the ability to access and channel the whole spectrum of emotions.

Chapter 2

WHEN IS POWER A CHALLENGE AT WORK?

"You may encounter many defeats, but you must not be defeated. In fact, it may be necessary to encounter the defeats, so you can know who you are, what you can rise from, how you can still come out of it."

–MAYA ANGELOU

N ow that we've examined power in its many forms and how you can access the whole power spectrum, let's explore times when you'll need to access power the most, specifically challenges that can threaten to derail you at work. Forewarned is forearmed and it makes sense to understand all the barriers that might come your way and how you'll need to Power Up to overcome them.

As women, there are times when opportunities are lost and our potential is compromised. A woman's career is littered with roadblocks that she has to grapple with along the way. As a result, her career progress is rarely just linear; sometimes we may veer off-track for months or even years, as we try to navigate our way around the challenges we face. Sometimes these challenges can be so extreme that we drop off the career ladder altogether. On the other hand, trying different paths and stepping stones can be more enriching in the long run than a one-track career.

For some, being powerful can be seen as deeply unfeminine and unattractive. For others, taking on a position of power comes with too many strings, as evidenced by the paucity of women holding positions of authority. At a global level, despite the fact that in 2017 the number of female leaders more than doubled since 2000[6], we are still a long way from parity with men, with fewer than 10% of the U.N. member states having ever been led by women[7]. At an organisational level, the latest research shows that women only make up 19% of boards[8] and represent only 22% of senior management teams[9]. Personally, I've met many women who have stepped off their career ladder because it was simply too hard to meet ever-increasing demands, particularly when juggling other responsibilities.

COMMON CAREER CHALLENGES FACED BY WOMEN

So why is this? Although men and women both encounter career challenges, today's working environment and cultural norms make it more challenging for women to steadily rise through the ranks and achieve the recognition they deserve. If you think I am overstating this, then let me ask you how many of these you can relate to personally, or have observed in others?

Not being recruited

It's a role you're keen on and you definitely have at least some of the qualifications listed on the job spec, but there's something that's stopping you from applying...

Despite companies' best interests to make job advertising gender-neutral and overcome unconscious bias, research has shown that the language used to describe roles can impact on whether men or women are more likely to apply, depending on whether it's a role that's traditionally been performed by one gender over another[10]. Not only that, the applicants' word choices also impact on how they are perceived and whether they'll be invited for an interview. In my Gravitas masterclasses, I ask participants to describe their leadership strengths and it's fascinating to compare the words used by women: *caring, team-player, hardworking*, with words used by men: *strong, result-driven, powerful*. If these descriptors are reflected in CVs, they will inevitably influence the sifting process. And that's even before there's been a face-to-face meeting. I was recently shocked to learn that women regularly hide their engagement or wedding ring for interviews because they worry that potential employers might be put off if they suspect the candidate might be having children at some point in the future.

Missing out on a promotion or pay rise

You work hard, you're diligent and conscientious, you're hitting all your targets. How come other people get rewarded and you don't?

Despite equal capability and competence, research shows that, whether they're going for a promotion, putting themselves forward for a project or saying they're experienced at a particular task in an interview, men are far more likely to say 'yes', even if they only have limited experience, compared to women, who will only say 'yes' if they are more than qualified[11]. Becky McOwen-Banks from creative agency FCB Inferno put this beautifully in a TEDx talk[12] that she gave in 2016 when she talked about how it was most often her male colleagues who offered to take on the high-profile pitches, which would then win the lucrative contracts and, in turn, bring them greater recognition and promotion. As a result, fewer women are promoted to highly visible, senior positions, which means there are fewer female role models for other women to look up to and be inspired by.

Pay, as well as promotion, is a big issue for women. Research shows that women are less likely than men to ask for a raise and even when they do, men are more likely to get a higher pay rise than their female counterparts[13]. And with the gender pay gap that currently exists, women's work is effectively valued less on average than men's. This is not only about equal pay for equal work, but also about the type of work that women do (e.g. care work, nursing, teaching) being valued less than typically male-dominated work (e.g. finance, engineering, science). For women who work just as hard, but are paid less than the men in their lives, the knowledge that their work is valued less by society is disempowering.

Not volunteering for high-profile projects

An exciting opportunity comes up at work, or a new project is initiated: how come it's often a man who's first in line?

Women are just as ambitious as men at the start of their career, but data shows that for a variety of reasons, their ambition dwindles the more senior they get. According to a report by McKinsey & Company, for all the focus on breaking glass ceilings, a notable percentage of women surveyed were less interested than men in becoming top executives.[14] So why is that?

In her book, *Lean In*, Sheryl Sandberg talks about the temptation for women to 'lean out' of their careers and avoid promotions for fear of putting themselves under too much pressure with family on the horizon. Feelings of unfulfilled potential can affect our self-worth and lead to 'little me' self-deprecating behaviour, putting us even less in the running for future opportunities.

Becoming a working mum

'Congratulations on your new baby!' says the card from the office. So how come you get the feeling your pregnancy and new status as a working mum is an inconvenience to your employer?

Companies vary enormously in how they handle this, but judging by sites like *Pregnant Then Screwed*[15], working mums are discriminated against all too often, and this can be hugely disempowering. If you're not kept abreast of developments in your department, you can't return from maternity leave fully informed and may well feel like a spare part when you're back at your desk. Negotiations over your working hours and flexibility to fit with childcare drop-offs and pick-ups can be fraught with difficulty.

Being side-lined

This is a common one, post-maternity leave. You return to your company to find that someone else is doing your job while you're given a less exciting role.

Although many companies look after the working mums among their employees, some women find that while they still have a job, it's become one that makes them utterly miserable. Women also find themselves side-lined at other times in their career – during restructuring, for example, or when a new head of department takes over. It pays to be aware that these practices are sadly quite common – and that hanging on by your fingernails when your interests are clearly not being protected is not always the most empowering way to operate.

Being made redundant

Perhaps one of the biggest career challenges is being made redundant. While these decisions are usually made for business reasons rather than personal ones, it can be the ultimate disempowering experience, and it's hard to rise above it and keep hold of a sense of your worth. Yet many women find they rediscover their true power post-redundancy and become the mistress of their own destiny in ways they'd never even anticipated.

Being self-employed

Women who work for themselves may struggle with their identity. If they've got a lifestyle business but their husband is paying the mortgage, it can affect their sense of self-worth. If they don't necessarily need to work, it can feel like they're just playing around at it and that affects their ability to fulfil their potential. Unless you can see evidence of your success or your worth, you've got nothing to work with; and this can lead to a drop in confidence.

As for the many self-employed women whose work pays the bills, the pressure to keep up a steady flow of income and the challenges of operating in isolation can lead to a wobbly sense of self-worth.

And there is still an expectation foisted on women to be successful in their work while also being perfect homemakers, leaving us with a constant sense of failing to make the grade[16].

Overcoming personal challenges

It can knock us sideways if we suffer a personal blow. Serious health issues, bereavement, a break-up or divorce can take a long while to overcome. While our career is not our main focus as we roll with the punches of life, it can be a real struggle to get it back on-track afterwards. We can feel directionless for a while, and, if we don't have the right career support, this can leave our sense of purpose and power in disarray.

As you've been reading through these career roadblocks, I wonder how many of them have struck a chord with you and how they make you feel? Throughout my career, both in corporate communications and setting up my own business, there have been many times when I've struggled to keep going. I don't think we'd be human if we didn't have the occasional wobble, or even a full-blown crash!

But although some of these roadblocks are beyond our control – who can predict when a life-threatening illness will hit or know how they're going to handle post-baby blues? – we can be in control of how we predict and react to challenges, as well as how we navigate around them.

Unfortunately, there are times when our own lack of emotional strength, assertiveness or personal power prevent us from communicating our needs, seeking support or calling out when the playing field is uneven. So much so that we can sometimes be our own worst enemy, and it's important to understand the various ways we get in our own way so that we can learn how to overcome them.

"

IN MY OPINION, IMPOSTER SYNDROME IS AN OVERUSED TERM TO DESCRIBE WHAT HAPPENS WHEN YOU'RE BRAVE ENOUGH TO LEAVE THE SAFETY OF YOUR COMFORT ZONE BEHIND.

COMMON POWER BLOCKERS

So why is this the case? There is a whole myriad of reasons, some cultural, some psychological, which affect our own sense of self and can block our ability to achieve our goals. In my experience of working with women at all stages of their careers, I've found that the most common are:

1. Not being heard

2. Imposter syndrome

3. Behaving as we 'should'

4. Needing to be liked

5. Hiding our light

6. Giving away our power

7. Needing to be perfect

8. Expectations around sexuality

As you read through these power blockers, reflect on which ones resonate most with you because the more you know what they are, the more ready you will be to overcome them.

Blocker 1: Not being heard

In my research, I've found that one of the biggest barriers to women fulfilling their potential is getting their voice heard, whether that's contributing to meetings or group discussions, asking a question from the floor or delivering a talk from the front of the room. And it's not just about speaking up, it's also knowing how to deal with interruptions and get your point across when you're being talked over or ignored.

According to a study by RADA,[17] women are 68% more likely than men to never feel comfortable when expressing themselves in a work environment.

I see this played out all the time and have lost count of the courses I've run, where it's a man who speaks up in a Q&A discussion or volunteers to lead a break-out session in spite of being surrounded by brilliant women who are often vocal in more informal situations, with the irony being that many of those courses are about leadership communication and team dynamics!

Aside from the fact that women are often in the minority, research shows that men's voices tend to dominate. Aside from their willingness to contribute, they have a biological advantage, as they often speak more loudly than women with a deeper timbre which cuts through generalised discussion. Men are also more likely to raise their volume for emphasis while women are more likely to raise their pitch. This can come across as unpleasantly shrill and makes it less likely that people will listen to or value what they are saying. And it's not just that men's voices can drown out women's.

Incredibly, the perception is that when a woman speaks – if only for a brief time – she's dominating the discussion[18].

A study conducted by the University of Sussex found that in a group in which almost twice as many men as women had spoken, participants reported that the majority of speakers had been female.

And so, when women do pluck up the courage to say something – just to feel like they've contributed – they don't necessarily perform at their best because, in their rush to blurt something out, their contribution is fuelled not by conviction but a sense of obligation.

Blocker 2: Imposter syndrome

Imposter syndrome occurs when we believe we haven't legitimately achieved the position we're in, that we don't belong and that someday, someone will find us out and tell us to leave. Much has been said about this condition, which applies to both men and women, but it perhaps affects women the most – at all levels, right up to CEO. The syndrome is prevalent and likely to be a blocker for everyone, whatever stage they're at in their career, and this is how it plays out: "I don't have a right to be here, I'm probably not good enough and I'm bound to get it wrong, so I'd better keep schtum."

In my opinion, imposter syndrome is an overused term to describe what happens when you're brave enough to leave the safety of your comfort zone behind. It's no wonder you feel like an imposter because you'll be most likely trying on a new version of yourself and behaving in a different way: and how powerful is that?

The problem is that many women are scared of leaving their safety blanket behind and therefore miss out on the growth, power and freedom that come from embracing a continually challenging environment.

Blocker 3: Behaving as we 'should'

Women struggle to feel comfortable with the notion of being powerful, and we don't have to look far to understand why.

For a start, the word 'power' is perceived as masculine – it suggests going into battle, winning and overcoming. These are not words traditionally associated with femininity, which is usually aligned with softness, nurturing and vulnerability. Traditionally, girls are brought up to be compliant. Well-behaved girls don't show off or take up too much space and they always play fair. I remember regularly being told to 'keep still', 'don't fuss' and simply being ignored when adults were speaking. On the other hand, boys are often encouraged to 'win' through sport, releasing testosterone through running and shouting. You only have to look at the difference between Barbies and Power Rangers for a plastic illustration of gender bias in action.

As a result, girls don't necessarily get the opportunity to take risks, put themselves in unfamiliar situations or try out the whole range of powers as they're growing up. Because they're conditioned to be nice and play by the rules, they don't get to practice putting themselves out of their comfort zone, making friends with their imposter, behaving assertively or exercising those bold, decisive behaviours.

And yet the world is not always a nice place, and not everybody plays nicely, so women can shoot themselves in the foot by playing fair in a world that just isn't. Simply put, they are not equipped to fight. And as those girls grow up, society's expectations continue to dictate how they 'should' behave.

Combined with girls' conditioning to be 'nice' is society's views, whether conscious or unconscious, on how women 'should' behave. We only have to look at newspaper headlines, covering everything from the world of politics to business, to see that the world as a whole disapproves of women who don't conform. Forceful, powerful women are portrayed as being unfeminine, ruthless, mad, manipulative or worse. Who remembers *The Daily Mail's* 'Never Mind Brexit, Who Won Legs-It!' headline, belittling a high-powered meeting between Nicole Sturgeon, leader of the SNP, and the then Prime Minister, Theresa May, to discuss the United Kingdom's future?

When female prime ministers are discussed more in terms of their legs than their legacy, it's clear that strong women will be derided.

As a result of this, there's a tendency for women to stick with what feels comfortable – the softer end of the spectrum of power rather than the harder, more aggressive end, where they won't scare the horses.

One of the reasons it's hard for us to exercise our power and explore its full range is the sense that society as a whole can't quite handle powerful women. From Churchill to Trump to Johnson, powerful men are allowed to be flawed human beings, to be admired for their positive traits and forgiven for their less appealing ones, but woe betide a strong woman if she puts a foot wrong.

Madonna has been showing us a certain feisty kind of female power since the early 80s, but is often more criticised or ridiculed than praised. Female MPs get ripped to shreds and threatened with rape on social media for even existing. This is not new. Historian Mary Beard explains in her book, *Women and Power*, "When it comes to silencing women, Western culture has had thousands of years of practice." She goes on to chart how strong women from Athena, Goddess of Wisdom and War, to Hilary Clinton and Serena Williams have been depicted negatively. They are often masculinised or shown to represent danger, like the Medusa with her hair of snakes and killer stare. To this day, there aren't many female role models who simply stand in their power without being derided.

Blocker 4: Needing to be liked

And what about our desire for approval and affirmation?

While society struggles with the notion of strong women, women, in turn, struggle with coming on too strong because of an overwhelming need to be liked.

Whether they realise it or not, women are fearful of unleashing a monster if they access their full range of power. They might not like themselves very much once that genie's unleashed from the bottle. Worse still other people might not like them either. It just doesn't sit well with how we think of ourselves.

So we avoid saying 'no' because we don't want to upset people, we don't challenge or disagree because we're worried people will take it personally, and we don't say what we really think.

The workplace environment often plays into this, with outspoken, assertive women being described as "bossy", "a bitch" or "pushy" when they display characteristics that would be praised in men. And who wants to be known as a bitch, especially if we've been brought up to play by the rules?

Unfortunately, I've observed across all sectors that whatever your gender, if you prioritise being liked over being valued for what you do, it can severely compromise your leadership potential. As you move into more senior positions, there will be times when you have to communicate unwelcome news, deliver negative feedback and strongly disagree with others' points of view. Being respected as someone who tells it like it is, who doesn't fudge issues, and is prepared to stick their neck out for what they believe in will inspire greater 'followship' than someone who's nice to everyone but wishy-washy in their style.

Blocker 5: Hiding our light

Linked to our desire to be liked is hiding our light. We can sometimes be our own worst enemy when it comes to putting ourselves out there. Have you ever met a woman who, in spite of having a fantastic job and a degree of responsibility, privately admits to hating being in the spotlight or avoiding 'showing off' at all costs? I have – many times.

I've lost count of the number of women who discount or minimise their intelligence for fear of being branded a show-off. Never daring to say (or even think) 'Actually I'm brilliant at this', or 'I'm the best person in this room to talk about this' or simply, 'I have something to say' means we are holding ourselves back when we should be moving forward.

However competent we may be, and however brilliant our ideas, we still have a fear of exposure. For some women, sticking their head above the parapet is akin to walking around with their skirt tucked into their underwear; it feels like they're an open target and laying themselves wide open to attack. What if people think you're showing off? What if you get it wrong, or get ridiculed for drawing attention to yourself? Women are used to hiding their light, even if their light is very shiny indeed, for fear of making themselves too visible.

Being appointed to a position of power implies a certain level of competence and confidence. And yet women often avoid sharing their expertise – even when they're in leadership positions or have won countless awards. They may look comfortable with the power their position denotes, but inside, they may be cringing with embarrassment. So they avoid the town hall presentations, which would raise their profile with a large audience, they don't put themselves forward for roles that will increase their exposure, and they attribute all successes to 'the team', saying that 'we did it' rather than 'I', and avoid putting themselves in a position where they will have to 'win over' others.

So why is it that we have this tendency to avoid standing out? Tough lessons are often learnt in our teenage years and young womanhood, leaving emotions and patterns of behaviour that are never fully resolved. From being bullied to longing for approval, to getting ridiculed for being 'too' confident and clever, we soon learn that being outspoken is neither liked nor welcomed. Incidents in life where we are belittled publicly – 'Who does she think she is?' – leave their scars. So we learn to hide our light. These are powerful lessons learnt at an impressionable age. And they are lessons that stay with us, blighting our adult behaviour.

Blocker 6: Giving away our power

If you give too much of your power away there's nothing left. We've all worked with women who, in spite of their brilliance, are prone to self-deprecation. Perhaps they say, 'Oh, don't mind me, I'm just waffling,' if you ask them to give you clarity on an idea they've just pitched, or joke about themselves and their scattiness/technophobia/nervousness at every opportunity. There are also self-sacrificing women who say 'yes' to every request, working ridiculous hours rather than pushing back. This kind of minimising behaviour is typical of a woman doing everything to avoid looking like a show-off, intent only on making everyone else feel comfortable. It does not serve anyone well. Although it may feed into this need to be liked, accepted and not viewed as a threat by colleagues of either gender, it undermines every good thing we do.

And what of the trend to trade on our insecurity, to make it part of our authentic self? The notion of sharing our vulnerability as a route to authenticity, as popularised by the speaker and author Dr Brené Brown in *The Power of Vulnerability: Teachings on Authenticity, Connection and Courage*, can backfire. A trainer friend once tried this at the end of a workshop she was delivering, when she admitted to the delegates that she'd found them challenging. The subsequent feedback from the company showed that by doing so, she had simply laid herself open to more criticism, giving the difficult crowd more ammunition to attack her. Allowing people to glimpse beneath our armour can leave us dangerously exposed and demonstrate too much vulnerability, meaning that some people 'smell blood' and go in for the kill.

So while there's a place for humility and humbleness, which can be charming and attractive characteristics, it's important to use them carefully. Deciding which bits of your personality you choose to reveal and which parts you want to keep private keeps you grounded and in control.

Blocker 7: Needing to be perfect

Another part of our conditioning as girls growing up is the need to feel 100% certain of ourselves and 110% right before we offer an opinion because of the fear of getting it wrong. Whereas men tend to shoot from the hip, say what they think without needing to check every single fact first, women will sit quietly in meetings for fear of saying something that they can't fully back up.

Statistics from a Hewlett Packard report show that men will apply for jobs even though they can fulfil only a fraction of the skills on the job description, whereas women in the same situation won't apply unless they can tick every box[19]. This is partly due to a need to operate from a place of certainty, coupled with insecurity about being found 'wrong'.

But there's also a need for approval. For many schoolgirls, a key need to be a 'good girl' stems from only receiving praise when they get straight As. The good girl cult leads to perfectionism, which means we won't share an unfinished thought or concept – it has to be perfect before it comes out of our mouths. And of course, speaking as a recovering perfectionist, perfection is an ideal that can never be achieved.

Blocker 8: Expectations around sexuality

And what about the power that comes from our sexuality? Girls who learn from an early age that approval is based on their looks ("Aren't you a pretty girl!") instead of their brains, actions or personality quickly find that their self-worth is dependent on them. Not having the right support around us when our sexuality is awakening can lead to confusion about how to employ it. If our looks are all that we're noticed for, we can unwittingly start to use them to get the desired result – in life, at school, in the office. This can lead to the belief that flirting is the way forward, whether through revealing clothing, fluttering your eyelashes, a little girl voice or making passes at colleagues.

So much of this is influenced by popular culture and social media. Our sexuality is a potent form of power that's so often misused in order to boost our self-worth. Using it to get what you want often backfires, creating an opportunity for men to win power back from women. How often does someone illicitly admiring your low-cut top lead to an unwelcome pass at a team away day? How many times has a friendly arm around the shoulders been misinterpreted as an invitation for something more? It's incredibly unwise to be more admired for your physical attributes than, say, your decisiveness or creative ideas. So flirting as power is a dangerous tactic.

While it's a positive force in many ways, social media has a lot to answer for. Our news feeds are jam-packed with per-fectly curated brands portraying passive images of female perfection, rather than powerful images of womanhood. By contrast, there are also images of famous women in pow-erful poses who happen to be wearing very little, sending out mixed messages about who has the power: them or the voyeur.

The Internet is a place where some people think it's OK to be highly negative and critical, but increasingly dangerous to have a point of view, especially if you're a woman. The Everyday Sexism Project was launched in 2012 by journalist Laura Bates to document examples of sexism from around the world and has been mercilessly trolled. Women should not be silenced for their views or threatened with violence for daring to voice them. But the conclusion may be that it's far safer to comply and conform, which in turn, can compromise women's ability to see themselves as powerful and feel comfortable in powerful roles.

FINDING A SOLUTION TO THE POWER CONUNDRUM

If you've been frustrated by this roll call of power blockers, #MeToo. I've found it hard to acknowledge all the ways that our worth can be compromised and all the reasons why it's harder for women to be powerful. But knowledge is power, and if there's one thing I know from listening to all these stories, is that now is the time to make a change.

So how do we construct a solution? I truly believe that we are at a turning point in history – a vacuum has been left wide open post-#MeToo, post-Weinstein, post-umpteen other sexual harassment cases where men and women no longer know how to behave. In this new normal, women are harnessing their power by challenging disparity and sexism.

And men are, mercifully, challenging their own preconceived ideas about appropriate behaviour too.

I recently met a young woman who works for an engineering company. Every time she went on site, she got wolf-whistled. Instead of letting herself feel small and embarrassed, she started countering it with similar energy, shouting back and giving as good as she got, disarming the wolf whistlers. It didn't take long for them to realise that their behaviour was unwelcome and the whistling stopped. Positively influencing our own mental environment impacts our actual environment. Applying strategies to fight back, beat people at their own game or rise above negative behaviour will change the culture we're in.

Organisations are also waking up to the potential of diversity and inclusion through initiatives to support equality for everyone – regardless of their characteristics. And global brands like Gillette are embracing the movement, calling out toxic masculinity and replacing their 30-year tagline "The best a man can get" with "The best men can be" in a campaign that's been both praised and highly criticised.

The old rules are being broken, social mores have been thrown up in the air and people are more cautious than ever. Sexism is taboo, more people are embracing the notion of gender-fluidity and there's a move towards androgyny and not putting people into boxes at all. We are questioning how to behave and that can only be a good thing, if we can come up with some good answers.

As we learn to navigate this new world, we need to learn to define a new kind of success, based purely on our merits. From there, our sense of power will come. Because allowing our careers and sense of success to be solely defined by our boss and place of work can be dangerous, especially when the day comes when we don't get that promotion or are told we're no longer required.

Achieving your potential and making the most of your latent power is not necessarily about becoming a CEO or even having a career; instead, it's about fulfilling your potential, whatever that means for you.

It's important to acknowledge that a lot of women will walk away from careers that leave them feeling small and reinvent themselves, discovering a whole other form of power. Marina Gask, editor and co-founder of audreyonline.co.uk, a platform for midlife women who are giving their life a reboot, says: "It's heartening to see the number of women who are taking a step into the unknown, redefining themselves by taking charge of their own careers and becoming mistresses of their own destiny."

And so this presents women with a choice: do you want to collude with what's come before, stay small and only access a fraction of your power? Or do you want to Power Up and unleash your potential?

History is full of examples of brave women who have decided that enough is enough and risen up to fight for change, from Emmeline Pankhurst to Oprah Winfrey. For years, the women who accused Bill Cosby of rape and sexual assault were afraid of speaking up and not being believed. But it took one woman, Andrea Constand, to waive her anonymity, and soon there were hordes of victims who joined the queue behind her to raise their voices against him. Once one spoke out, it empowered all the others.

Accessing power is an act of leadership – being the lone voice so others will follow. We need to take inspiration from Andrea and all the women who've had the guts to access their power, even though they knew it may attract criticism or even the threat of worse.

So let's change the paradigm. This doesn't have to be a battle, nor a walkover. There wouldn't be any need for one behaviour to win over another if all of us, whatever our gender, had access to all the types of power on the spectrum, from the soft glow of intuition right through to the blazing flames of indignation. And got comfortable with using them.

We have the power if we believe we have the power. We need to tread our own path, be brave and fulfil our own potential, opening doors for others to do the same. We need to power up.

EXERCISE 1:
POWER: WHY YOU NEED IT AND WHEN

Now that we've explored why and when women need power, it's your turn.

- Start by reflecting on the word Power and the words you would use to describe it.

- Think about why you chose to pick up this book, what attracts you to the word 'power' and what you want to achieve as a result of powering up.

- Project yourself forward to when you've finished reading this book. How would you like to feel when you've fully stepped into your power?

- What will be different for you and the people around you?

- What will be different in the way that you experience the world?

EXERCISE 2:
PREPARING FOR
THE ROADBLOCKS

Now think about all the forces that could prevent you from living your most powerful life. Go to the list of career blocks earlier in this chapter and identify all those that resonate for you, whether you've experienced them personally in the past or predict them in your future. Note them down in the table below.

Then write down how your 'low power' self has behaved or would have behaved in each situation in the first column and how your 'high power' self will behave in the next column along. An example might be coming back from a career break to find that your job has been taken over by a more junior colleague. A low power response would be to accept this and pick up on the tasks that have been neglected while you're away. A high power response would be to hold a meeting with your manager and HR to discuss a new role which will maximise your skills.

If you're wondering how you'll move from a low power to a high power response, don't worry, the rest of this book will give you guidance on exactly that!

Career Roadblocks	Low Power Response	High Power Response

Behaviour is a choice. Thinking about the different ways you might react to challenges in your career and life and learning from this is a great way to ensure that when curveballs do come your way, you'll make the more empowered choices.

IN SUMMARY

★   Women encounter a range of roadblocks, which can hinder their career progression, unlike men, whose career path tends to be more linear.

★   Common challenges include recruitment bias, missing out on a promotion or pay rise, not feeling comfortable volunteering for high-profile projects, becoming a working mum, being side-lined, made redundant and becoming self-employed.

★   There are also cultural and psychological blockers that can prevent women from communicating their needs, seeking support or calling out when the playing field is uneven. These include not being heard, imposter syndrome, the pressure to behave as we 'should', needing to be liked, giving away our power, perfectionism and when sexuality backfires.

★   Achieving your potential and making the most of your latent power is not necessarily about becoming a CEO or even having a career, but about fulfilling your potential, whatever that means for you.

★   Understanding the different ways you might react to challenges in your career and life and learning from this is a great way to ensure that you make the more empowered choice when curveballs come your way.

Chapter 3

THE POWER UP MODEL

"I do not wish them to have power over men; but over themselves."

–MARY WOLLSTONECRAFT

Now that we've examined why power is such an important resource for women, let's move onto what you can do to power up! In this chapter, we're going to explore the six sources of power that will unleash your potential and guarantee success in your personal and professional life.

The Power Up Model© is a unique tool which I've designed to help you assess your personal strengths and track progress on your route to personal power. It's based on research into the qualities that truly powerful women have honed and developed to be successful in all aspects of their work and life.

If you look at the model below, you'll see that the right-hand side of the star represents your *internal* power and includes *Intuition*, *Knowledge* and *Resilience* and that the left-hand side represents your *external* power: *Magnetism*, *Relationships* and *Assertiveness*. At the centre of the model is the word 'Purpose', which is the force that propels you forward.

As you begin to develop your personal power, working on the internal sources will give you inner confidence, strength and the resolve to act; working on the external sources will give you the skills to express your power to the outside world. As you connect with your purpose, you will harness conviction, determination, drive and energy, all of which will power you forward.

THE POWER UP MODEL

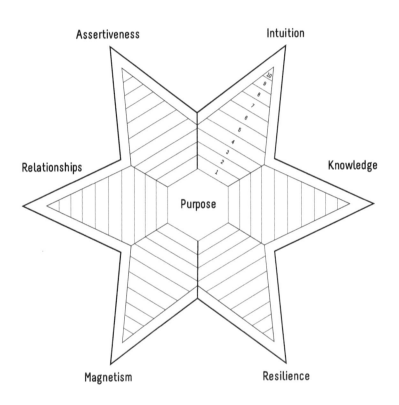

The internal sources of power are:

Intuition: the ability to trust your innate wisdom and gut instinct, giving you the freedom and impetus to act. Intuition has nothing to do with divine intervention or 'trusting the universe' and everything to do with tapping into your conscious, lived experiences and the power of your subconscious mind. Being able to access the power of intuition leads to greater emotional intelligence, the ability to quickly 'read' situations and people, a willingness to trust your own judgement and the confidence to make decisions without overthinking.

Knowledge: the ability to use the unique information and skills you possess to add value and demonstrate your worth. Knowledge is the practical complement to Intuition, giving you the evidence to state your case and the confidence to speak. Although knowledge is infinite, you only need to know slightly more than the people around you to be powerful. When clearly and intelligently expressed, knowledge will denote authority and credibility, essential if you want to get your voice heard.

Resilience: the ability to stay strong in the face of adversity, bounce back after setbacks and manage self-limiting beliefs, which can stop you from fulfilling your potential. Developing resilience is about knowing how to maintain a healthy mind and body so that you can navigate the many roadblocks and challenges that threaten to push you off course. With resilience, you have the inner resolve to handle difficult situations and people with ease and you will be able to keep your head when all about you are losing theirs.

The external sources of power are:

Magnetism: the ability to attract attention to yourself and make a powerful impact, essential in a world that remembers the shiny and forgets the dull. Developing the power of magnetism is about understanding the unique qualities that represent your authentic personal brand and knowing how to 'switch on' your most magnetic self through using your attitude, body language, voice and word choice. The power of magnetism is what will draw people to you when networking, in meetings, from the stage and online so that you can influence them and inspire them to say 'yes'.

Relationships: the ability to build and prioritise bonds with people around you. The saying, 'It's not what you know, it's who you know' works on both an emotional and practical level and is just as relevant in today's digital age as it was when the only way that people could communicate was face to face. We need strong relationships with people we can trust because sometimes it's too hard to do it alone. Building supportive relationships and knowing how to create a powerful network is the most effective – and enjoyable – way of getting things done at work, as well as surviving the knockbacks in life.

Assertiveness: the ability to make our wants, needs and views met, using our mind, body and voice to confidently stand up for what we believe in. Many women are hard-wired to avoid saying 'no' because we hate being 'difficult' and want everything to run smoothly. Unfortunately, the world isn't always fair and we can end up sacrificing our own needs and wants for others. Assertive behaviour is honest, direct, clear, expressive, self-enhancing, persistent and respectful.

It's what enables us to speak our truth, walk knowingly into conflict and live fully in the world.

Over the coming chapters, we'll examine each power source in detail and explore what you can do to harness them to achieve your goals.

EXERCISE 1:
HOW TO DEVELOP YOUR OWN PERSONAL POWER

If you're looking to develop your personal power, a useful first step is to examine which sources of power are strongest in you, and which might be holding you back. In my experience of working with this model, I've found that it is very context-specific. For example, there will be situations when you're fully able to communicate *Assertively* and demonstrate your *Knowledge*, and other times when you find it harder. Likewise, there are occasions when you feel fully connected to your *Intuition* and others when you don't.

For this reason, as you complete the model, start by understanding which context/s you want to work on and exactly what you want to achieve by powering up, the challenges you're currently facing and the objectives you'd like to accomplish. You can then assess your power sources against these criteria and prioritise the time you spend on each.

1. Start by establishing the context you want to work on and identifying the goals you'd like to achieve (see the goal setting exercise in Chapter 1 to help you with this).

2. Then, work around the star clockwise, starting with Intuition, the first internal source of power. Mark up where you currently see yourself against each of the sources, taking the centre of the Model as 1 and the outer edge as 10. For example, if you feel like you have a considerable amount of *Knowledge*, but find it difficult to build Relationships, you might score yourself 8 and 4 respectively. If you have spent considerable time listening to your intuition but find asserting your opinions challenging, score yourself 9 for *Intuition* and 3 for *Assertiveness*. You can use the brief descriptions of each power source above as your guide or turn to the corresponding chapters for a more detailed explanation.

3. Then consider how you would ideally like to score yourself against each power source, given your goals and the context you're working on. For example, if your goal is to get promoted to a role you feel highly qualified for in the next six months, but are struggling to get the recognition you deserve, you may want to prioritise maximising your external sources of power by increasing your *Magnetism,* building new *Relationships* and developing *Assertiveness* so that you can ask for what you deserve.

4. As you complete your ideal power profile, bear in mind that the goal is not to score 10 for each – in fact, someone who scores themselves 10 in each

component would probably experience too strong a power surge and spontaneously combust! Using the Power Up Model© is context-specific and there will be times when one source is more appropriate than another. The real goal is to identify which sources of power are inherently strong in you and which, if further developed, will enable you to overcome your challenges and fulfil your goals.

5. Once you've completed the Model, consider the following questions:

- Which sources of power do you currently score highest in?

- Which sources of power do you currently score lowest in?

- Are you stronger on the inner or outer sources of power?

- Which sources of power could you make more of to fulfil your goals?

- Which sources of power would you like to develop further?

- Where are the greatest gaps between your existing and ideal Power Profile?

- Given your goals, which gaps do you need to prioritise?

Now that you have identified your Power Profile, you can use the chapters of this book to focus on those areas you would like to develop. In each chapter, we explore the six Power Sources in turn, starting with the internal sources – the foundation of your power – and ending with the external sources – how you express yourself to others.

USING THIS BOOK

Within each chapter, you will find a range of models and tools which, when applied, will enhance your *Intuition, Knowledge, Resilience, Magnetism, Relationships and Assertiveness*. In applying these learnings, you will expand your power range and develop the skills to make an impact and achieve your objectives. I've also created a downloadable workbook which you can access via the Power Up website: (**www.womenpowerupbook.com**). This includes all the exercises in each chapter for you to complete in one place to aid your learning.

As you make your way through the chapters, you'll see that each segment of the Power Up Model© is interconnected and interdependent: for example, if you increase your *Knowledge*, you'll find it easier to be *Assertive*. If you tap into your *Intuition*, you'll have greater *Resilience*. Your *Magnetism* will enable you to attract a wider span of *Relationships*.

Although all the components are interconnected, it is not necessary to read each chapter in turn. If you prefer, you could begin with the areas which are a priority for you and go back to the other chapters afterwards.

Once you've read this book and completed the exercises, you'll have a solid understanding of your unique personal power and have, at your fingertips, a wealth of tips and techniques that you can use to fulfil your potential.

IN SUMMARY

★ The Power Up Model© is a unique tool to help you assess your personal strengths and track progress on your route to personal power. It's based on research into the qualities that truly powerful women have honed and developed to be successful in all aspects of their work and life.

★ The right-hand side of the model represents your *internal* power sources and includes: *Intuition*, *Knowledge* and *Resilience*.

★ The left-hand side of the model represents the *external* power sources: *Magnetism*, *Relationships* and *Assertiveness*.

★ At the centre of the model is the word 'Purpose', which is the force that propels you forward.

★ If you're looking to develop your personal power, a useful first step is to examine the sources of power that are strongest for you and which might be holding you back. You can then use the tools, techniques and exercises in this book to build on your strengths and develop areas of weakness.

PART TWO

THE INTERNAL POWER SOURCES

INTRODUCTION TO PART TWO

Now that we've explored the six power sources encapsulated in the Power Up Model©, let's begin by focusing on the three internal qualities: *Intuition*, *Knowledge* and *Resilience*, which when combined give you inner confidence, strength and the determination to act.

Intuition is an underestimated source of power often attributed to women. Knowing how to tap into your inner wisdom and trusting it will give you greater confidence and ease. By honing your intuition, you'll become more decisive and in control of your own destiny. Through applying the techniques in this chapter, you will find it easier to speak and act authentically because you will second guess yourself less. And you will be able to read people more easily, knowing who to trust and who to keep at a distance.

The phrase 'knowledge is power' is well known and goes way beyond any letters after your name. When powerfully expressed, knowledge will convey your authority and credibility, essential if you want to have your voice heard. This chapter will explore not only how you can hone your knowledge, but also how you can use it to increase your visibility, thereby enhancing your worth and status.

However much we try and avoid it, there will be times when our inner resolve is compromised. The power of *Resilience* – strength through adversity – will help you to stay strong, bounce back when under pressure and learn from knockbacks to emerge even more powerful than before. When you know you have resilience as a back-up power source, you're much more willing to take risks and live life to the full.

Let's go!

Chapter 4

INTUITION

"I've trusted the still, small voice of intuition my entire life. And the only time I've made mistakes is when I didn't listen."

–OPRAH WINFREY

THE POWER OF INTUITION

Intuition is a valuable source of power, which is there whenever you want or need it. I'm a big believer in the power of intuition – that hidden ability to read and react to situations and people, if only we allow ourselves to do so. We call on our intuition to make decisions, assess risks, take action (or not), read people, identify friends or foes, sense when danger is lurking and to let us know how to stay safe.

While we all have a rough idea of what intuition is, it's difficult to define or rationalise it. Pretty much everyone has experienced a gut feeling – that unconscious reasoning that encourages us to do something without telling us why or how. If we trust the power of intuition, we can allocate the same amount of time and energy to making decisions, irrespective of their size, whether it's saying 'yes' to a date or a marriage proposal, buying a chocolate bar or an apartment, investing in travel insurance or a new car. If we tune into our intuition, decisions can be made in the blink of an eye.

Intuition can sometimes be viewed negatively: a flaky unsubstantiated force akin to 'asking the universe', unfounded on evidence and logic. And yet, many of the world's most successful leaders attribute the power of intuition to their success.

Steve Jobs called it "more powerful than intellect," whereas Oprah hailed it as the instinct that's driven all her best business decisions.

Richard Branson said, "In the same way that I tend to make up my mind about people within thirty seconds of meeting them, I also make up my mind about whether a business proposal excites me within about thirty seconds of looking at it. I rely far more on gut instinct than researching huge amounts of statistics."

"Often you have to rely on intuition," according to tech guru Bill Gates, especially when there is no obvious right or wrong, no black or white, which is so often the case.

In my case, I have learnt to love my intuition, aka my sixth sense or 'spidey sense', a term originally attributed to the comic-book superhero Spider-Man. Having in the past wasted time fretting on decisions where there was no black or white answer, these days I get a small thrill from putting my trust in snap judgements. People are often surprised at how quickly I can accept or reject a proposal and although this may on the surface appear to be flighty, I know that those lightning-fast reactions are, in fact, based on a lifetime's experiences.

Intuition in action

Seven years ago, shortly after launching my first Gravitas course, I was approached by a woman about running one in Dubai. The programme was my brainchild, so the idea got me very excited. I had visions of my fledgling idea escalating beyond my wildest dreams: massive audiences, thronging fans, a TV deal! But somehow, deep down, it just felt wrong. This was still a new baby and the idea of giving it away before it had even started to crawl felt irresponsible, dangerous and foolhardy. On top of that, I had two very young children and didn't want to spend too much time away from home. After some internal wrangling, I politely declined.

The fact is I'd known the second she'd started talking that it was a no. But when the pound signs started flashing and my ego started dancing around at the prospect of a global deal, I very nearly said 'yes'.

By contrast, the other day I was approached by another woman about running a programme, once again in Dubai. This time it felt different. As we talked I knew within the first couple of minutes that I could trust her, and said 'yes' without further thought. What was it that made me struggle to say 'no' first time round and 'yes' decisively the second? Intuition. In the intervening years, my 'spidey sense' has become more acute, and I knew with certainty that this opportunity was right for me. Listening to intuition means we don't waste time on 'coulda, woulda, shoulda' because we know when something is right and when it's definitely not.

Intuition not only makes sound business sense, it can keep us safe. As women, we occasionally find ourselves in situations where we sense that something's not quite right, but may not be able to explain why rationally. Often these situations take us by surprise and require rapid action, and so it's vital that we learn how to tune into those feelings and act on them, as illustrated in this story as told to me by one of my friends. Her experience is sadly only too common.

It was Saturday night and she was on her way home. She had had a few drinks but was still sober enough to walk in a straight line and pick up on her surroundings. It was dark, cold, the street was deserted. As she made her way towards the station, she could sense someone walking up behind her, hear footsteps and see a shadow approaching hers.

She turned around and there he was. His smile seemed innocent enough, but there was something she didn't like about the hunch of his shoulders. He began to walk alongside her, matching her stride-for-stride and asking about her night out. As she pulled her coat closer, she noticed a small movement out of the corner of her eye. Glancing down, she realised that he was exposing himself to her.

She felt sick to the stomach and broke into a run. As she entered the busy station, she felt violated, embarrassed. She wondered whether she'd had more drinks than she thought and if she'd brought the situation on herself. She wanted someone to tell her everything was going to be OK, but everyone was intent on their own journeys home. She took a deep breath and got her ticket from her purse.

★ ★ ★

There will be times when we ignore our intuition, allowing the loud voice of reason or authority to influence our judgement, only to regret it later. We've all felt those footsteps coming up behind us, but how many of us have chosen to ignore those hairs prickling at the back of our neck and how many of us have chosen to run, even if we did feel silly?

How does Intuition relate to Power Up?

Intuition may not seem the most obvious power weapon. It certainly doesn't have the loudest voice in the Power Up Model©, but its quiet guidance will be by your side your entire life, not only keeping you safe but also propelling you forward. If you trust your powers of intuition, you will make quicker decisions, freeing up time and brain space to achieve your goals. You will find it easier to speak and act authentically because you will second guess yourself less. And you will be able to read people more easily, knowing who to trust and who to keep at a distance.

In general, women are thought to have stronger intuition than men, hence the term 'women's intuition'. However, the fact that we tend to be more risk-averse may mean that we ignore our intuition more often than we should. In academic and corporate environments, intuition is often undervalued: too sensitive, emotional and dramatic to be trusted compared to what might be perceived as the more masculine powers of empirical evidence, rational thought and logic. This is a shame because attitudes like this make us doubt our excellent judgment and ignore all those powerful instincts.

"

WE IGNORE OUR INTUITION AT OUR PERIL. NOT TRUSTING IT CAN BE SERIOUSLY CAREER-LIMITING.

Why do we need it?

Many of us are bound up by indecision and massively risk-averse. We tend to hesitate before taking action. For fear of looking foolish or getting it wrong, we second-guess ourselves. When choosing tiles, even if I like the first ones I see, I'll still look at all the tiles in the shop, before finally going back to the ones I liked in the first place! This is not the end of the world when it comes to home decoration, but in the workplace and in life, it can have enormous implications for our success.

Right now, I can think of at least four decisions I need to make which I would be able to make far quicker if I just used my intuition.

1. Deciding which supplier to use for a major event I've got coming up.

2. Deciding whether to pick up the phone and call a friend I've lost touch with.

3. Choosing who to ask for advice about a new project.

4. Deciding whether to confront a family member about an issue that's been bothering me.

I've been putting off making all these decisions because I've wanted to allocate what I perceive to be 'sufficient' time to make them. But if I'm honest, whether I made a snap judgement right now or spent half a day reflecting on it, I don't think the decision would be any different. How much more productive would I be if I chose to listen to my intuitive brain even more than I do already?

That's what makes it a power we need to learn to use with confidence.

I was recently coaching a young woman, let's call her Carley, who'd been offered three different work opportunities and was struggling to make a decision. The problem was, she was focusing on the potential negative outcomes of each. One involved working on a really exciting pitch and all she could think was, "What if we lose and it reflects badly on me?" My response was, "Yes but what if you win?" Sometimes we can be so risk-averse that our brains go straight to the negative. At the time, Carley wasn't listening to her intuition.

We ignore our intuition at our peril. Not trusting it can be seriously career-limiting, preventing you from offering your opinion, sharing your ideas and saying 'yes' to opportunities. It can hold you back from building vital relationships and waste valuable hours caught at a crossroads, dithering over which way to turn.

CASE STUDY

Darshana Ubl is a serial entrepreneur, investor and co-owner of Verve Rally, a sports club that provides luxury adventure holidays with GT/Supercars.

I was curious to know where her success came from, as well as the lessons she's learnt along the way. When I asked her what her one power was, she replied: "intuition". But that it had to be combined with energy, because anyone can have a gut feeling, but you have to act on it to be successful. This is her story.

"When I was growing up in India, my parents moved around a

lot. I found it hard because each time we arrived in a new place, I had to make new friends. But I learnt very quickly to use my intuition to work out who I could trust. That has helped me enormously in my business, because so much of what I do is about relationships.

"My dad, who was an entrepreneur, used to pick me up from school and take me to the share market and then the bank, before going to get ice cream. That was my favourite part of the day. He treated me as an equal. I didn't realise it at the time, but that experience made me comfortable talking about money, a skill I later used when I put myself forward to be an economics spokesperson for the BBC. My mum had different ideas. She wanted me to conform to a traditional role. When I was 14 or 15, a week before my exams, she decided I needed to learn how to cook, while all my friends' parents were encouraging their children academically. I knew I had to get out: I got good grades and used them to move to a university far away from home. Through my intuition, I learnt the importance of education and became fiercely independent.

"Despite that, my mum put me in an all-girls hostel which had been previously been used by the British as prison cells. I stayed there for a whole year, which was tough. I put posters of Michael Jackson and Madonna on my walls, which I was never allowed to do at home. And so to survive I used my inner wisdom and strength to create a happy space for myself.

"When I look back on that experience I know it gave me strength. I now know that my power comes from knowing myself, so I continue to build time into my busy schedule to do that.

"A lot of people wouldn't expect that was my story. Some people say, 'How lucky, she has a business in the luxury field!' Yes, but I created that from scratch. Part of my success is because I spend more time planning and less time executing. And I don't give up. So although I do base a lot of my decisions on intuition, my intuition is based on what I know and reacting to what's happening.

"In my experience, intuition comes from being in tune with yourself, listening and observing people. I'm not super detailed on spreadsheets, but I can pick up on people details. I listen, I remember, and through that, I can understand people's motivations. And if you listen to your higher self, it tells you stuff. For example, if you're doing something relentlessly in your business and there's no change, your intuition will tell you what to do next. Maybe you're not listening. Maybe the business model is wrong. You didn't arrive knowing everything. So you have to listen and learn."

What gets in the way?

The three main barriers that get in the way of intuition are lack of confidence, fear and immunity to change.

1. **Lack of confidence** to make decisions is tied up with knowing when to listen to our intuition. If we do not believe that we know the answer to questions or wonder whether we have enough information, it can sometimes be a sign of imposter syndrome, a term originally coined by psychologists Pauline Clance and Suzanne Imes in 1978 to describe being convinced that we don't deserve the success we have despite having adequate external evidence of accomplishment, a feeling that we're a fraud and don't have a right to be in that position in the first place.

2. **Fear** plays a complex role in all this. If that voice inside your head (AKA your intuition) is telling you to leave your toxic work environment and find somewhere that values your talents, the fear of the unknown can drown it out and stop you from taking action. Fear can also be disguised as intuition. You hold your tongue in meetings and rationalise your silence by saying to yourself that it didn't 'feel like the right time' when, in fact, you didn't want to say something foolish or risk sticking your neck out. How can we trust our fear to be telling us something that we need to know, rather than preventing us from acting? Observing the circumstances and asking yourself the right questions will help. For example, if you find it difficult to speak up in a meeting, are you pretending your intuition is telling you to keep quiet when, in fact, you simply feel overwhelmed by the

greater brains in the room? It might be time to override your fear and listen to your inner cheerleader instead who's saying, "Come on, you can do this."

One way to become more attuned to this is to notice how you feel after you've trusted your intuition and acted. So, after that meeting, are you berating yourself inwardly for not speaking up, which you would have done if you'd listened to your intuition? Or are you, in fact, thinking, "That was the right call, if I'd spoken I would have exposed my lack of experience in this area"? Notice your true feelings in these situations because that's your intuition talking.

3. **Immunity to change**. If your intuition is telling you to make a massive change and you're overwhelmed by the prospect, it may be that you're experiencing what Harvard Graduate School of Education professors Robert Kegan and Lisa Laskow Lahey call 'immunity to change'[20]. This is something which I've shared with many of my coaching clients who have wanted to achieve a certain goal but have found themselves resistant to taking the steps to get them there. We are hardwired not to make big changes and this goes back to cavemen times, when choosing to take a different route to the waterhole could have meant instant death because of a lurking tiger, unlike our trusty and predictable route. So although we may say, "'I really want to get promoted,' we don't put ourselves forward for senior positions because, deep down, we're frightened by the prospect of taking the next step up or an alternative path.

Trying to change behaviour when we don't understand the root cause of it never works. This isn't because of a lack of willpower, but rather the result of an emotional immune system that helps protect us from the fallout that can come from change – which when viewed negatively could be disappointment and shame.

As an antidote, Keegan and Laskow recommend putting our ability to change to the test by doing something small – nibbling the toenail of the elephant rather than eating the whole thing. If you try and do something big, the likelihood is that your intuition will work against you, telling you that change is hard and even harder to maintain. But if you choose one tiny task to complete and that goes well, you will be proving to your intuitive self that you can do it, which will then open up the floodgates to bring about more change.

Why has intuition got such a bad rep?

Often, the perception is that intuition can be a bit fluffy, one of those weird inexplicable things we dismiss as psychobabble in the same vein as fate, happy accidents and déjà vu. People who talk about trusting the universe and that everything happens for a reason can come across as naïve, like they're not living in the real world, in danger of abdicating responsibility for their lives, rejecting the need to be accountable for their actions and generally believing that life happens to you, rather than for you.

People who rely on the power of their intuition can be perceived in the same way: a bit woo-woo, the opposite of sensible, evidence-based people. Nothing could be further from the truth. In fact, becoming conscious of your intuition, tapping into your instincts and trusting yourself to act upon your inner wisdom is the opposite of this as it means you're consciously accessing your whole range of conscious and subconscious intelligence, rather than just what you can reach through your conscious mind. This will give you an advantage over the vast majority of people.

We have all experienced a sixth sense about a situation or a person, a hunch that they will be good or bad for us, or randomly thought of someone only to be contacted by them two seconds later. But what exactly is intuition, can we trust it as much as some people seem to, and if so, how can we hone and refine it to both accelerate our potential and achieve our goals?

WHAT IS INTUITION?

The word intuition comes from the Latin 'intuir', meaning knowledge from within. The dictionary definition is the ability to understand something instinctively, without the need for conscious reasoning. Based on her research at the University of Houston, the author and professor Brené Brown defines it as "our ability to hold space for uncertainty and our willingness to trust the many ways we've developed knowledge and insight".[21]

This indicates that we have access to a vast spectrum of intelligence, including the most obvious intellectual kind (which we'll explore in more detail in the *Knowledge* chapter), as well as the more subtle kind, found in our subconscious.

INTUITION ISN'T JUST AIRY-FAIRY NONSENSE. IT'S THE ENERGY WHICH PUSHES YOU TO TAKE RISKS.

Intuition isn't just airy-fairy nonsense. It's the energy which pushes you to take risks – and not just calculated risks, but the jumping-out-of-an-aeroplane-just-because-you-want-to ones. It's the antidote to fear, hesitation and being stuck.

Closely linked to emotional intelligence, intuition is the impetus we need to trust, be open and be vulnerable with others, or not. And the fact is, intuition doesn't just come out of thin air. It is based on knowledge, lived experiences and the ability to trust oneself and one's own judgement.

"Even when we're not at a fork in the road, wondering what to do and trying to hear that inner voice, our intuition is always there, always reading the situation, always trying to steer us the right way. But can we hear it? Are we paying attention? Are we living a life that keeps the pathway to our intuition unblocked? Feeding and nurturing our intuition and living a life in which we can make use of its wisdom, is one key way to thrive, at work and in life."

–'THRIVE', ARIANNA HUFFINGTON

Where does it come from?

The nature of intuition has inspired centuries' worth of research and inquiry in the fields of philosophy, psychology and neuroscience. From a scientific perspective, research tells us that the human mind is wired to seek patterns. Not only does the brain process information as it comes in, but it also stores insights from all our past experiences. It therefore follows that our intuition is a natural by-product of a complex sorting mechanism occurring within our brains. As we make our way through life, all our experiences get stored in a mental 'filing system' in our subconscious mind. This means that our intuition has been developing and expanding since we were born. Every interaction, happy or sad, is catalogued in the mental filing cabinet (AKA our memory). Whenever something happens where we're required to act, our minds swiftly refer to this filing system to pull out any relevant data for our reference, without us even realising it. Intuition draws from that deep memory well to inform our decisions.

Steve Jobs explained this process during his commencement address to the graduates at Stanford University in 2005 in terms of 'connecting the dots' between our past experiences and the conclusions we have filed away for future use: "You can't connect the dots looking forward; you can only connect them looking backwards," he said. "So you have to trust that the dots will somehow connect in your future... Because believing that the dots will connect down the road will give you the confidence to follow your heart, even when it leads you off the well-worn path; and that will make all the difference."

When we subconsciously spot patterns, our bodies respond, firing neuro-chemicals in both the brain and gut, which we sometimes experience physically. This gives us that instant sense that something is right, or that it's 'off'; for example, that queasy sensation when we meet someone who gives us the creeps or that headache we get when under stress. These automatic processes are faster than rational thought, which means that intuition can help us make decisions when time is short and traditional analysis may not be possible.

An example of its helpfulness is when someone speaks over you in a meeting or dominates a conversation. You might be irritated by their rudeness and feel your pulse starting to race, but feel uncomfortable calling it out for fear of being disrespectful. Your intuition can help you decide whether to act or not, based on what you've done in similar situations and the outcome you'd like to achieve.

Of course, your intuition may be ill-informed because you don't have all the dots you need. As you call on your intuition, it's worth bearing in mind that it's purely based on the sum total of your own experiences, which may or may not be enough. Or it could be that you are putting more emphasis on one dot rather than another – for example, the views of someone you trusted in the past, which may no longer be relevant to you now. Memory isn't just the recollection of events that have occurred, it's based on the meaning that we attributed to those events at the time. And because past experiences can be rewritten each time they're recalled, they are by definition subjective, rather than balanced and objective.

As well as the scientific approach, another view of intuition is what we 'feel' subconsciously as opposed to what we consciously observe. While some people may take comfort from referring to 'the universe' or another power telling them what to do, intuition is born out of all the experiences that we've had, and we have our own brain to thank for offering us its wisdom, based on years of observation on our behalf. And if you just ignore it, by dismissing it as 'woo-woo', you're missing a trick. Trust your intuition: it's real.

Female intuition versus gut instinct

Intuition is often perceived as a female trait, but is 'women's intuition' real, or is it just a myth? Do women have some sort of 'psychic' ability to pick up on what others are thinking?

The ability to tap into what might be perceived as our intuition and read other people comes from women's traditional position in society. Evolutionary factors are believed to play a part, with the development of our brain circuitry being based on our ability to anticipate the needs of children, seek out potential mates and avoid danger. Women have become adept at 'sizing up' a person or situation quickly for survival reasons and have an edge when it comes to reading people. There is also evidence that women are seen as more empathic than men, and that they are more likely to see themselves that way.

Contrary to popular belief, it's not just women who possess this mysterious instinct. According to Judith Orloff, MD, assistant clinical professor of psychiatry at UCLA and author of *Guide to Intuitive Healing: Five Steps to Physical, Emotional, and Sexual Wellness*, 'Men can be powerfully intuitive – they have the same capabilities as women... But in our culture, we view intuition as something that's warm and fuzzy, or not masculine, so men have often lost touch with those feelings.'

Women, on the other hand, are encouraged to be receptive to their inner thoughts, so it appears that they have more intuition than men. "The reality is, girls are praised for being sensitive while boys are urged to be more linear in their thinking rather than listening to their feelings," Judith Orloff says.

But what about gut instinct, which is sometimes seen as the male equivalent to female intuition and is perceived as visceral, manly and strong? Is this any different to intuition? Neuroscience tells us that we have a 'second brain' in the gut, with hundreds of millions of neurons connecting the brain to the enteric nervous system. And this second brain – the gut – informs our state of mind and influences our emotions, hence the fluttery 'butterflies in the stomach' we experience when we're nervous or the urge to use the loo when scared.

While intuition is often seen as a feminine trait and therefore softer and less trustworthy, gut instinct is seen as tougher and more masculine, something that you simply trust and act upon. And, of course, both intuition and gut instinct are driven by exactly same thing.

www.webmd.com/balance/features/power-of-female-intuition#1

When can you use it?

Intuition can be used in a wide variety of circumstances. Because it's often unconsciously accessed, it's something that we have to work on and develop, like a muscle, so that we can use it at will whenever we need to.

An example of when it can be particularly useful is when you move to a different team or organisation, where the culture or the 'way things are done' is different, and it's only by careful observation that you can intuit how best to operate. I recently worked with a female leader from Sweden, where there's far greater equality between genders and women are empowered to be stronger. While speaking about the challenges she faced with her UK team, she confessed to being unable to fully express herself and the need to rein in the 'strong leader' aspects of her personality in order to be seen as less of a threat by her team members and peers.

Intuition tells you when it's totally OK to shine your light – to be loud, direct the conversation and become the centre of attention – and when it's better to dial it down and let someone else shine. Sometimes this is about your intuition, letting you know whether or not it's 'safe' to speak up or you're in danger of being shut down. Sometimes it's a sense that you need to quieten down to let others take a turn in the limelight.

Back to Carley who I mentioned earlier in this chapter, and her three job choices. After exploring all the options fully, she decided to use the logical approach and applied specific evaluation criteria to them all, weighing the pros and cons of each. But you know what? She didn't like the 'winner'. How often has that happened to you when assessing a situation? The scientific approach is not always enough.

In Carley's case, I advised her to sleep on it so her subconscious could sift through the information and come up with an answer based on feeling, not logic. The following morning she emailed to say that she'd decided to go for the option where she would lead the new business pitch. And the good news is, they won. The scientific approach can only take you so far; you have to trust your intuition and inner wisdom to be sure.

"The intuitive mind is a sacred gift and the rational mind is a faithful servant. We have created a society that honours the servant and has forgotten the gift."

–ALBERT EINSTEIN

HOW CAN YOU DEVELOP IT?

Now that we understand more about what intuition is and where it comes from, let's explore how you can tune into your own intuitive powers. We're going to break this down into three sections:

- Developing your own intuition

- Using intuition to read people

- Intuitive decision-making

Developing your own intuition

Now that we understand that intuition is intelligence accessed via the subconscious, how can we create the right environment so that we can tap into it at will? Based on my research, there are three steps, which I call ACT©, that will help you to connect with your intuition and make the most of its power.

 Accept it's real

 Create the right environment

 Tune in

★ Step 1: Accept it's real

The first step is to accept that intuition is a legitimate source of information, just like Oprah Winfrey, Brené Brown, Steve Jobs and Richard Branson have. See it as your trusted advisor who can help you take your success to the next level. Notice the times when you're using your intuition and when you're not, and then compare the outcome of your intuitive versus evidence-based decisions (both of which have their place). Learn to hear that little voice which tells you that deep down you want to do something, even when your logical brain is saying 'no'.

★ Step 2: Create the right environment

Once you've accepted it's real, the next step is to create an environment that encourages your intuitive insight to come forth. We all like to think that we are fully aware of what we're capable of and what we need. But, like with any relationship, there are times when we are not in the best place emotionally and can become disconnected from ourselves. I find I lose confidence in my intuitive powers when I'm over-emotional, defensive, tired, outside my comfort zone, intent on impressing or pleasing someone, trying too hard or feeling alone. By contrast, I listen to my intuition when I'm relaxed, feeling safe, well-rested, supported and content within myself. Look after your emotional and physical health and your intuition will be more able to look after you.

As we've already established, our brains see connections and join the dots where we can't. But it needs the time and space to be able to do this. We've all had the experience of 'just knowing' the right answer when we wake up or just dropping off to sleep; we often have our best ideas at random times like in the shower or when walking the dog. Those moments of insight happen when we put our brainwaves in alpha frequency. This is when we slow down the brain a little; for instance, when daydreaming, during light meditation or, by contrast, during aerobic exercise[22].

Just like Carley's approach to writing down all her job options and then sleeping on it, the best approach is to weigh up all the information available, then give your brain a break. Although we may berate ourselves for taking our mind off the task at hand (just like a teacher scolds a child for daydreaming when they 'should be' concentrating), ironically, the very act of taking our mind off a complex challenge is often the best strategy for coming up with a solution. As we're giving our brain a break, it will continue to mull over the problem on our behalf, sifting through the mental filing cabinet and combining past experiences with new facts. Our intuitive brain becomes better at joining the dots if we provide it with the information it needs and then leave it alone to come up with the answer.

★ Step 3: Tune in

Having accepted that intuition is real and then created the right environment for it to thrive, the final step is to tune into the information it brings. You won't let your intuition flourish if you don't allow that inner voice to come out.

In order to do this, it's important to create opportunities to be with yourself, away from the frenetic world of your work or home life. Seek out solitude and quiet, create space in your life where you do nothing. When you're not sure what to do, or how to think, take yourself on a walk. Don't take your phone or anyone with you, just your brain. All kinds of stuff bubbles up when you're out in nature, so let it do its stuff.

Staring into space and letting your mind drift is how we let stuff surface and make those clever and sometimes surprising connections between fact and feeling. Mindfulness can be very powerful, as this technique stills our brain's churnings and enables us to see situations more clearly. Through meditation, we become more detached from our feelings and see things from a distance, enabling us to make a better judgement.

Another way to tune into our subconscious is through dreams and tapping into that feeling you get when you wake up and 'just know' something. Although dream imagery may seem random, it isn't at all. What's freshest in our conscious mind tends to show up in our dreams, like relationship angst or work stress. Many of the bizarre dream images we experience are just distortions of normal scenes, sounds and observations from the previous day. So if you're feeling overworked and repeatedly dream that your boss is a vampire, it could be your subconscious mind telling you that your current role is bleeding you dry and you need to move on!

The body can also be a powerful source of information, if we choose to listen to it. Our thoughts, emotions and bodily experiences are inextricably linked, which means that your mind and body are not separate entities but mutually influencing. When we get itchy feet we know that we need to move and take action. When we say someone's a pain in the neck, we can get an actual pain in the neck. Intuition comes through our bodies as well as our brains, and we need to learn to 'listen' to it.

EXERCISE 1: USING ACT TO DEVELOP YOUR INTUITION

One of the best ways to maximise your intuitive powers is to become more aware of when you could use them and how.

Identify a problem or challenge you're facing and decide that you're going to use ACT to overcome it. Start by writing the problem down. Then ACT:

1. **A**ccept it's real: start the day by telling yourself that you're going to use your subconscious mind to tackle the problem, as opposed to using a logical, rational approach.

2. **C**reate the environment: block out a 15-20 minute slot during your day where you set your intuitive mind to work on the problem through using the techniques above. Remember, this will not involve focusing on the problem itself, but leaving your mind free to wander.

3. **T**une in: as you become aware of your intuition at work, note down any insights or thoughts that come to you. Notice also which environments are most conducive to intuitive thought.

Finally, consider how you can make intuitive thinking part of your everyday life.

Using intuition to read other people

Now that we've established how to develop your intuition through ACT, let's explore how to use its power to understand people better.

Why is the ability to read people a valuable skill? If you've ever been in a similar situation to the woman at the beginning of this chapter, you'll know why it's important, particularly as a woman, to develop the ability to read signals sent out by others. But it's not just about keeping yourself safe. Examples of times you'll want to read people accurately include dating or meeting new people, agreeing to a deal, interviewing candidates or when you what to share something personal.

How will you know if you can trust that person or not? Who will you choose? Often, we'll get a feeling about people – whether positive or negative. Sometimes that feeling proves to be right, other times, the person we trusted or suspected turns out to be quite different from our first impression.

As we know, intuition is often perceived as a female trait, closely linked to emotional intelligence. Women tend to tune into their feelings and pick up on nuances in behaviour more acutely than men. For example, some of us can even detect when another woman is pregnant, without any outward clues.

Whether this heightened female ability is real or simply attributed more to women doesn't matter. What's important is that you use it to your advantage.

So how can we hone our 'spidey sense' about people?

"

USING YOUR INTUITION
TO 'READ' PEOPLE IS
NOT ABOUT JUMPING
TO CONCLUSIONS OR
MAKING ASSUMPTIONS.
GIVE PEOPLE THE
BENEFIT OF THE DOUBT
BUT MEANWHILE,
BE A DETECTIVE.

Asking questions

One of the quickest routes to sussing someone out is by asking lots of questions and *really* listening to the answers. Some people hold themselves back from asking too many questions for fear of being perceived as nosy. However, being genuinely curious about people and keeping an open mind about them and their intentions is an effective route to building rapport because they will often respond to your questioning with questions of their own about you and before long, you'll be connecting deeply with their level of thinking. By asking probing questions, you will also inform your intuition more profoundly; as a result, you'll know if they are someone you can trust, someone you need to with-hold judgement on or someone to steer clear of.

Using your intuition to 'read' people is not about jumping to conclusions or making assumptions. Give people the benefit of the doubt but meanwhile, be a detective – ascertain what they are about, as well as their underlying motivations.

You can find out so much by asking the most mundane ques-tions, especially if you put a finger on a nerve. Subtle 'tells' (also known as emotional leakage) can give the game away.

Getting behind the poker face

Although some people hide their emotions behind a 'poker face', you can get behind it by picking up on the subtle emotional messages we are all sending out all the time, sometimes without even realising it. Psychologist Dr Paul Ekman is an expert in micro-expressions. These are subtle facial expressions that occur within a fraction of a second and expose a person's true emotions. As there is no way to prevent them from occurring, learning how to detect

133

micro-expressions is invaluable for emotional intelligence and detecting deception. As these expressions often occur so rapidly, in half a second or less, they are more likely to be picked up via the subconscious rather than consciously, and so will directly inform your intuition.

So what can you read from someone's behaviour? What are their micro-expressions, facial expressions and body language telling you? Picking up on these subtle cues takes practice, but if someone's smile doesn't reach their eyes or if they say they're happy, but the subtle frown and drooping shoulders say otherwise, take note. They may look confident but if they're stroking their shoulder or twirling their hair, this may indicate insecurity.

Sometimes it's dangerous to equate body language to certain messages – not everyone who puts their hand over their mouth is lying. But when there's congruence between what someone's saying and doing, it's more likely that you can trust them. And when there isn't, you need to wonder why. Look for patterns of congruence and dissonance in your relationships. When we're in rapport, there's a natural mirroring of body language. But when someone does it deliberately – a well-known persuasive technique – it lights up the same part of the brain that activates when we step on dog poo. We need to listen when we feel something's 'off' and take note.

EXERCISE 2:
READING PEOPLE

Noticing the power of your intuition when reading people can be a game-changer. To make this part of your Power Up repertoire, I encourage you from now on, whenever you meet people, to adopt an attitude of curiosity as described above.

In your interactions with friends, family and people you meet out and about, decide to connect with them intuitively. Pay attention to how they express themselves, their facial expressions, body language and what it tells you about them.

The benefits of this will extend far beyond intuition and feed into the power sources of *Relationships*, *Magnetism* and *Assertiveness*, all of which we'll explore in more detail in the rest of this book.

Intuitive decision-making

How many decisions do you think you've made so far today? Just ordering a coffee is a minefield and deciding what to wear can sometimes be such a stressful experience that it throws you off track for the rest of the day!

Researchers at Cornell University estimate we make over 200 decisions each day on food alone. As your level of responsibility increases, so does the multitude of choices you have to make.

It's estimated that the average adult makes about 35,000 remotely conscious decisions each day. And each decision carries certain consequences with it that are both good and bad[23].

There are three interrelated issues that often get in the way of decision making, especially at work.

1. **The pressure of time** – a looming deadline or someone standing over you waiting for a decision.

2. **The complexity of the decision** – you're often operating in a VUCA environment (a term originally coined by the military which stands for Volatile, Uncertain, Complex and Ambiguous) where decisions are rarely black or white.

3. **The information available** – it can be difficult to gauge when you have enough information to make a decision: too little data and you could be missing a vital piece of insight, too much and you run the risk of overwhelm and analysis paralysis.

Tapping into your intuition will help you make decisions faster. Having a decisive nature and feeling confident that the decisions you make are the right ones will increase your power at work. People will rely on you to get things done and will find your clarity of thinking refreshing. We all hate working with a manager or leader who sits on the fence and can't make a decision without canvassing the opinion of five people, by which time it's too late to act anyway. Being decisive will also make you more effective in the rest of your life. Why waste a whole weekend deciding on which shade of grey to paint your hallway when you can make the decision in a split second if you need or want to?

So how can you use your intuitive powers to help you make better decisions, and are there times when intuition lets you down?

The psychological study of intuition may be traced back to the Swiss psychiatrist Carl Jung, who argued that people either take a "bottom-up" approach to life, in which data drives their decisions, or a more "top-down" approach where they let their own thoughts and feelings take command.

Emotional and rational decision-making are often seen as opposing forces. Daniel Kahneman describes them as two separate systems of thinking in his book, *Thinking Fast and Slow*, with the emotional and intuitive process happening first, followed by the slower and more analytical process of rational logic.

Instead of two separate systems, recent research by Antonio Damasio[24] suggests they are, in fact, closely linked, and that harnessing the emotional and intuitive aspects of a decision can lead to better outcomes, including quicker decisions, by making sure you act based upon the wisdom of past experiences, rather than just assessing the facts in hand.

EXERCISE 3:

INTUITIVE DECISION MAKING

To hone your intuitive decision-making power, I have devised the following four steps. Identify a decision on the horizon and apply them, reflecting on how intuitive thinking is powering your thought processes and actions:

Four steps to intuitive decision making:

1. Define your question
2. Source appropriate information
3. Seek input from others
4. Let your intuition do the rest

★ Step 1: Define your question

The first step to effective intuition-based decision making is defining the question you'd like answered. Ask a wishy-washy question like "What do I want?" and you'll get a wishy-washy answer. Our unconscious mind loves a challenge and will work on our behalf until it has found answers. Remember those situations when you've forgotten the name of a film or book, only for the answer to pop up in your mind a few hours later – that was your unconscious mind.

However, the unconscious mind only does what it's told. If we ask it, "Why do I find networking so awkward?", then it will search for all the reasons why you find networking awkward. Conversely, if you ask yourself, "What can I do to make networking events more enjoyable?" or "How can I go into networking events feeling more confident?" – your unconscious mind will go looking for answers and serve up some valuable insights for you. Of course, there are some decisions that are best made rationally, so make sure, when applying this approach, you ask a question that warrants an intuitive response!

When is intuition useful?	When is it not useful?
When there are multiple courses of action	When there is only one course of action
Dealing with an ambiguous situation	Following instructions or specific advice (for example from a trusted financial or legal representative)
Navigating multiple pathways	Crossing a busy road

★ Step 2: Source appropriate information

In the Knowledge chapter, we'll explore how you can access valuable information to enhance your power. For intuitive decision making, it's important to know when you have enough to make the right choice. As John Naisbitt, author of *Megatrends: Ten New Directions Transforming Our Lives*, put it: "Intuition becomes increasingly valuable in the new information society precisely because there is so much data." An excess of information can make clear thinking tricky and we can take it too far when it comes to sourcing information.

To put it simply, if you know, you know.

Instead of going into 'analysis paralysis' (which is often linked to a need for control and perfectionism) ask yourself, "Do I have sufficient information to make up my mind or will I miss out on vital facts if I stop now?" Nine times out of ten, your answer will be you have enough.

Another approach to applying the right amount of information for intuitive decisions is a heuristic technique. This is a practical, short-cut approach to problem-solving which isn't guaranteed to be perfect, logical, or rational, but is sufficient to reach an immediate goal. Examples include developing your own rules about what you share on social media so you don't spend hours deliberating over whether a particular photo will enhance or detract from your personal brand, having a rule-of-thumb estimate of the amount of time it takes you to perform various tasks so you can plan your time more efficiently, and making some educated assumptions about a new colleague by looking at their LinkedIn profile.

★ Step 3: Seek input

It's sometimes good, when making big decisions, to have a second opinion to 'sense check' your thinking. Whether you're changing jobs or launching a new venture, hearing someone say, "Yes, I was thinking that too," or "OK, but have you thought about this?" can make all the difference.

If you're more on the extroverted spectrum, you may find you do your best thinking by talking things out, so find a trusted friend to listen to you and build in sufficient time to do this. Although seeking others' opinions is valuable, you also need to create a gap to allow your inner wisdom to come forth, otherwise you won't be using your intuition, and instead, be basing your decision on the last thought that went through your head – or somebody else's.

★ Step 4: Let your intuition do the rest

Having defined your question, sourced appropriate information and sought input from others, your intuition should have all it needs to provide you with a decision. A final step to encourage your brain to serve you up with an answer is to ask yourself self-coaching questions (see examples in the box below). These are usually open-ended rather than questions that are answered by a fact or a simple yes/no. These can help to open up your thinking and refocus you from the problem to the solution.

Self-coaching questions

- What's the opportunity/challenge here?

- What does an ideal outcome look/sound/feel like?

- What's still unclear and how can I gain clarity?

- What else is relevant?

- What's stopping me?

- If I could do anything I wanted, what would I do?

- What would [insert your favourite film star/sports legend/author/performer] do?

- What will I think about this in a year's time?

- What's my next step?

- What would be my decision if I had to make it right now?

The best way to coach yourself is to find a quiet place where you won't be disturbed and are not under time pressure. Relax your mind, read through the questions in the box above – and others you can create which work for you – and let the answers emerge, jotting down your replies as they occur to you.

When intuition gets it wrong

It would be inappropriate to finish a chapter on the power of intuition without acknowledging that however valuable, it can sometimes get it wrong.

There are many reasons for this including not having access to all the information you need, being too emotionally attached, or making assumptions based on past experiences that may not be relevant to the situation you're facing now.

For example, women can feel threatened by powerful women, viewing them with envy and mistrust. Your fear, disguised as intuition, is telling you that they are a threat and so you consciously or subconsciously, actively or passively, avoid or undermine them. Recognise this feeling. Know where it's coming from your own fear and lack of self-belief. Say thank you to it but move on. Don't resent powerful women. In fact, ask yourself what you can learn from them and how you can befriend them. Remember: we are far stronger together.

INTUITION CONCLUSION

Ultimately, to tune into your intuitive instincts you need to do whatever works for you. Harnessing this superpower is about keeping a cool head, giving yourself the time, increasing your self-awareness about your emotional triggers, as well as tapping into the other powers in this book.

As Oprah often tells her friends: "When you don't know what to do, do nothing. Get quiet so you can hear the still, small voice – your inner GPS guiding you to true North."

IN SUMMARY

★ Intuition is the ability to trust your innate wisdom and gut instinct, giving you the freedom and impetus to act.

★ Accessing the power of intuition leads to greater emotional intelligence, the ability to quickly 'read' situations and people, a willingness to trust your own judgement and the confidence to make decisions without overthinking.

★ Intuition has nothing to do with divine intervention or 'trusting the universe' and everything to do with tapping into your conscious, lived experiences and the power of your subconscious mind.

★ If you want to develop your intuition use ACT©:

  ▪ A = Accept it's real: see intuition as your trusted advisor who can help you take your success to the next level.

  ▪ C = Create the right environment: give your intuitive brain the time and space to work on your behalf, create opportunities for daydreaming and engage in meditation.

  ▪ T = Tune in to its power: allow intuitive thoughts to surface and listen to the messages being transmitted to you from your subconscious.

★ Emotional and rational decision-making are often seen as opposing forces. However, the latest research suggests that they are, in fact, closely linked and that harnessing both can lead to better outcomes by accessing past experiences, as well as assessing the facts.

Chapter 5

KNOWLEDGE CHAPTER

"A wise warrior is better than a strong one, and a man of knowledge than one of strength."

—PROVERBS 24:5

THE POWER OF KNOWLEDGE

K nowledge and education are a pretty reliable route to power. At the time of writing, an incredible 20 UK Prime Ministers went to Eton and three-quarters of them went to either Oxford or Cambridge. Conversely, a lack of 'recognised' knowledge is a huge barrier to confidence. I know many people with a massive chip on their shoulder because they haven't got society's accepted badge of intelligence, a university degree, or didn't go to the right school. Society has had a very narrow view of what intelligence should be and how knowledge in all its forms can be turned into power.

Knowledge in action

I clearly remember dumbing down my intelligence at school. In a mixed comprehensive, it just wasn't cool to put your hand up with the answer, get high grades or win awards. Education is different today, but I still notice that the stock answer to a question for my teenage daughters and their friends is, "I don't know." No one wants to be branded the clever one, the goodie two-shoes, even though 'the geeks', on the surface at least, are proud to be branded that way.

Knowledge, and the associated intelligence that may come with it, can form just as powerful a barrier between people as class. I have deliberately camouflaged my knowledge, simplified my phraseology, not corrected people and stopped myself from sharing facts or opinions when I've known I'm the most 'educated' person in the room. This is for fear of making other people feel stupid or them thinking that I'm superior, or worse, that I think I'm superior. Equally, I've stayed quiet during political discussions, wishing that I'd paid more attention during *Question Time*!

Many women have a fear that they are not clever enough and the impact can be very damaging. In spite of their skills and talents, they're scared of offering an opinion. Not wanting to take up too much airtime, get called out for being wrong, or forgetting crucial details halfway through recounting something, they'll just stay schtum.

I have coached many people whose low self-esteem is based on a belief that they're not clever. Perhaps a teacher told them that once and it stuck. I remember being made to feel like a total idiot for not remembering how many weeks there were in a year. I have a complete mental block when it comes to maths, was in the lowest stream and have to be very careful not to pass that 'can't do' mindset onto my daughters.

How does Knowledge relate to Power Up?

We've all had that disempowering feeling when someone asks you a question and you know how you want to answer it, but you don't quite have access to the information that will help you to state your case.

Knowledge is a powerful weapon. It's the evidence that people use to rate you and the passport to expressing a valid opinion.

Knowledge – broadly speaking the accumulation and application of facts and skills – provides a power boost to the other components of the Power Up Model©, a practical complement to the wisdom that comes through your *Intuition*. Understanding and valuing your unique knowledge will enable you to remain *Resilient* in the face of challenge, provide common ground with which to strengthen your *Relationships* and enable you to become more *Assertive* through the confident articulation of your opinions and desires.

"

AS WELL AS INCREASING YOUR CREDIBILITY, KNOWLEDGE OPENS UP YOUR MIND, GIVING YOU A WIDER PERSPECTIVE, AND STOPS YOU FROM BEING ONE-TRACK OR SMALL-MINDED.

Why do we need it?

The phrase 'knowledge is power', commonly attributed to philosopher, Sir Frances Bacon, is well known and goes way beyond any letters after your name.

- Knowing your stuff gives you an inner certainty that whatever the world throws at you, you will have the ammunition to strike back.

- Making your point in a discussion and knowing that if you hadn't spoken, the group would have been less well informed is hugely empowering.

- Knowing that you've articulated your opinion in an engaging way can give you a massive confidence boost.

- Winning an award or landing the next plumb role because of your intellectual prowess can give you a well-deserved sense of pride, as well as the knowledge that in achieving your goals, you've inspired others.

- Using your knowledge and holding your own when someone disagrees with or interrupts you or talks to you in a patronising way is one of the best feelings in the world.

Research conducted by Dr Robert B. Cialdini found that people perceived to be knowledgeable have greater authority, prestige and influence than those who don't. In his book, *Influence, the Psychology of Persuasion*, he noted that we respond differently to people who are a recognised authority on a subject. If you have letters after your name, have published papers, authored a book or been invited to speak on stage, your status will naturally elevate.

As well as increasing your credibility, knowledge opens up your mind, giving you a wider perspective and stops you from being one-track or small-minded.

Knowledge gives you more choices: when faced with a decision, the more evidence you have to weigh up, the more you know about the pros and cons, the more likely you are to make the right one and stick by it.

Having knowledge also makes it easier to make connections with people: if your mind is restricted to a limited pool of thinking, you will only feel truly comfortable with a small group. Whereas the greater your breadth of knowledge, the wider your network. Knowledge gives you a seat at the table and the right to join a conversation and express your opinions.

What gets in the way?

Unfortunately, acquiring knowledge and letting it be appreciated by others can be challenging. Although wearing glasses might make you look clever, the antiquated phrase 'men don't make passes at girls who wear glasses' still rings true for some. Too many times, I've seen intelligent women morph into blinking does when faced with a thrusting, straight-talking man. Bright, sparky, capable women will turn to their male companion or husband to make a decision or answer on their behalf. Why is this?

1. **Historically, brighter women have a harder time.** Historically, men have been relied upon to weigh up the information at hand and make decisions and women have been called upon to be the deferential ones who say what they feel rather than what they think. When we think of the four March sisters in Louisa May Alcott's *Little Women,* Meg is the pretty subservient one and her sister Jo the intelligent opinionated one who ultimately finds it harder to get on in life and find a husband. The one with the most knowledge is seen as the least 'womanly'.

   Research by Dr Maria do Mar Pereira from the University of Warwick's Department of Sociology indicates this is unfortunately still an issue, 150 years on. In the course of her research, she found that girls feel they must downplay their own abilities, pretending to be less intelligent, and that boys, by the age of 14 had acquired the belief that girls of their own age should be less intelligent.

   "There are very strong pressures in society that dictate what is a proper man and a proper woman," argues Dr Pereira. 'Young people try to adapt their behaviour according to these pressures to fit into society. One of the pressures is that young men must be more dominant – cleverer, stronger, taller, funnier – than young women, and that being in a relationship with a more intelligent woman will undermine their masculinity.'[25]

2. **Lack of clever female role models.** There's also a lack of visible female role models who exemplify knowledge in public life. In a recent video from Microsoft in which schoolgirls were asked to name famous inven-

tors, they could cite plenty of male ones, but drew a blank with female inventors[26]. They were then amazed by a long list of female inventors, like Sarah Mather, who made the underwater telescope, and Ada Lovelace, responsible for the first computer algorithm. So while there are plenty of female models, actresses and Instagram influencers for girls to look up to, it's clear that we don't have enough visible female role models who are famous for their knowledge. And that makes it harder for girls to aim high because if you can't see it, it's so much harder to be it.

3. **Lack of belief that we can improve our abilities.** It doesn't help that conditioning gets in the way. Research by Carol S. Dweck, author of *Mindset,* and Lewis and Virginia Eaton, Professor of Psychology at Stanford University, has shown that girls are brought up to believe their abilities are innate and unchangeable, while boys believe that they can develop their ability through effort and practice. This means that when bright girls are given something tricky to learn, they give up quickly, whereas bright boys see it as a challenge and feel energised by it, trying harder.[27]

This plays out in adulthood. A 2018 study by Arizona State University School of Life Sciences found that men working in STEM subject areas overestimate their own intelligence and credentials and underestimate the abilities of female colleagues, and that as a result, women themselves doubt their abilities — even when hard evidence such as grades say otherwise.[28]

4. **Undermining ourselves.** Women can also unwittingly undermine their own intelligence and knowledge. Although they may be the most knowledgeable person in the room, they may be perceived as the opposite because of behaviour which could be seen as dumb. Dumb in this context can mean not practically-minded, lacking in common sense, not being street-wise or savvy, being naïve or absent-minded, or even just blonde. None of these things indicates a lack of intelligence or knowledge, but society can draw these lazy conclusions, particularly when they are associated with women, unless we provide evidence otherwise.

We may, of course, play down our intelligence because that's what we've been brought up to do. If we're told as children that "no one likes a know-all," our need to be liked can take precedence over our need to be right. And what of using humour and jolly japery to make ourselves likeable? Undermining our knowledge and being self-deprecating is an all too common practice. We get everyone to laugh because we're more comfortable with that than showing our intelligence.

And what a waste! Think of all that hidden knowledge, latent intelligence and untapped potential. Knowledge is only valuable if you have the confidence to use it.

Ditsy and bubbly

Recently, I was coaching someone, let's call her Rose, who had just joined a company. Before leaving her old one, she asked for feedback. Although the majority of it was extremely positive, there was a common theme running through it. Colleagues felt that the initial impression she gave – of being a little ditsy and bubbly – was different from how they saw her after having worked with her for a while. She had a depth that she initially kept hidden. Rose found this hurtful – she is naturally a fun, positive person and didn't want to lose her authenticity in the workplace. However, she realised that being fully herself at work was sometimes undermining her intelligence, particularly with drier, more serious colleagues who didn't respond well to what they saw as an overly-bright communication style.

Rose's challenge is a common one. How can we be ourselves AND be knowledgeable and feel comfortable with that combination?

Let's start by breaking down the 'ditsy' label... Ditsy is an exclusively female term which often conveys a lack of intelligence, with the dictionary definition being 'flighty and easily confused; mildly or harmlessly eccentric'. Women can be branded as ditsy either because they genuinely do display these characteristics or they're mistakenly labelled as such due to a range of behaviours (that are sometimes linked to a drive to be liked) which together lead people to make that conclusion. Maybe you can identify with some of the following?

- You don't want to bulldoze people when you first meet them, so you start out soft and friendly in order to win them over.

- You deliberately downplay your intelligence because you don't want to draw attention to yourself or be seen to be showing off.

- You do the self-deprecating thing: 'Oh, silly me! I'm new here, no idea what's going on!' in order to appear unthreatening.

- You want to build rapport so you start out by fishing for easy, lightweight things in common, leaving people unaware that you are capable of greater depth.

- Your accent may play a part, sadly. Research shows that different accents can convey intelligence or not[29]. If you've got a twangy nasal accent you're going to have to fight much harder to be seen as intelligent.

If these pieces of 'evidence' are compounded with cues that don't project intelligence – i.e. quirky, kooky or overly glamorous/revealing clothing, soft hair, blondeness, a babyish voice, or appearing very young, the conclusion drawn could be that you're ditsy or not knowledgeable. Unfortunately, if you're perceived as ditsy you may then 'act into' that expectation – it becomes part of your brand – which means that you're then perceived as 'nice' but not 'knowledgeable'.

Although being known as ditsy or bubbly may bring you attention, having that persona means you compromise your power – people will underestimate your value, they will give you less airtime and won't take you as seriously. Any points you make will be ignored only to be fervently agreed with when made by someone else more powerful.

And the sad thing is that some people only need to detect one or two of the traits listed above to then paint you with the ditsy and bubbly brush. An example of this was Claire, a warm and outgoing surveyor I met recently at a female empowerment event I chaired, whose first comment was

"I'm a hugger" as she embraced everyone she met. I really warmed to Claire, as she put everyone at ease and had a hugely engaging communication style, even though she admitted she'd found being on stage quite nerve-wracking. However, it was clear that there were times where her bubbly nature, combined with society's biases around her profession, could undermine her authority. She spoke about the times, particularly at the start of her career, when she would arrive at clients' houses ready to survey their house, only to be greeted with the question, "When's he arriving?" because the client couldn't accept that she was the professional and was expecting a male colleague to arrive. My concern was that it wasn't just the clients' biases which were standing in her way, but her overly bubbly style which made her appear less credible and authoritative than her male colleague.

So how can you overcome the ditsy stereotype?

In the *Assertiveness* chapter, we'll focus on how to express yourself eloquently and powerfully. For now, let's focus on what you can do to avoid the ditsy label.

Firstly, we need to avoid sounding dumb, in our own heads and in the heads of our audience. We need to ensure that our knowledge is respected and heard. As Michelle Obama has said: "In every room of power I've sat in, I've had to learn that my voice has value or else what's the point of me being in the room." And: "A lot of times what you find is, when you sit and listen in a classroom or a boardroom or an office, you'll hear men talk and talk and talk. And if you listen, many of them aren't saying anything. And what you realize is they're not really saying anything more important than what's going on in your head, then you develop the courage to put what you're thinking on the table right with them."

Secondly, we need to overcome our self-doubts. Sadly, just being female can work against us. While talking about girls' education in general, Michelle Obama told a US Glamour panel for Let Girls Learn: "Sometimes we have to be better. Sometimes we have to work harder. Sometimes we have to come back from those negative thoughts in our heads about who we are and how we look and how people feel about us. So many of us are haunted by the voices of other people who tell us what we can't do, and that's something you have to work on every single day. Every woman you know is working on this. I am still working on it."

Sian Richardson is sometimes described as a bubbly blonde. An actor who specialises in helping business people maximise their personal presence, she has learnt how to transcend people's preconceptions and be her authentic self: "I often got told when I was younger not to wear pink or wear heels, both of which I wear (pink suits a paler complexion and I'm 5 foot 2 inches, so heels help me feel taller and more in control). I really believe this came from people who were wanting to help me be taken more seriously, but I didn't change what I wore and never have. I just learnt how to wear them well!" Speaking about her natural communication style, she adds, "People mirror what they see and being with people who exude confidence and are upbeat and positive is difficult to ignore. We naturally feel good about ourselves when with people like this. I've had to learn to like being me. If I feel self-conscious others will doubt me. You just have to be careful you don't 'overplay' who you are. I know I get enthusiastic and this can sometimes mean I rush and speak at speed. I have learnt to slow down."

Lisa Conway Hughes is a Chartered Financial Advisor, member of MENSA and a published author who just happens to have blonde hair. In her opinion, the best way to deal with people's negative perceptions is to rise above it: "In some ways, if people start with low expectations of you, I find that when you really impress them, it has an even bigger impact".

WHAT IS KNOWLEDGE?

Knowledge is defined as an accumulation of facts, information and skills acquired through experience or education; the theoretical or practical understanding of a subject. Although the saying states that 'knowledge is power', what makes it powerful is its application. It's not enough to learn new facts, what's valuable is how you join those facts together and interpret them to make a relevant, cohesive and valuable whole. Think of a Monet painting. Close up it's just a load of dots; from a distance, it's a beautiful picture.

According to Howard Gardner, Professor of Education at Harvard University, we have nine different types of intelligence, present in differing amounts, which act as the foundation of our knowledge[30]. These include:

- **Verbal-linguistic**: well-developed linguistic skills and sensitivity to words

- **Logical-mathematical**: ability to think numerically and capacity to discern numerical patterns

- **Spatial-visual**: capacity to think in images

- **Bodily-kinaesthetic**: ability to handle objects skilfully

- **Musical**: ability to appreciate rhythm, pitch and timbre

- **Interpersonal:** capacity to detect and respond to the moods and motivations of others

- **Intrapersonal**: capacity to be self-aware and in tune with our inner feelings, beliefs and thinking processes

- **Naturalist:** ability to recognise objects in nature

- **Existential**: capacity to handle deep questions about human existence.

If you're looking to develop your knowledge in a particular field, it is helpful to know which of the intelligences from the list above you are strongest in, as this will help you to focus your time and attention on related subjects that are most likely to interest you. You will also have a better understanding of which roles you should pursue at work or which projects you are best suited to. For example, if you're someone with a high logical-mathematical intelligence you will be most at home in an analytical role.

Where does knowledge come from?

Knowledge can come from multiple sources, including academia, on the job training and personal study, but what's even more valuable is your own unique knowledge bank, amassed through the acquisition of information and filtered through your life's experience, which results in your own unique interpretation.

Although the acquisition of knowledge in whatever form could take you anywhere, society unfortunately still has a very narrow perception of what intelligence is. We might judge someone who can't spell as unintelligent when they may be dyslexic but have so many more gifts. People with learning disabilities will often find they're dismissed as unintelligent.

In my experience of working with people from a variety of educational backgrounds, I've found that even though academic qualifications will take you a certain way, the knowledge you gain from life experience is infinitely more valuable and transferable.

Examples of successful women in the public eye who didn't go to university aren't exactly plentiful, but here are a few: *Vogue* editor-in-chief Anna Wintour, who didn't finish secondary school. Oprah Winfrey, who got a job reading the news on-air while enrolled in a drama class in her last year at high school. Ellen DeGeneres, who dropped out of university after one term and eventually found her way into comedy. Baroness Karren Brady, who got four A-levels but made a conscious decision not to go to university, wanting to get out in the world and make her mark.

However, things are changing, and as part of my research, I've spoken with a number of extremely successful women who rejected the typical school-college-uni route because they were hungry to begin a career and wanted the power and independence of a regular salary. What I noticed was that, even though some of them had gone down the corporate route, the majority of them had ended up forging their own, entrepreneurial path and so I wondered whether choosing independence from an early age led to increased bravery and a willingness to rely on knowledge picked up through experience rather than in the classroom.

CASE STUDY

Sarah Matthew is a senior advisor and mentor to business leaders and one of the most inspirational and knowledgeable women I know. Sarah left school at 18 to pursue a career in marketing and went on to found one of the most admired communications consultancies in its field, become a C-Suite Executive of a global board and advise some of the biggest companies in the world on building and maintaining their reputations.

Speaking about her choices, Sarah said: "Career advice at school had directed me to study law, but after experiencing a taster session at my intended university, I knew it wasn't for me. Not any of it – the subject or continuing to be a student. I was impatient to get out into the world and what I really wanted to learn about was marketing, so on seeing a newspaper advertisement for a role with Johnson & Johnson, which I actually wasn't qualified for, I applied and must have said something interesting enough to spark their curiosity. On attending the interview, I was amazed to be offered a job on the spot and the company even encouraged and supported me to complete my higher education through day release to college across the next five years. From there, I went on to do all sorts of roles that seemingly on paper, I didn't have the qualifications to do. My advice to others would be to never let that be a reason to stop you and most importantly, always trust your instincts and follow your own path."

HOW CAN YOU DEVELOP IT?

Having explored what knowledge is in its many forms, let's examine how you can further develop and articulate it so that you can use it to power yourself forward, at work and in life in general. We're going to do this in five steps:

1. Defining your niche

2. Profiling your knowledge

3. Honing your knowledge bank

4. Expressing yourself with confidence

5. Handling challenges

1. Defining your niche

One of the quickest routes to powering up your potential is creating your own niche. Although it can be tempting to want to know a lot about many things, this will take an extremely long time and could simply position you as a Jill of All Trades, but Mistress of None.

Gary Keller, author of *The One Thing: The Surprisingly Simple Truth Behind Extraordinary Results,* says, "The key to success is figuring out your ONE most important thing in your business/ career/life over the long-run. Think of this as your 'someday' goal. Once you've figured that out, you need to identify how many dominoes you need to line up – and then knock down – in order to achieve it." He advises identifying what is most important to you and then giving it your undivided attention.

BECOMING A SUBJECT MATTER EXPERT IMMEDIATELY ELEVATES YOUR AUTHORITY.

"What's the one thing you can do such that by doing it every-thing else will be easier or unnecessary?"

Twelve years ago, I set up my business with the aim of deliv-ering world-class leadership development programmes. Although we were successful, the business only came into its own when I decided to ditch the generic content and design a unique programme focusing purely on Gravitas. It was only when I had identified my 'one thing' that the business really took off and my profile as a thought-leader began to grow.

Becoming a subject matter expert immediately elevates your authority, as it differentiates you and increases your visibility, thereby enhancing your worth and status.

Daniel Priestley, the international speaker and author of *Become a Key Person of Influence,* says to be truly successful we need to claim a niche – or even better, a micro-niche, and become known as the go-to person of influence in that field. "Now is the time to claim your micro-niche. It's time to say, 'I won't try to be all things to all people. This is exactly what I do and this is my unique take on things.'"

A great example is Mary Portas, who is claimed to be one of the UK's foremost authorities on retail and brand communi-cation. Mary's career trajectory started with a Saturday job at Boots, after which she created window displays at Harrods, before joining Topshop as display manager. She then became creative director of Harvey Nichols, before launching a suc-cessful creative communications agency and now regularly travels around the world advising on retail strategy. Her 'one thing' throughout has been understanding retail and brand communication. She has created a reputation as a fearless, no-nonsense thought-leader and everything she has done has enhanced her reputation as an expert in that field.

A key consideration when identifying your niche is whether it fires you up or not. This goes back to your wider goals around why you want to Power Up in the first place. Whether it's because you want to be known as the number one authority in your field, you're ready for the next promotion or you simply want to communicate your views with credibility and impact, acquiring knowledge will be far more enjoyable if it's in an area that you love.

Sometimes we forget why we do what we do, we lose our mojo and when the going gets tough, we think about throwing in the towel. This happens to all of us, but it will happen far less if we've chosen a field that we're passionate about and we keep that fire alive by stoking the flames through acquiring more knowledge.

EXERCISE 1:
DEFINING YOUR NICHE

If you want to define your niche, the first step is to identify which aspects of your role you find most interesting and
what you're best at:

- Maybe you want to be the only 'go-to' person in your
  organisation who understands a particular system or
  tool.

- Perhaps you want to become a subject matter expert
  in a particular field.

- If you run your own business, perhaps there's a gap
  in the market for your unique skillset.

- If you're new to a role or organisation, and there are
  a number of people at the same level as you, what
  can you do to deepen your knowledge and stand out
  from the crowd?

Consider too what might be your 'one thing', as defined by
Gary Keller. What do you enjoy most about your role? How
does your role relate to your overall purpose? As part of this
process, you might like to revisit the Power Up goals you
defined in Chapter 1.

2. Profiling your knowledge

Having identified the niche that you'd like to call your own, the next step is to profile the knowledge that you currently have that will power you towards your goals. As you're reading this book, I'm making the assumption that you have amassed a considerable amount of knowledge. If you've been working in your field for years, it's likely that you know far more than the people around you – and probably far more than you realise! You may take that knowledge for granted because you haven't noticed yourself learning it: you've just assimilated it and you're now an unconscious expert.

To find out what you know – and what is of significance to other people – start by taking stock of what you've got. If you work in an organisation that conducts appraisals, take a look at your latest feedback. If you haven't received any for a while, ask five people, both in work and outside, to provide you with specific pointers on your strengths and capabilities.

Another useful tactic is to get someone to record an interview with you talking about what you do. Transcribe it, and then pick out the key themes and your thoughts on them – you'll be surprised at how eloquent you sound and all the knowledge that you possess.

The next step is to assess, as objectively as you can, the knowledge you possess and where there are gaps. This is a valuable exercise at any point of your career, but particularly useful if you're considering a career change or returning to work after a break. Taking stock of your strengths is a great way to offset concerns around technological and industry advances that may have occurred while you were away.

You will also gain confidence through acknowledging that although there will have been some technical changes, fundamentally your knowledge and experience are still valuable in your workplace, however much it's evolved.

EXERCISE 2: PROFILING YOUR KNOWLEDGE

A great tool for assessing your knowledge is the **SWOT**, a classic business planning tool that profiles your Strengths and Weaknesses (which are about you), as well as the Opportunities and Threats (related to the environment you work in).

To create your own knowledge SWOT, you can use the guiding questions below.

Strengths:
internal traits that propel you forward (S)

In which areas of your role are you particularly knowledgeable? Consider subject matter expertise, skills, personal qualities.

In which areas are you confident?

In which areas of your role do you consistently receive positive feedback?

What do you consider to be your greatest strengths?

In which areas is your knowledge different from that held by others?

Opportunities:
external factors that could support you (O)

What changes are occurring in your industry and how can you take advantage of them?

Is there an unmet need in your company/marketplace that you could fulfil with your unique knowledge?

What opportunities are there for you to deepen your knowledge base?

How can your professional network support you in achieving your goals?

<u>W</u>eaknesses:
internal traits that hold you back

In which areas of your role do you lack knowledge? Consider subject matter, skills, personal qualities.

In which areas do you lack confidence?

In which areas of your job do you consistently receive negative feedback?

What do you consider to be your greatest weakness?

In which areas do you have the same or similar knowledge as others?

<u>T</u>hreats:
external factors that could hinder you

What obstacles do you currently face at work which relate to your lack of knowledge?

Is your role, function, department or company changing in a way that doesn't match your knowledge or skill set?

Are technological changes threatening your position?

Are any colleagues competing with you for work or roles?

Knowledge buckets

In addition to the SWOT, it can be helpful to think about your knowledge more broadly. As we've established, knowledge comes in different forms and it's important to value them all. To enable you to do this, I've identified six work-related 'knowledge buckets', as illustrated below.

As you think about your past, present and future career, mark up a line on each bucket to show how full they are, giving yourself a score of 1 to 5 with 1=low and 5=high for each. You can use the description of each bucket below to guide you.

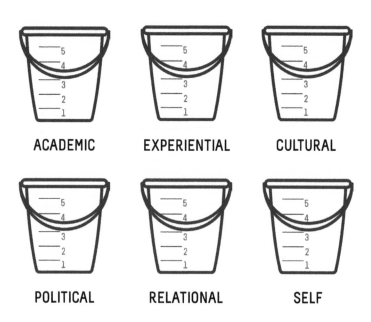

ACADEMIC   EXPERIENTIAL   CULTURAL

POLITICAL   RELATIONAL   SELF

- **Academic:** the qualifications, courses and CPD (Continuing Professional Development) points that have earnt you your position and got you to where you are today.

- **Experiential:** the amount of time you've spent 'on the job' which leads you to feel confident about what you do and may earn you a promotion to more senior positions.

- **Cultural:** your understanding of and involvement in the vision, mission and values which drive your organisation – also known as 'how we do things around here'.

- **Political:** your ability to read and navigate your organisation; your understanding of the systems and relationships within your organisation. People tend to think 'political' is a dirty word but, in fact, knowing how to play organisational politics is a very powerful skill to have.

- **Relational:** what you know about the people you work with/for: what's important to them, what they need, how they like to be communicated with, what keeps them up at night. Although the assumption may be that the most powerful person in an organisation is the MD because of the knowledge that is required to get there, the person with the most power is often the PA/receptionist because they have the most touchpoints with, and knowledge of, the greatest number of people.

- **Self:** we can't ignore self-knowledge in all of this – a crucial ingredient in the quest for power. Self-awareness, emotional intelligence and intuition (as discussed in the previous chapter) have to be used in combination with knowledge for you to be truly effective. As Lao Tzu said: "Knowing others is intelligence, knowing yourself is true wisdom. Mastering others is strength. Mastering yourself is true power."

Assessing your knowledge level against each of these criteria so that you know where you're excelling, competing or struggling compared to others is a valuable exercise because it helps you to acknowledge where you're powerful and where you're weak – and work out what you're going to do about it.

Having marked up your knowledge levels against each bucket, make a note of where there are gaps (or leaks!) and what you might do to fill them – there's more on this in the next section.

"

ALTHOUGH KNOWLEDGE IS INFINITE, YOU ONLY NEED TO KNOW SLIGHTLY MORE THAN THE PEOPLE AROUND YOU TO HAVE AN EDGE.

3. Honing your knowledge bank

Once you've defined your niche and profiled your knowledge levels, you'll be in a position to build out from your strengths and address the gaps in your knowledge which might hold you back. True expertise is attained through many years in a chosen field. In his book *The Outliers*, Malcolm Gladwell famously quotes a study by Anders Ericsson which estimates that it takes 10,000 hours to reach a level of greatness.

Although knowledge is infinite, you only need to know slightly more than the people around you to have an edge and get your voice heard, which can be particularly encouraging if you're feeling a touch of imposter syndrome or just starting out in your chosen field.

EXERCISE 3:
HONING YOUR KNOWLEDGE BANK

To hone your knowledge, start by identifying how you best acquire it, whether that's reading, trying out new skills or discussing new concepts so that you know which activities will accelerate your knowledge acquisition.

Now take a look at the recommendations below, which I've created to help you deepen your knowledge in your chosen field. Make a note of which actions you plan to take over the next six to twelve months to Power Up your knowledge in that area.

- **Training and development**: identify which skills-based courses, leadership/management development programmes, CPD points and qualifications you need to enhance your knowledge. Request any relevant on-the-job coaching and mentoring that's available and be specific about the support you'd like from your manager.

179

■ **Personal study:** create a regular diet of news and information: books, magazines, special interest journals, blogs, vlogs, podcasts and create a daily ritual where you scan the news for relevant developments in your field.

■ **Create a system for gathering and categorising information:** a useful example is PEST, which stands for Political or Psychological, Environmental, Scientific or Systems and Technical knowledge. For example, if you are preparing for a job interview, you could research how recent political changes have affected the company, observed the working environment to understand how you'd fit in; you might investigate which systems they use and which technical skills you will be required to demonstrate in the role.

■ **Spend time with people who challenge you:** as the saying goes, if you're the most knowledgeable person in the room you're in the wrong room. To accelerate your potential, seek out special interest groups, both within your organisation and externally, which focus on your target area and challenge yourself to hone your unique point of view. Identify thought-leaders you admire and immerse yourself in their material: podcasts, webinars, books, interviews and TED Talks – and consider what you would say (or will say!) if you were in their place.

■ **Build your mental filing system:** as you acquire all this new knowledge, it's helpful to create a system to help you organise your thinking and build memory. The famous London black cab drivers get tested on 'The Knowledge' which is a mix of memory and mapping. For information to become truly 'sticky', it needs to move from your short-term to your long-term memory. To aid this process, here are some techniques:

- Decide to become fascinated in what you're learning. If this is your niche, that shouldn't be too difficult, but if you're finding a particular subject challenging, think about how you can relate to it personally, or even what aspects you find funny/touching/exciting.

- Create a Mind Map. Popularised by the author of *How to Mindmap,* Tony Buzan, these capture the 'shape' of a subject, the relative importance of individual points and how facts link to one another. As opposed to the traditional list, a map can hold a large amount of information on one page, making it easier to review and for our minds to recall. An alternative is the memory tree, which shows the big branches first, then the leaves. Both these techniques enable us to 'chunk down' large pieces of information into smaller sections which can be more easily remembered and recalled.

- Another effective technique is creating mnemonics and acronyms. For example, in my Gravitas programmes, I talk about my OPRAHS© technique, which stands for Objective, People, Role, Attitude, Hear and Say, which is a proven, highly effective technique for planning for meetings. This is explored fully in the *Magnetism* chapter.

While you may need to put the hours in to become a world-renowned expert, it is possible to be seen as a source of knowledge after a relatively short space of time if you have a perspective that's valued by others. This is import-ant because some knowledge has a sell-by date – what you know now about technology, for example, will be obsolete in ten years' time and many of the jobs our children will be doing don't even exist yet. Even those at the top of their pro-fession need to keep up with the latest advances to maintain their position.

While we should always keep learning, it's important to acknowledge when you have sufficient knowledge and that knowledge is relative – you may be the most junior person in a meeting, but if you are the only person who has access to knowledge that is required by the group, you will be the most powerful person there. In these cases, it's particularly important to share it!

4. Expressing yourself with confidence

Once you've identified how your knowledge will bring you power, it's crucial to demonstrate it confidently. So how can we get comfortable expressing what we know and overcome the pressure to hide our light under a bushel? We have a brain and should feel comfortable using it.

Although men have traditionally used knowledge, evidence and information to express their opinions, women tend to use emotion and feelings. This obviously doesn't need to be the case, and the most powerful people are the ones who use both, in turn, to influence and persuade. In the film *The Iron Lady*, after being asked by a doctor how she feels, Margaret Thatcher says, "Don't ask me what I feel, ask me what I think."

Love or loathe the Iron Lady, she certainly broke the mould for women demanding to be taken seriously for their intellect.

Expressing Your Knowledge: The 4 'I's

To help you hone your own, unique perspective – drawing on both your intellect and emotions – I've developed the 4 'I's method. This is a four-step process which takes you from amassing to synthesizing to revealing your thoughts. We will go through these steps one by one.

- Inquire
- Inform
- Insights
- Illustrate

★ Step 1: Inquire

The first step to confidently expressing your knowledge is developing a forensic inquisitiveness about your chosen topic. This will enable you to amass relevant information and give you an edge. Rather than being inquisitive about everything, start by identifying what you want to be inquisitive about and why – what is the purpose you'd like to fulfil through expressing your knowledge? We all know how irritating it is when someone pontificates for hours, meandering around a subject without any apparent destination point. So write down the problem that you'd like to overcome and the information you'd like to find out. To avoid regurgitating everyone else's views, steer clear of social media (which is often an echo chamber where everyone sounds the same). Seek out new people and opinions instead, go where no one in your niche goes and learn how to ask powerful questions that other people don't ask.

Journalist Marina Gask, whose job is to create articles that bring a fresh perspective, advises: "Be prepared to ask the 'dumb' questions – as though you knew nothing whatsoever about the subject. This is how the truth comes out."

Business speaker and author of *Watertight Marketing*, Bryony Thomas agrees: "Always ask the 'elephant in the room' questions; for example, if jargon is being used that you don't fully understand, or if a topic that should be on the agenda doesn't seem to be." Bryony's nickname in her corporate role was The Elephant Spotter and AOB became 'And, Over to Bryony' because, as she puts it: "Over the years, I've come to a place of confidence in my own intelligence that not knowing something doesn't scare me. I've found that simply saying, 'I think I understand xyz acronym' to mean 'what you understand by it, but can you please clarify for me to make sure I'm not getting the wrong end of the stick,' or at the end of a meeting, using the AOB (Any Other Business) to bring up the current tension in the office rumour mill has served me well."

Another route to hone your Inquisitiveness and avoid simply taking facts at face value is to ask the five whys, which were originally developed by Sakichi Toyoda and extensively used by Toyota Motor Corporation. Here's how the five whys work:

Using the 5 Whys for Inquisitiveness

Statement	Why Question
"I'm feeling really deflated today."	*1. "Why's that?"*
"I've been passed over for promotion."	*2. "Well, why's that?"*
"They gave the job to someone else."	*3. "And why's that?"*
"Because they were more qualified."	*4. "And why's that?"*
"Because I haven't gone on the right courses."	*5. "And why's that?"*
"Because I don't feel like I'm worthy, capable or confident enough to do so."	

And there you have the real reason this person has been passed over for promotion. Asking the five whys is a powerful way to demonstrate your commitment to the truth and you get to the root cause of – and solution to – any challenge or situation.

"I have no special talents. I am only passionate and curious."

–ALBERT EINSTEIN

★ Step 2: Inform

The second step to expressing your knowledge with confidence is to seek out information that others don't have. Get a wide-reaching grasp of the facts but also a breadth of opinion. Avoid the quick fix of a Google search as there will be a trail of people before and after you who will have trodden that well-worn path. Likewise, beware the Wikipedia/fake news trap. Of course, any search for information can start with Google, but it's vital to cast your net wider to get a true breadth of understanding and question what you are learning. Go to recognised and reliable sources to find out what the facts are, explore contradictory opinions so you can see things from both sides and weigh them up, but also talk to relevant experts to get their take on things.

★ Step 3: Insights

Once you've collated the relevant information through Inquire and Inform, the next step is to draw your own conclusions – the 'which means that'. Your ability to draw insights from all the knowledge that you've amassed and demonstrate your unique take on it will make you stand out from the crowd and increase your perceived value. I often use the following questions to help me identify key insights when I'm researching a new opportunity or designing a new course:

- What's the biggest issue we're facing?

- What's the most critical thing that needs to happen now?

- What do I now know that I didn't know before?

- What questions remain unanswered?

- Which actions need to happen and when?

★ Step 4: Illustrate

Knowledge is useless if it just stays in your head. The next step is to work out how to illustrate your hard-won knowledge so that it can help you to achieve your goals and power up. One of the most memorable techniques to illustrate your knowledge and make dry data come alive is through storytelling. This isn't about 'once upon a time', but sharing an anecdote, case study or example which your audience will relate to.

Another powerful technique is to create your own model to make your point. An example of this is the Power Up Model©. Rather than simply listing the six power sources, I've designed a graphic that encapsulates all six in one place, which can also be used as a profiling tool.

5. Handling challenges

As we identified at the start of this chapter, there are a number of challenges that get in the way of ensuring our knowledge is appreciated by others. The most common barrier is getting your voice heard. Whether it's because you feel like you have less right to speak than them (perhaps they're more experienced or senior) or because they, for some reason, feel their voice has a right to overpower yours, the outcome is that you don't end up having an equal say, which is an extremely disempowering position to be in.

We will explore a whole range of communication and body language techniques in the *Assertiveness* chapter, but for now, here are some specific tips to get your voice heard:

- Firstly, prepare in advance: write down a few bullets summarising what you plan to say – this will keep you focused on your main points and stop you from waffling. Know who will be there, what they're likely to say, and consider how you can build on their points as a way of encouraging them to build on yours.

- Get your voice heard in the room early on. If you leave it too late, people will assume you've got nothing to say and therefore find it easier to interrupt you when you do speak up.

- Sometimes if we're nervous or enthusiastic, we can rush through our points and speak too quickly. Instead, breathe deeply and keep your delivery slow and deliberate.

- Use the numbering technique: this draws people in and prevents interruptions; if you say you have three points to share, they will be unlikely to stop you at one and a half!

- Avoid devaluing your knowledge through phrases like "Does that make sense?" or fillers like "sort of", "if you know what I mean", "kind of", or "maybe".

- As well as making your points, ask questions and wait patiently for the answer, rather than jumping in too quickly to fill the silences.

And what about a lack of knowledge? We can't know *everything* there is to know, so it's important to learn how to feel comfortable with the gaps and know how to handle getting put on the spot when you don't know.

- **Don't fudge it:** 'fudging' it can only take us up to a certain point. Many people bend the truth on CVs to bump up their credentials or skirt around an issue when they're not fully apprised of the facts. But it's a dangerous strategy to take. Who can forget Joey from Friends having to teach a dance class after he lied on his CV that he'd been to ballet school? And there are few things more damaging to your credibility than being exposed for having misappropriated the truth, whether deliberately or not.

- **Always check your facts:** I've witnessed many professional speakers share facts that are out of date or 'research' which is unsubstantiated. To avoid this, seek out the primary sources for all your facts rather than relying on Wikipedia and make sure you quote where your data comes from. A great way to convey authority in a particular subject is to 'borrow' it by quoting from an expert, but make sure that if you're sharing someone else's expertise, you give credit where it's due.

■ **Don't draw lazy conclusions**: at the start of my career, I made the mistake of 'just thinking' it would be OK not to create name badges for journalists attending an event. In our debrief, my terrifying dragon lady boss screamed in my face, "You assumed that was OK?!!!! Write down the word 'assume.'" She then grabbed the pen out of my hand and scratched two lines across the word, shouting: "Assume makes an ass out of u and me!" It was a horrendous lesson, painfully learnt. But, of course, she was right. You can never assume anything or you'll end up with egg on your face. Don't just take things at face value. If someone tells you something, or you hear it somewhere else, don't just believe it's the truth – check it.

■ **Be comfortable with not knowing**: pretending you have all the facts or trying to deflect attention can easily backfire, so it's important to be honest about your levels of knowledge. Never feel ashamed that you're not a walking encyclopaedia. Sometimes the person with the least knowledge asks the best questions because they don't get lost in the weeds of an argument. Work out when it's OK for you to say, "I don't know" and when it isn't. Or be the person who takes the conversation in a different direction.

Handling a clash

To finish our chapter on Knowledge, let's explore what we do when there's a clash of opinions, to ensure that your voice still gets heard.

Different ways of seeing the world can lead to some pretty ugly clashes, as social media wars have shown us. But having a different world view, a different perception of how things should be, doesn't necessarily mean there can't be common ground. When the former president, Republican George Bush, passed Michelle Obama a cough drop at Senator John McCain's memorial service, it emerged that they had a long history of chumminess – in spite of strong ideological differences. When challenged, she made it clear that while they are from opposite ends of the political spectrum, ultimately, there are a number of causes they're united on.

■ **Look for common ground:** you may have a markedly different view on parenting than another woman, or you may, for example, be firmly against corporal punishment, but realising that you come from the same place of wanting the best for your children means you need to be comfortable with different perspectives. Mediators in high-level disputes have to find common ground, where common interests are shared. You might not agree on corporal punishment but do agree that you want better behaviour from your children.

■ **Listen:** it's in these situations that we have to have the higher intelligence to listen – negotiations fail when someone becomes entrenched in their own view. The bigger your world view and the wider your perspective, the easier it will be to listen to the other person, find common ground, get your points heard and manage situations of conflict, which will ultimately enhance your power. (For more on combining your power of Knowledge and Magnetism to influence and persuade, take a look at the Magnetic Influence section in the Magnetism Chapter.)

KNOWLEDGE CONCLUSION

While we're waiting for society to catch up and develop an appreciation of knowledge and intelligence in its many forms, we need to take control to ensure we have as much *relevant* knowledge as we can, and that we can express it appropriately and confidently, in order to stand out from the crowd and do ourselves justice. Knowledge is power, yes, but this needs qualifying: having knowledge in a unique area gives you an edge. But it's not the one with the most knowledge who has the power, but the person most capable of articulating it, as well as the emotional intelligence to understand how it can be applied, which is where the other sources of power covered in this book come in.

IN SUMMARY

★ Knowledge is the ability to use the unique information and skills you possess to add value and demonstrate your worth.

★ Knowledge is the practical complement to Intuition, giving you the evidence to state your case and the confidence to speak.

★ Although the saying states that 'knowledge is power', what makes it powerful is its application. It's not enough to learn new facts; what's valuable is how you join those facts together and interpret them to make a relevant, cohesive and valuable whole.

★ Although knowledge is infinite, you only need to know slightly more than the people around you to be powerful.

★ Developing your unique knowledge can be achieved in five steps:

   1. **Defining your niche**: consider what your unique niche might be, based on the aspects of your role that you find the most interesting and what you're best at.

   2. **Profiling your knowledge**: objectively assess the knowledge you possess and where there are gaps.

3. **Honing your knowledge bank**: take action to build on your knowledge through professional development, personal study and spending time with experts in your area.

4. **Expressing yourself with confidence**: this can be achieved through using the 4 Is: Inquire, Inform, Insights and Illustrate.

5. **Knowing how to handle challenges**: it's important to learn how to feel comfortable with the gaps in your knowledge and how to handle it when you're put on the spot.

Chapter 6

RESILIENCE

"You may tread me in the dirt but still, like dust, I'll rise."

—MAYA ANGELOU

THE POWER OF RESILIENCE

Resilience, also known as inner strength, resolve or grit, plays a vital role in our ability to Power Up again and again, throughout our professional and personal lives. Resilience is what we rely on when there are more bumps in the road than smooth bits. We can all play our 'A' game on our best days, but how do we perform when the wheels are threatening to fall off? Can we withstand pressure, criticism and the inevitable knocks that come with success and live to fight another day? This is a quality to nurture and cherish because there's nothing more powerful than a strong and resilient woman.

Resilience in action

It's ironic that I find myself writing about resilience at the end of one of the most challenging times of my life. Last year, I lost my dad. It's only just beginning to dawn on me what a huge deal this has been. Coping with grief and a sense of loss while supporting others through theirs has seen me burying myself in work to avoid dealing with it. But, of course, some levels of pain can't be ignored. It turns out that the whole world tilts on its axis when one of your most significant anchors is snatched away. And it's at times like this that we really learn about ourselves and how resilient we are.

These are the times in all our lives when we have to dig deep and look within for resolve and strength. I like to think that my major challenges have made me a tough cookie. But they've also made me, at times, brittle and unreachable to the world around me. I've just thought 'look at me with my first-world problems' – with so much anguish in the world, in the hierarchy of suffering, who was I to make a fuss? And perhaps those early experiences of feeling lost and voiceless gave me the sense that I had to soldier on alone, and just, well, toughen up.

And therefore, in grief this past year, my inclination has been to shut down and turn inwards, rather than open up to those who can support me. But I've discovered that this time I just can't do it alone. The fact is, losing my dad is on a whole

I KNOW NOW IT'S FAR MORE DIFFICULT TO DEAL WITH CHALLENGES WHEN YOU'RE THE LONE WOLF WHO DOESN'T SEEK HELP.

other scale to all the other difficult things that have happened to me before. This tough cookie well and truly crumbled. And it's impossible, when crumbling, to shut down and build resources from within, as I normally would. I've had to accept help and support from outside.

I know now it's far more difficult to deal with challenges when you're the lone wolf who doesn't seek help. And that when you join the pack, open up to people, share some of your vulnerabilities and insecurities and ask for support and advice, the world gets warmer. Your openness acts like a magnet and likeminded people are moved to help you. As a result, you move through suffering far more smoothly.

This year has encapsulated resilience for me. I don't think we ever become fully resilient, but through building strategies to get through difficult times, I've learnt how to 'live with' difficult feelings, and become more adept at rolling with the punches and drawn strength from that.

How does Resilience relate to Power Up?

So why is developing resilience so important for powering up? Aside from our conditioning that we should put the whole world before us on our list of priorities, our heightened powers of intuition and superior levels of emotional intelligence mean that we women pick up on subtle cues far more than men. We feel things more deeply and read much more into them than our male counterparts. This can pick away at our strength, undermine our resilience and sap our energy so that it's harder to just get on with the day.

It's this mindset that can make you feel like a failure when you come out of a meeting without landing a single point.

In your head you're either bad or brilliant – you can't be in between, or just having an off day, or have nothing particular to say on that subject, or only be there to listen. If you're insecure, you may interpret this as a failure on your part, when most men wouldn't think twice about putting on a similar performance and deeming it a success.

Some women can be extremely sensitive, hold onto harsh words and cruel actions far longer than men. We can blow these things up out of all proportion. We find it difficult to let go of stuff. Those hot, tear-igniting feelings of being misunderstood, not being heard or respected, of being misjudged, of not being enough –which can linger and erode our self-esteem. They can be so powerful that they can tarnish our resilience and get in the way of our fulfilling our potential. Because in this frame of mind we're just hearing the bad stuff, not the good, and we come out feeling we haven't done ourselves justice – or that we are rubbish anyway. As a result, we may shy away from assertively expressing our knowledge for fear of being shot down, or simply disagreed with. We instinctively avoid forming new relationships because we're fearful of rejection. We steer clear of experiences that will draw attention to ourselves because we don't want to look stupid or out of place.

When resilience is compromised it negatively impacts on all the other sources of power in the Power Up Model©. This becomes a negative spiral because if we don't put ourselves out there in these ways, we become less adept at doing so, which will make us even less resilient because we'll be in fewer situations where we have to toughen up and 'bring it'. We need to learn this because colleagues are not always nice, the world isn't always fair and it pays to know how to roll with the punches. So what do we need to do?

When faced with a challenge, we can either let it consume us, let it hold us back or, alternatively, we can find a way to overcome our feelings of self-doubt by keeping things in perspective and developing strategies to overcome them.

To be crystal clear, this isn't about 'putting on our big girl pants' (an expression I despise as much as telling a man to 'grow a pair'). This is about learning how to maintain our power, even in the face of adversity. If you do yoga, think 'warrior pose' (as opposed to 'worrier pose'!): standing strong, arms outstretched, feet planted, looking in the direction of your outstretched hand. You feel that unwavering power, not just when things are bad but all the time. Like a centurion whose strength is maintained through war and peace, our weapons are not our sword and shield, but our own inner strength. Our resilience.

Why do we need it?

How do you respond to setbacks, failure and negative feedback? Do you allow them to paralyse or overwhelm you? Or do you spring back? Perhaps it depends on the circumstances? Maybe a couple of knockbacks are do-able, but the relentless drip-drip is what threatens to drive you over the edge?

Resilience increases your sense of self-worth. Not only that, it will help you to identify those moments when life threatens to topple you and give you the foresight, strength and confidence to do something about it.

Before I launched my business, I had a leadership role in a global communications firm. Although my main driver to leave was because I wanted to do something different, the relentless juggle of global travel (which may sound glamorous

but so wasn't!), sorting out childcare and pretending to clients that I didn't have a home life definitely had a negative impact and, in the end, wasn't sustainable for me.

I remember very clearly the moment I decided enough was enough. Sitting on a plane bound for Chicago, with crippling cystitis because I'd sacrificed time on the loo for time at my laptop, I realised that however strong I was, for me, at that time in my life, I needed something else. It had got to the point where my work commitments had chipped away at my resilience to the extent that it was affecting my physical and mental health. The balance had tipped too far in favour of my career and everything was suffering as a result.

I've lost count of the number of female colleagues who left the industry for similar reasons, either choosing a simpler life at home, setting up their own businesses or becoming consultants. And although companies are waking up to the specific challenges faced by women as they juggle their various work and home responsibilities, they're not changing fast enough.

What gets in the way?

As we navigate our way through life, there are times when our sense of self can be knocked sideways and our resilience compromised as a result. How many of these do you recognise, or have you observed in others?

1. Career roadblocks

Women face significant roadblocks throughout their career which can threaten to derail them, so much so that many give up on the journey altogether. Very few careers can be represented by a smooth upward curve trajectory, but the roadblocks and milestones many women experience can make for a very bumpy ride indeed! We go into common career challenges in detail in Chapter 2 so you might want to revisit the list and consider how they might negatively affect your resilience.

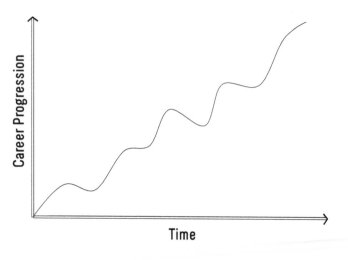

2. Events outside our control

However prepared we are, there will be times when the proverbial hits the fan and we come out badly through no fault of our own: redundancy, company buy-outs, downsizing, your industry declining. There are other times when you've put your heart and soul into a longed-for opportunity, maybe a job application or hoped-for promotion, and it didn't go your way. Or times when you've been criticised, side-lined or let down at work, or even publicly ridiculed. As you think about your own career, it helps to acknowledge that these challenges will be an inevitable part of your history and to think about what you can do to stay strong. This isn't only about how you feel about yourself during these times, it's how your organisation responds to you. In some cases, you'll have to be extra tough and fight extra hard to secure opportunities; for example, if your work status has changed, you may be battling against the perception that you will be less able to deliver than before.

3. Everyday knocks

As well as career roadblocks, there are other more day-to-day setbacks which may not seem like a big deal in isolation but when repeated over time, can build up to become the straw that broke the camel's back. I've found with my coaching clients that it can sometimes be those little things which consistently bring you down that can have an extremely negative impact on their general wellbeing and motivation at work. These include:

■ **Treatment by others:** harsh words, strange looks, abrasive attitudes and being taken for granted may be figments of our imagination. The person in question may just be having a bad day, you may just have caught them with a scowl on their face or they may be thinking about something else entirely. Whatever the reason, when we lack resilience, we blow it up into something else, or worry that they may genuinely have a point.

■ **Minor slip-ups:** from using the wrong word to going into too much or too little detail, to losing your place in a presentation, to saying something that didn't go down well in a meeting or having someone react negatively to a piece of feedback. If we lack resilience and get drawn into overthinking, these little slips that may not be picked up on by others and certainly don't reflect our lack of ability, can blow up in our minds into a major source of worry. This is when we can often over-read people's reactions and interpret everything as a negative.

■ **Dealing with difficult situations/people:** giving someone bad news or delivering negative feedback are conversations that you avoid if you lack resilience because you simply don't have the strength to deal with the fallout. Unfortunately, these issues can escalate until you've got a major problem on your hands. Making someone redundant or handling a disciplinary are challenging conversations which can be very difficult to let go of at the end of the working day if you don't feel resilient. They can seriously tarnish your equilibrium if you're not careful so it's essential to know how to handle them and get the support you need.

4. Unhelpful thinking

Aside from the external challenges, we can compromise our own resilience through unhelpful thinking patterns which often become more extreme when we're unwell or feeling under pressure.

■ **Comparison and competition:** when comparing ourselves with others, we often put ourselves in a lower position than them. We might think of ourselves as less experienced, less articulate, less confident, less attractive. This can be futile and damaging. Or we may put ourselves above them and think of ourselves as superior in some way, which can come across as arrogant and brittle. So comparison is not great – but neither is competition.

I often find that when people join an organisation they ask themselves, "What do I need to do to get on?" or "Who do I need to prove myself against?" They then identify those who appear to be the most successful and decide to either compete with or emulate them. Why compete with others? It may mean you 'win' a new opportunity, but because it often requires you exerting power over others, it can end up as a pyrrhic victory because they end up resenting you or shutting you out.

A more constructive approach is to look inward and focus attention on who you are and where you want to go. Rather than obsessing over someone else's promotion or the award they've just won, find ways to redirect your energy to your own path. When you choose to believe there is room for everybody, you don't waste as much energy worrying how you're going to win over other people or how they're leaving you behind. Power should be about how you propel yourself forward, regardless of where the others are. They may be on different paths, this is about travelling along yours. And just because they're good doesn't mean you're less good.

■ **Perfectionism:** often fuelled by comparison, constantly seeking perfection can negatively impact on your resilience because, like the pot of gold at the end of the rainbow, it's unachievable. Although a large percentage of my high-achieving clients are perfectionists, I am careful to point out that if unbridled, it can be a risk factor for a range of mental health conditions, including obsessive-compulsive disorder, eating disorders, social anxiety and workaholism, as well as physical problems like chronic stress and heart disease.

Speaking as a recovering perfectionist, it can be a powerful driver if applied to selected areas of your life – maybe you are on a quest to bake the perfect chocolate cheesecake or develop a best-in-class product. However, it can become destructive when applied to everything. It is time-consuming and energy-sapping, hinders productivity and fuels self-loathing because nothing is ever good enough.

To counter perfectionism, my advice to clients is to differentiate between 'gold-plated, Rolls-Royce projects' and those that will pootle along nicely as a 'Mini Metro', so you can direct your perfectionism at the things that matter, not every single item on your to-do list, and in general, care less about being perfect, and more about getting the job done.

■ **Self-sabotaging:** linked to perfectionism, self-sabotage is another powerful factor which can seriously undermine our confidence and erode our resilience. This is where we consciously or subconsciously create problems in our lives that interfere with our long-standing goals. According to business psychologist and founder of the Tame Your Inner Critic programme, Jess Baker: "Underlying all self-sabotaging behaviours are self-critical thoughts like 'I don't deserve good things' or 'I am not good enough' or 'I'll only mess it up'. These negative judgements are usually unconscious, irrational, and often based on something someone said that our brain has latched onto it as if it were true." To override self-sabotaging behaviour, Jess recommends firstly, noticing that you're doing it; secondly, talking to someone about it; and thirdly, 'reframing' the negative beliefs about the situation to something more practical. For example, if you catch yourself having a self-sabotaging thought like: 'If I make one mistake in that presentation I'll be fired!' you could reframe it to: 'I'll give it my best shot, practice in advance, and if I make any mistakes, I will learn from them'.

5. Identity changes

Managing your mindset can be particularly challenging during times when your identity is shifting or in a state of flux, including happy life events where you start to question, "Who am I now?" And so to improve your resilience, it makes sense to be aware of all the potential challenges and shifts in identity you'll face, and think about how you'll harness power in all its forms to positively evolve through them.

EXERCISE 1:
STAYING RESILIENT THROUGH IDENTITY CHANGES

Take a look at the life events described below, whether you've been through them already or have some of them on your horizon. Consider how these events could affect your sense of identity and how this might compromise your resilience. Knowledge is power and the more you can predict and pre-empt these life changes, the more you'll be able to enjoy the happy ones and live with the negative ones.

■ **Marriage:** getting married may fill you with joy, but it can also make you feel differently about yourself and how you're treated – where once you were an independent single woman, a free agent, you may find yourself thinking, "Oh, I'm just an old married lady now." Being someone's wife (a wife!), a Mrs, and agonising over whether to take your new husband's name, keep your own or go double-barrelled – these can all affect your sense of self.

■ **Motherhood:** although a wonderful, life-affirming gift, having babies can be overwhelming. You may have been used to planning and controlling everything, but conception can't be guaranteed when it suits you (if at all). There's no volume button on a screaming new-born and no amount of planning can get your cranky offspring off to sleep at the required time. There's also the loss of identity after having kids. You're no longer a career girl, but a mum. You're responsible where before you could be entirely irresponsible. Your body's changed, so you may feel you're no longer sexy and glam, just a pram pusher.

■ **Sickness and bereavement:** prolonged periods of worry and responsibility in the light of a family member's ill health can leave you fretting over how you're going to fit visits and health appointments in alongside work, family and home. Spending so much time caring for someone can take its toll on our self-worth and mental wellbeing no matter how badly we want to look after them. And our own health can suffer, especially in the case of serious, long-term, chronic conditions. The loss of a friend or loved one can shake us to our very core, especially if they make up part of our system of 'anchors'. At its worst, grief can leave us feeling uncertain of who we are and how we can carry on.

■ **Changing work status:** we may go from full-time to part-time, from employee to self-employed and struggle with the change of status. Promotion can thrust us into an unwelcome spin of self-doubt and imposter syndrome – "Oh, so I'm supposed to be in charge now?"

And so many aspects of being an employee can knock your inner confidence – missed promotions, appraisals, difficult colleagues, negative feedback, the project/presentation/call/meeting that went wrong... Equally, we may struggle to rediscover our confidence after a career break to raise children or may have multiple 'careers' and ventures all jostling for our attention, all performing at different levels, meaning our self-esteem can rise and fall depending on the day.

"

RESILIENCE IS A SECRET WEAPON IN THE FIGHT FOR POWER. IT ISN'T ABOUT NOT FALLING DOWN, IT'S ABOUT GETTING BACK UP AFTER YOU'VE FALLEN.

WHAT IS RESILIENCE?

Resilience is defined as the capacity to recover quickly from difficulties or the ability of a substance to spring back into shape. If we think about it from the perspective of physics, resilience is an object's ability to withstand pressure from an outside force. Glass is less likely to shatter if the load is spread across the surface, rather than concentrated in one place. In human terms, we might spread the load of an outside pressure or blow by talking to people (a problem shared is a problem halved) or seeing the bigger picture. Skyscrapers are built with foundations that move, rather than being rigid, which stop them collapsing in an earthquake. This translates into our ability to be flexible in the face of adversity and adapt our approach when required.

Personal resilience is about toughening up; for example, standing up for yourself when you need to, walking knowingly into conflict and speaking your truth, even though you know it will hurt, and dealing with the consequences. But it's not just about being tough, having a shield or letting things bounce off you. It's also about having the mental and emotional tools to help you ride through challenging times. It's about knowing it's OK to falter and that it's possible to live with difficulty and still flourish.

Resilience is a secret weapon in the fight for power. It isn't about not falling down, it's about getting back up after you've fallen. It's about knowing that when wounded, you will heal; when at a low ebb, you will find the strength to Power Up and that when there's a storm, you will yield to its force knowing that when it's passed you'll rise again.

When you know you have resilience as a back-up power source, you're much more willing to take risks and live life fully than if you're scared of what might happen and hide in the shadows of life.

Where does it come from?

Resilience comes from our ability to manage our physical and mental state to make the best of situations, whatever they may be. We are naturally conditioned for resilience and we become most aware of its power when it is tested to its limits.

Our body's natural response

We are, of course, built to respond to threats. Our body knows just what to do when we meet a sabre-toothed tiger – or the modern-day equivalent, an aggressive colleague or a nasty deadline. Says Dr Lynda Shaw, author of *Your Brain Is Boss*: "When we are in a stressful situation, the brain secretes the hormone adrenaline which makes us run or get ready to compete, turning off some areas of the bodily systems which are not immediately needed to help us deal with the stressful situation. The cortisol pathway can also be activated. Exposure to cortisol in small amounts is actually good for us; it helps us survive, keeps us on our toes and helps us stay alert." It therefore follows that being in stressful situations can actually be good for us, as long as we see the situation positively and react accordingly.

Freedom to choose

Viktor Frankl's 1946 book, *Man's Search for Meaning*, in which he chronicles his experiences as a prisoner in Nazi

213

concentration camps during World War II, talks about how, as humans, we have the privilege to be able to choose our thoughts and feelings in response to anything that happens to us: the epitome of resilience. We all have a choice: we can catastrophise, and our lives can stop in the face of trouble, or we can move through it. When I find myself stressing over something that's happened or worrying about something coming up, I remind myself that, by comparison to many, I have had an incredibly fortunate life and remind myself of Frankl's quote, which has had a profound effect on how I manage my emotional state.

"Everything can be taken from a man but one thing: the last of the human freedoms – to choose one's attitude in any given set of circumstances, to choose one's own way."

–'MAN'S SEARCH FOR MEANING', VIKTOR E. FRANKL

Not sweating the small stuff

A friend used to date a man whose response to any adversity was to catastrophise. He just wasn't chilled about anything. If he spilt his coffee on the rug, it was the end of the world, with lots of swearing and drama. If he missed his bus, cue a big strop that everyone else had to hear. He would blame other people, panic about the consequences and throw his toys out of the pram. Needless to say, the relationship didn't last long, but my friend learnt a valuable lesson. "Accidents happen, buses get missed. If you let it get to you like my ex did, your whole life becomes a crisis, which means when something

214

really bad happens you just go to pieces. You just have to have some perspective when things don't go your way, deal with the fallout, learn from it and move on." As Rudyard Kipling said in his famous poem, if we can 'keep our heads while all about us are losing theirs' we will have greater resilience.

Persistence

The ability to keep going after a setback rather than giving up will serve you so many times in your life and career – as it served Steph. She was in one of my Mastermind groups years ago and having worked so hard for many years to design a piece of software, was on the brink of giving up. She admitted to having a history of giving up at the last minute, but this time, we urged her to stand firm. Luckily, she listened because she's gone on to sell the product across the whole of the Middle East and to speak on stages worldwide about her new technology. As Steph's story shows, when you're at the point of giving up, that's when you need to stand firm and attack with renewed force.

The same goes for athletes and all professional sportsmen and women. Finding the strength and will to carry on, day after day, is crucial to their success. It's when you're on the floor eating mud, totally spent, that you have to somehow stand up and carry on.

"With a defeat, when you lose, you get up, you make it better, you try again. That's what I do in life, when I get down, when I get sick, I don't want to just stop. I keep going and I try to do more."

–SERENA WILLIAMS

Losing the curse of perfectionism

Developing your resilience also comes from overcoming the 'good girl' curse of perfectionism. If we can get comfortable with being a bit messy and learn to love, rather than hide our weaknesses, trusting our own voice rather than doubting whether what we're saying is 'right', we can start to make friends with our own imposter syndrome and even use it to our advantage. Because no one has all the answers, no one is perfect, and embracing our flaws can be truly liberating. It's at those times when you're on the cusp of personal change and things are feeling harder than ever before that your true resilient character emerges. If you welcome your imperfections and learn to be kind to yourself through difficult times, you will progress even more.

Understand the role of vulnerability and detachment

So what do we do when we are at a low ebb? How do we find the strength and courage to show up and give our all when our self-belief and sense of purpose has a wobble?

I've often felt conflicted by the notion that 'in vulnerability there is strength,' which is espoused by the academic and thought leader Brené Brown. My conflict has been that if people are looking to us to be strong, how are we going to be believable if we're sharing our vulnerability? And yet, I've come to realise that being a rounded human being, complete with vulnerabilities, has a huge impact on how you deal with difficult things and how people relate to us. Because we all go through challenging periods when we go wobbly and suffer emotionally; it's just humanity and doesn't make us any less strong.

My own experience of this in the last few months has been an eye-opener. Because when I've felt my own strength weakening in the face of my own grief-related emotional challenges, what I've really needed is comfort from others and to understand what other people value in me. If people are used to you being invincible and not needing support, they won't necessarily offer it. So we need to learn how to ask for feedback, compliments or affirmations because sometimes we really need to hear them. And if we never show our vulnerable side, people think we're so strong that they don't bother to tell us how great they think we are.

People who are ruthlessly sure of themselves are just unbearable, and we tend to view them with distrust. Whereas being able to get under the skin of how people feel means you've been there yourself – and that makes you not only more effective, but also more admirable.

So the fact that I will have written this book during my most difficult year is a gift because it's meant digging very deep in order to acknowledge these things and frame them positively. It's enabled me to write about resilience in a totally real way.

HOW CAN YOU DEVELOP IT?

Having explored what resilience is, let's now look at how you can develop it so that you can access it to handle both the everyday knocks, as well as those times when the proverbial truly hits the fan.

We're going to use the analogy of a car journey. Whether you drive or not, you'll know that in order to arrive at your destination, it's important to know where you're going and that you will need to vary your speed on the way there, from the exhilaration of the fast lane to the stop-start of a traffic jam.

Although I'm naturally impatient and want to get to places as quickly as possible, I know that being too hasty is danger-ous for me and unnerving for others, so I have learnt to enjoy both the fast lane and pottering along in the slow. As with resilience, if you attack life at breakneck speed continually, you will eventually run out of fuel and burn out. And if you get immensely frustrated at traffic lights, the only person who'll blow a gasket is you.

There are four steps you can apply to make your journey through life as smooth as possible:

1. Planning your journey: taking control

2. Getting in the driving seat: choosing the right mindset

3. Ongoing maintenance: building resilience into you daily life

4. Knowing what to do when the wheels fall off: staying strong through adversity

★ Step 1: Planning your journey

Central to resilience is the unwavering knowledge that you know where you're going and are in control of how you're going to get there. If you don't have a destination point in mind, the chances are your car won't even leave the driveway.

Any personal growth carries within it the feeling of moving into unchartered territory, and because we've been pro-grammed since cavemen times to stay safe, we can uncon-sciously sabotage our progress by avoiding what lies beyond our comfort zone, such as being brave and trying new things.

219

"

FEAR AND WORRY CAN BE VERY POWERFUL BLOCKERS TO TAKING ACTION... THEY MAY BE EXERTING A POWERFUL EFFECT WITHOUT US EVEN REALISING IT.

Plans keep fear and worry at bay

Fear and worry can be very powerful blockers to taking action, and because they reside in our subconscious, they may be exerting a powerful effect without us even realising it.

When we lack resilience fear and worry can knock us off course.

This means that before you've even put your key in the ignition – by, for example, deciding to talk to your boss about a pay rise – your subconscious mind may be working overtime, conjuring up all the reasons why that's a bad idea – they'll think you're being too demanding, will say 'no' or realise they've been paying you too much – all of which may overpower your resolve and chip away at your resilience.

When you have a determined plan, you will feel in control and stronger. You will be able to override negative thoughts and design the life you want to lead rather than reacting to the one that's happening to you.

Map out your life

To override our natural instinct for self-preservation, the first step is to 'start with the end in mind', as Stephen Covey said in his book, *Seven Habits of Highly Effectively People.*

When I'm working with my coaching clients, the first question I ask them is: "What goals would you like to achieve from working together?" Although this is a pretty basic starting point, they're often so wrapped up in delivering their work projects that they haven't given it a second thought! Establishing what you want to achieve and setting the right goals to get there represents the 'Smart' in the title of this book. It not only sends a powerful message to your brain that you're worth it, but also helps to give a 'point' to everything you do, enhancing your motivation and giving you the strength to power through challenges.

Once we've established the 'big' goals, I'll work with my clients to map out the day-to-day goals. This will often spill into work and personal life because one inevitably affects the other. If I'm working with a client who wants to do more public speaking, for example, we not only consider how they'll get more time on stage, but also the amount of travelling involved and how this will impact their home life. In my experience, it pays to be as specific as you can about how you spend your time, including the what, where, who, how and why. That way, you're more likely to get there and less likely to regret having taken the wrong path in retrospect.

A great example of the benefits of mapping out your life is financial planning, given that money worries are top of many people's list of things that keep them awake at night. According to Lisa Conway Hughes, Chartered Financial Advisor, founder of misslolly.com and author of *Money Lessons*: "The short-term consequences of good money habits are rewarding and hopefully liberating. However, the long-term impact of financial savviness is life-changing. It's the difference between living a life where you use money to achieve the things that are important to you and make you happy, rather than money dictating how you will live your life."

Predict the bumps and be flexible

As well as having a plan, it's important to predict the bumps in the road; as Mike Tyson said: "Everyone has a plan until they get punched in the face." Resilience is also about how you prepare for and respond to knocks, or as the author of the Jack Reacher novels Lee Child put it: "Hope for the best, plan for the worst."

Although it's important to have a plan, resilience is also about developing flexibility and recognising those times when you need to change your plans, revise your goals or choose a different direction altogether. For example, if, having spoken to your boss about a pay rise, it becomes clear that career progression won't be possible in your current role, the most resilient response is to look at alternative options.

And how about if the bumps are of your own making? Bringing your subconscious fears into your conscious mind and looking at them for what they are is a great way of mitigating negative thinking. A great children's book called *The Huge Bag of Worries* by Virginia Ironside features a girl who ends up lugging a huge bag of worries around until one day, when she meets an old lady who helps her sort her worries into groups. She ditches all those that belong to other people and notices how much less overwhelming each worry seems when brought out into the light of day.

Asking yourself, 'What's the worst thing that could happen?' is a great way to put your fears into perspective, but a better question to ask is, 'What's the best thing that could happen?' as it moves your thinking into a more resourceful, energised and resilient place.

CASE STUDY

Claire Norwood is a property developer. We met at a women's networking event, and she opened up about how she had struggled to find her way in the world, particularly since having a family, and how challenging she had found getting her voice heard. Her story is one of resilience and shows that reinvention can be possible after a career break. I went on to coach Claire, to help her become a speaker and share her inspirational story.

"I've never had a game plan. After doing a business degree, I fell into PR. From then on I just did whatever work came along. Then, by the time I'd met my husband, I had this romantic idea about making shoes, so I used my savings to train as a cobbler.

"Although I became quite well known and got my shoes on catwalks and in Vogue and Elle, I made no money at all. When our children came, I kind of bottled out of the whole career world and threw myself into giving my kids the best childhood ever. We moved to the country and for many years I was taken up with motherhood.

"Once the boys were in their teens, we moved back to London and I hit a wall. I needed to earn money to contribute to the family finances. Meanwhile, the boys needed me less and I missed my country friends. I felt like life was going on without me. I couldn't stay in my small, domesticated world. It was now or never.

"So in my late 40s, I started retraining in property. It gave me a real sense of hope and excitement. After doing a course, I ended up working for one of the guys who taught it, and although I was paid next to nothing, it gave me the opportunity to reinvent myself. Here I was, a middle-aged intern, but being allowed to part-run a company, design a website, talk to clients, deal with solicitors, organise refurbishments and design interiors. And I loved it. I could see that there was a life out there for me and I had value – it gave my self-worth such a boost.

"Now, I have my own property development company and I love it. My role is all about solving problems and building relationships. I use my background of creativity, my life skills and my experience. And being older means I come with automatic credibility; because I've been around the block and done so many things, people listen to me.

"I've come into my own in my 50s. It's like, for the first time, I have power. I'm being acknowledged and noticed and respected. This is like round two of my life, and it's better than the first time by a long stretch.

"Antoinette was the first person to really listen to me, and to identify what lit me up. It was as if she'd given me permission to own my abilities, and honestly, I never looked back. That's not to say it's been easy, but working with Antoinette gave me a glimpse into a world of possibility I never thought possible. Once you've visualised yourself being someone with a contribution to make, it's difficult to go back to your old, small self."

This interview appeared in full in www.audreyonline.co.uk, a website for women looking to reinvent their lives.

★ Step 2: Getting in the driving seat

Take responsibility

Having planned your journey, the next step to resilience is acknowledging that you are the one in charge of your own life. When you are in the driving seat, you are no longer passive but the one responsible for moving in the right direction. So, instead of moaning that your boss overworks you, you realise that you're allowing yourself to be over-worked, either by saying 'yes' too often or not saying 'no' often enough. Approach your work in a different way and have the assertiveness and self-confidence to flag up when you're stacked. If you don't get the response you need, let the negative comments slide off you and remember, no one is forcing you to stay and you can always leave.

Our ability to 'go with' the challenges that life throws at us, rather than catastrophise, is key to power and success. Getting in the driving seat is a mixture of learning how to be hard, like a diamond, but also bouncy, like a ball.

Be diamond hard

Women often focus on likeability at the expense of respect. For many, it's more important to please people and make everything OK over their own needs and wants. Being diamond hard is about setting boundaries, disagreeing when you need to, giving challenging feedback and showing your grit and determination, even if that means displeasing some.

My personal trainer, Abbie Benjamins (AKA Abs Abbie) is a great example of diamond hard. She has no problem marking out her boundaries. When we're working out together in the gym, people will often unintentionally encroach on our space, attempt to set their mats out in readiness for the next class or come and ask her for advice on how to use the equipment. Instead of letting it go or pandering to their requests, she will state out loud, in no uncertain terms, what needs to happen. People sometimes react in a shocked or annoyed way because they're just not used to a young woman being that way, but she is unapologetic and they just do what they're told!

A great technique here is to literally imagine yourself sur-rounded by a protective coating which will allow you to be and say whatever you want. One of my coaching clients runs a virtual assistant business and was finding it difficult to negotiate higher fees for projects that went over budget. When I asked her how she saw her role, she described herself as a guide dog, which reflected her responsibilities but limited her ability to push back. She now imagines herself surrounded by a protective orange glow whenever she goes into negotiations and has been far more successful with fee generation as a result. For more advice on how to communi-cate with power, take a look at the *Assertiveness* chapter.

Don't let other people's comments throw you off

Resilience is also how you choose to respond to other people's comments, whether they are well-intentioned or not. As a speaker, I'm regularly offered feedback – some of which I'll value, some not – and I've learnt to look objectively at the person and consider whether they represent similar values to me or have the skills to make their comments worthy of listening to, or not. This is about being open to feedback, but not allowing the sharp claws of criticism to cut so deeply that they draw blood. So when someone makes a comment about you, take what they say seriously, but don't take their views so much to heart that they knock you off course. As well as imagining being as tough as a diamond, you can also imagine having a Teflon-coating, so that negative comments which don't serve you literally slide off.

Bounce back

To counterbalance being diamond hard, you must develop bouncebackability. Avoid thinking of yourself in the 'put upon' role, even in a jokey way, as this will cast you in a victim role and contain you there. Instead, remind yourself of all the times when you've recovered after a fall and the factors that helped get you back on your feet.

Think about how you hold yourself after a setback. The phrase 'you look like you're carrying the world on your shoulders' is telling and you can often spot people who are going through a hard time because their whole posture has collapsed in on itself, head bent, shoulders stooped and body closed in, as though reacting to a physical pressure or blow.

Poor posture will compromise your ability to take a deep breath and could even affect your mood. And what can happen with people who allow this posture to become their default is that their overall attitude to life follows suit and they become the kind of glass-completely-empty person who no longer notices the good stuff and only fixates on the bad.

"If there is tomorrow when we're not together, there is something you must always remember... You are braver than you believe, stronger than you seem, and smarter than you think. But the most important thing is, even if we're apart, I'll always be with you."

-'WINNIE THE POOH', A. A. MILNE

To cultivate bouncebackability, identify your mood boosters and make sure you access them regularly, particularly after a setback. Listen to music, dance, go for a windswept walk, get your hair done, buy a new top, reread old diaries, potter around in a junk shop, go to your favourite coffee shop or lie on the sofa watching reality TV – whatever. If it works for you and recharges and nourishes your soul – do it. Also, think about your posture. Make the effort to stand up tall, shoulders back, head up. Look up and out at the world rather than down at your feet – you'll be amazed at what this fresh perspective brings.

Developing a strong network is also vital to bouncebackability. As I found in this last year of grief, it's essential to have support when the chips are down. Having your own group of cheerleaders – be they friends and family or a business network, a netball team you play with, your dog walking pals or a book club – will act as an emotional safety net, a bolster through tough times, as well as a way to laugh at the absurdity of life and work.

And when people ask how you are, rather than the usual bright and breezy "Fine!", be real, soften up, let people in, and admit it when you're finding things tough. At a particularly low point, asking a friend, "Can you help me understand what you value in me because I don't know what that is anymore?" was one of the bravest things I've done. It was an important lesson because it forced me to be what I would have previously labelled self-absorbed and selfish, and taught me that being real and asking for what you need is a key part of resilience.

EXERCISE 2:
GETTING IN
THE DRIVING SEAT

Two of the best ways to develop resilience are preparation and practice. This will not only power you up day to day, but also strengthen your ability to handle it when the going really gets tough.

1. Make a list of the situations in your life where you feel like you're compromising who you are and what you want to be doing.

2. Think about how you want to be in these situations and imagine a diamond-hard coating that will help you to toughen up and be that way. Think about what you will say and how people will respond.

3. Practice your diamond-hard approach on 'small' situations like correcting a friend or family member if you disagree with them and move up to more challenging situations like telling a colleague that you want them to stop bringing smelly food into the office. Reflect on how your diamond-hard approach is affecting your

resilience and what you will do to apply your techniques on other situations in your life. For more on powerful communication skills as a route to resilience, go to the Assertiveness chapter.

4. Identify three to five resilience cheerleaders who have your back and will support you through thick and thin. People love to be helpful but often need guidance on how. So if you're asking for help, be specific on what you need them to do.

★ Step 3: Ongoing maintenance

As well as having a map and being in the driving seat, to be resilient you'll need to look after the whole of you – you're not going to get very far in your journey through life if you haven't put fuel in the tank, topped up the water levels, charged the battery or checked the brakes.

How you show up on the outside reflects how you feel about yourself on the inside – they're symbiotic. If you are exhausted and look it, you will be telling the world you don't prioritise your own health and wellbeing.

So how can you make resilience part of your daily life?

Put the right fuel in

Getting the right fuel in is what will give you the energy for success. According to Mel Noakes, author of *The Little Book of Self Care*: "The way we nourish ourselves on a daily basis fundamentally impacts our lives. Nourishment comes in many forms from the words we say to ourselves, the food we put into our bodies, the amount of sleep we get, the way we move our bodies and the lifestyle and friends that influence us. If you continually put rubbish in, quite simply you get the same back out." According to Mel, looking after your physical health day to day means following the standard metrics, including aiming for 8 hours sleep, moving your body in any way that feels good, aiming for 2.5 hours of moderate physical activity every week, drinking adequate water (2 litres a day is the guide) and focusing on eating 'real food' rather than processed food wherever possible.

Don't run on empty

It's also invaluable to understand your peaks and troughs of energy throughout the day so that you can work with your body's natural rhythms, rather than against them. Unlike my husband, who needs three cups of strong coffee before he can have a conversation, I'm at my most productive first thing, which is why I've written most of this book before the rest of the family has even woken up. Likewise, while my husband can happily watch a movie until midnight, I will invariably be asleep on the sofa next to him, my energy fully spent. In this way, you can diarise work that requires concentration and creativity or those difficult tasks you've been putting off for times when your energy is at its peak. Leave the easier tasks for when your energy is at a lower ebb and give yourself a break when you need to.

As well as the daily peaks and troughs in energy, as women, we should not underestimate the impact that our monthly cycle can have on our energy and resilience levels. Dr Alison Grimston, functional medicine doctor and nutritional endocrinology practitioner, says: "It pays to learn to listen intuitively to our bodies. There may be times in our cycle when we need to rest more, or eat more cleanly, in order to be able to show up at work and be as productive as we would like. We often find that we need to slow down, particularly during a time of menstrual loss." Likewise, the menopause can also have a negative effect on our vitality. To counter this, she advises: "Pay attention to your work-life balance at this time, make as good food and lifestyle choices as you can, and if you are suffering, seek the help of a practitioner whom you feel you can trust."

"

SOME OF US ARE
SO DRIVEN AND
HARD ON OURSELVES
THAT, EVEN IF WE
DO NOTICE WE'RE
HEADING FOR A
CRASH, WE IGNORE IT.

Stay balanced

For ongoing balance, comedy performer, MC and Speaker Mentor Emma Stroud recommends the Rainbow Diary technique to make sure you find equilibrium in your day-to-day life. Using a box of highlighter pens (or colour tabs if you use a computer diary) with seven colours representing the different aspects of your life – for example, family, relationship, exercise, self-care, fun, work and a hobby – go through your week ahead and highlight each activity planned. When you've finished, check if you have a good balance of colours. If any of them are missing – if, say, you've left no time for pink fun or yellow relationship, or all you can see is green for work, you can take action. A good week should have all the colours in balance.

EXERCISE 3:

BUILDING RESILIENCE INTO YOUR DAILY LIFE

Having explored a range of resilience techniques, let's take a look at how you can use them to build resilience into your daily life.

■ Make a list of what energises and invigorates you: for example, exercise, food, music, films, favourite locations and make sure you diarise time to access them regularly.

■ Note down what your body and mind need when your energy is at a low ebb and how you will be gentle with yourself, allowing your energy to replenish and recuperate ready for another day.

■ Identify your resilience anchors, those people, places and things that keep you strong – and plan how you're going to make them a regular feature.

- Create an Energy Flow Graph, with your waking hours on the horizontal axis and a scale of 1 to 10 on the vertical axis for your energy levels. Mark up your levels of energy throughout a typical day, showing your peaks and troughs at different times. Consider how you can allocate time wisely to work with your natural rhythms.

- Create a Rainbow Diary in which you schedule your various activities – from things you *have* to do to things you *want* to do. Monitor which colours predominate, which are missing. Plan how you're going to create a multi-coloured life.

★ Step 4: Knowing what to do when the wheels fall off

Are you keeping an eye on you? And are you treating yourself with as much kindness as you would a friend?

Sometimes it's hard to notice when we're getting into a state of overwhelm because it can come on gradually or we become used to being in battle mode. Some of us are so driven and hard on ourselves that, even if we do notice we're heading for a crash, we ignore it.

As the fable goes, if you put a frog in a pan of cold water and gradually heat it up the frog will boil to death, whereas put it in the hot water and it will jump straight out. Preventing your frog from simmering is about continually checking in with yourself to ensure you're rolling with the punches – and if you aren't what are you going to do about it?

There are a number of powerful factors which can gnaw away at our resilience, many of which are self-created and, if left unchecked, can seriously impact on our ability to power up. We all have demons, whether it's our brain's habit of waking us up at 3am to remind us of our worst moments, the fact that we get The Fear every time we have more than two glasses of wine, or just a tendency to think 'I can't do this, I'm rubbish' whenever we face a challenging situation.

Speaker and resilience coach Pam Burrows talks about discovering your own 'Red Flags'; the clues that all is not well and you need to take action to avoid burnout. In her book, *Burnout Buster*, she describes thirty-three signs we sometimes spot but tend to ignore, like eating junk, too much coffee, loved ones telling you to slow down, or you saying things like, "I've got to carry on because there's no one else to do it!" Many of the women I work with have had a good handful of these red flags waving for years. Although each one may not seem that important, collectively they take their toll – I've seen this happen and unfortunately, it's often only when the person reaches crisis point do they take action because they are forced to. The two crucial parts to this are noticing your red flags and acting quickly. Pam suggests reflecting on why you drive yourself too hard, spotting your red flags and then taking time out to get things into perspective.

Here are some proven strategies which will help you cope with those unwanted or unexpected challenges that life throws at you:

Coping strategies for when the going gets tough

1. **Breathe:** when we are stressed and tense our breathing becomes shallow, which only increases our anxiety, as it lowers oxygen levels in the blood, which the brain senses as stress – making us breathe even faster and shallower. Holistic practitioner Jo Tocher recommends taking five deep breaths: "Get in a comfortable position, then ground yourself by taking deep breaths through the nose, all the way from the stomach up into the top of the lungs, then releasing it all out in long slow breaths out."

2. **Remember, this too shall pass:** a phrase that is believed to have originated in the writings of the medieval Persian Sufi poets can serve all of us when we are going through hell. Yes, it may be the worst thing

ever right now, but like all other major challenges, it won't last forever and you will survive. Emotions rarely remain at an intense level over a long period of time. Although you may feel engulfed by sadness, or wracked by grief, you can take comfort from the fact that the shape of your emotion will soon shift into something else if you encourage your mind to drift somewhere else.

3. **The rule of 10**: when you feel overwhelmed by a problem or adversity, get some perspective by applying the rule of 10, asking yourself: 'Will this matter in 10 years' time?' 'Will it matter in 10 months' time?' 'Will it matter in 10 weeks' time? 'Will it matter in 10 days' time?' 'Will it matter in 10 hours' time?' 'Will it matter in 10 minutes' time?' What seems enormous in the heat of the moment can often show itself to be relatively minor – because emotions, like buses or clouds, tend to all arrive together, clouding our view.

4. **Mindfulness**: a concept that originated in Buddhist culture, mindfulness is increasingly being recognised for its health and wellbeing benefits, as well as its relevance in the workplace. Through connecting with all your senses, it enables you to empty your mind of thoughts and distractions and become attentive, focused and aware of the present. As well as being a great way of pulling your attention to the here and now, it's a useful technique for calming the mind, overcoming nerves and building concentration. As you apply mindfulness to all aspects of life, notice how it enhances your ability to stay calm, focus on the task in hand and connect more fully with others – and the impact it has on your resilience and inner power.

5. **Compartmentalising**: being able to park or comparmen-
    talise difficult feelings so that we can perform effec-
    tively is an important part of being resilient. Think of
    the catastrophising ex-boyfriend and the way my friend
    learnt to take negative incidents in her stride, rather
    than picking up on his negative energy and throwing
    a strop. Or that colleague who's caring for a terminally
    ill relative but still manages to make everyone smile
    with their cheerful greetings at the start of every day. So
    you might have had a run-in with the office bully that
    morning, but if you let it ruin your day, it will stop you
    from performing at your best in the afternoon's meeting
    and take your attention from your to-do list, which
    will then increase your stress levels and productivity...

    A key part of resilience is rethinking and reframing
    life's challenges. There are many ways to do this:
    such as using humour in adversity – think Twitter's
    response to President Trump's unpopular policies. You
    can also choose diminishing words to describe a sit-
    uation in order to shape our experience of it – "well,
    that was a bit awks" – when describing that time you
    mistakenly said, "I love you" when saying goodbye to
    your boss. Or you could literally eject an uncomforta-
    ble feeling through making a comment or gesture like
    "bygones" or shaking out your hands or feet as though
    you were ridding yourself of something.

6. **Detaching**: this is the ability to remove yourself from
    what's happening as a coping mechanism, choosing
    when to get involved and when to steer clear. Finding
    ways to disassociate yourself from the emotion of a

situation, through distraction and keeping a sense of perspective can be an extremely powerful strategy when you need an increased dose of resilience. This can be particularly useful when you're under attack. When challenges arise, you just think, 'I don't need to hear/see this,' so in your head you just rise above it. The only danger with this skill of detachment is overdeveloping it, to the extent that you disassociate yourself from the pain or joy in your life and just become numb. This same is true when we numb out difficult feelings with drugs, food, alcohol or any other poison; yes, they may take the pain/boredom/frustration/unhappiness away for a short period of time but they will also cancel out our ability to feel the good stuff.

7. **Growing through change**: how we respond to major negative changes in our lives impacts enormously on our long-term resilience. In Sheryl's Sandberg's book, Option B: Facing Adversity, Building Resilience and Finding Joy, she explores her personal journey through grief after the death of her husband. "How you fail actually affects the speed and strength of recovery and growth. Resilience is about the choices we make in staying the course – and not being afraid to fail."

Author Sophie Sabbage has been living with incurable cancer, at the time of writing, for four years. In her book, *Lifeshocks*, she explores those very specific encounters with what we cannot control, predict or plan: 'There are moments in time when our internal perceptions are confronted by external events, when what is assumed, wished or imagined collides with what is...' Through sharing her own deeply personal story, as well as other case studies, she reveals how these lifeshocks can bring healing, transformation and peace if we take the time to decipher their messages.

EXERCISE 4:
MINDFULNESS

Mindfulness takes practice and becomes easier the more you do it. There are lots of apps available or you could try the steps below:

1. Start by removing all technological distractions from sight and earshot.

2. Take a couple of minutes to notice your breathing. Sense the air coming in and out of your body, watch your belly rise and fall.

3. Tune into all your senses. If you are sitting at your desk, what do you see around you, how does your body feel in the chair, what can you hear, smell and taste?

4. Take some time to just 'be'. If your mind wanders, gently bring it back to your breath and the present.

5. Notice when you tend to zone out and practice bringing your awareness back to the here and now.

6. Observe the world around you without anticipation or judgement: listen with an open mind and allow a deeper wisdom to emerge.

RESILIENCE CONCLUSION

There will always be roadblocks in our way, some massive, some more day to day – they are unavoidable. As George Bernard Shaw said, "Life is not meant to be easy, my child; but take courage: it can be delightful."

It's the courage and optimism of the second part of this quote that tells us what we need to know about resilience. Facing challenges bravely and with positivity and knowing that there will be more tricky moments along the way is the best way to survive.

IN SUMMARY

★ Resilience is the ability to stay strong in the face of adversity, bounce back after setbacks and manage self-limiting beliefs, which can stop you from fulfilling your potential.

★ Developing resilience is about knowing how to maintain a healthy mind and body so that you can navigate the many roadblocks and challenges that threaten to push you off course.

★ Resilience can be compromised by career roadblocks, events outside of your control, everyday knocks, unhelpful thinking and identity changes.

★ Sometimes, it's hard to notice when we're getting into a state of overwhelm because it can come on gradually, or we become used to being in battle mode. Some of us are so driven and hard on ourselves that even if we do notice we're heading for a crash, we ignore it.

★ There are four strategies you can apply for resilience to make your journey through life as smooth as possible:

  ▪ *Planning your journey*: taking control of where you're going and how you're going to get there.

- ***Getting in the driving seat:*** choosing the right mindset and acknowledging that you're the one in control of your own life.

- ***Ongoing maintenance:*** building resilience into your daily life by putting the right fuel in, not running on empty and making time for the things you enjoy.

- ***Knowing what to do when the wheels fall off:*** knowing how to stay strong through adversity is about knowing the clues which tell you all is not well and taking action to avoid burnout.

PART THREE

THE EXTERNAL POWER SOURCES

INTRODUCTION TO PART 3

Now that we've explored how you can tap into your internal sources of power (*Intuition*, *Knowledge* and *Resilience*), let's focus on how you can develop the three external sources: *Magnetism*, *Relationships* and *Assertiveness*, which together will allow you to express yourself powerfully to the outside world.

Firstly, we'll examine *Magnetism*, a star quality which enables you to draw attention to yourself in an attractive and compelling way rather than an 'all about me' way. By applying the techniques in the Triple A System©, you'll increase awareness of your unique personal brand and learn how to use your mindset, body language and voice to make a memorable impact and inspire people to say 'Yes'.

We'll then explore how to develop strong and wide-reaching *Relationships* so that you can access practical support and advice whenever you need it. In this chapter, you'll create a relationship-building strategy to ensure you prioritise time with the people who are most likely to support you in achieving your goals. As part of this, we'll focus on practical techniques for developing and nurturing relationships both on and offline in a way that benefits you both.

We'll finish with *Assertiveness*, the ability to get your wants, needs and views met, as well as confidently stand up for what you believe in. We'll examine how you can harness the whole spectrum of emotions and channel them for the common good. In learning how to be assertive, you will have the freedom to speak your truth, walk knowingly into conflict and live fully in the world.

Let's *do* this.

Chapter 7

MAGNETISM

"A girl should be two things: classy and fabulous."

—COCO CHANEL

THE POWER OF MAGNETISM

There are times when you need to command attention in order to get things done. This isn't necessarily about being liked or popular, but about compelling people to want to do things with or for you. Magnetism is about the art of attraction and standing out from the crowd. It's about being confident that when you open your mouth, people will not only want to listen, but also hang on to your every word. And because it's rare for anyone to accomplish anything without the support of others, it can be the difference between being successful in life, or not.

Magnetism in action

When was the last time you met someone who truly sparkled? When was the last time you shone yourself? This morning, I was at a networking event with about 20 women. And I can honestly say that every single woman in that room had an iridescent quality. Like a myriad of diamonds, they attracted light and attention and refracted it back. The room was like a rainbow.

Now, this isn't something that happens every day. A collective sparkle doesn't happen by accident. Yes, we were in a loft room and the light was spectacular, but it was more than that. It was to do with the atmosphere that had been created by the women themselves, many of whom knew each other well, all of whom had each other's best interests at heart. As a result of that level of mutual support, everyone felt able to relax and bask in the glow of each other's company. And their collective power was magnified.

I understood the importance of magnetism when advising a friend struggling to make her presence felt at her new job. Surrounded by big personalities, she played small, seemingly unable to be the feisty and hilarious woman I know her to be. She's far from shy, but somehow in this new office environment, she was sinking without a trace. Eventually, I gave her some coaching to get to the core of her self-limiting behaviour and tackle her loss of sparkle in this challenging situation. We had to dig deep to raise her awareness of her own brilliance and help her feel at ease with being herself (that is, her best self). As her confidence came back, her natural presence and humour started to emerge and she found herself being noticed for all the right reasons.

The dictionary definition of magnetism, when it comes to human behaviour, is the ability to attract and charm people. Although this might be one of the outcomes, its power brings so much more than that. Think of someone who just seems to know how to make life 'work' for them, who makes an impact on a room by radiating likeability and charisma, someone who irresistibly draws people to them, seemingly without trying. That's magnetism. And yes, some people are born with it (the lucky things) – they are the ones whose natural looks and talent mean that they have fewer hoops to jump through than the rest of us. But it's also a quality that we can all learn to switch on as required.

I was reminded of this at parents evening when discussing my daughter's progress with two teachers. One – let's call her Mrs M – was warm and welcoming and clearly knew my daughter very well. My daughter lit up when she spoke. Mr S, however, had a negative and unappealing air which sucked all the energy out of the room. As we sat there listening to him drone on, my daughter looked so uninspired and deflated, and I understood why because I felt the same way. No surprise that Mrs M gets far more positive results and engagement. Teachers can't afford to lack magnetism and neither can you.

Think about events you've been to and the difference between the speakers. They may be delivering an equally important message, but it's the ones with charisma that captivate you, that are most memorable, and whose stories stick in your mind. The rest? Meh. Your phone and that gif of a cat trying to start a fight with its tail suddenly appear far more interesting.

Every year, the matter of who wins *Strictly Come Dancing*, *The Voice* or *X-Factor* teaches us that it isn't necessarily the ones with the best technical skills who count. It's usually the ones who capture our hearts through their stagecraft, storytelling, the emotion they show and the journey they've been on.

With all these people, it's not just about the amount of energy they project. It's something else. It's not just about the level of expertise or technical ability they display. It's more than that. It's not just about the relevance of the stories. There's something more... It's an indefinable twinkle in their eye that makes the world fall in love with them and get on their side. And we could all do with a bit more of that.

How does magnetism relate to Power Up?

The irresistible quality of magnetism makes it an essential tool for anyone wishing to Power Up at work and in life.

In today's fast-paced, competitive world, being good isn't enough. You have to let it show. The fact is, the world doesn't notice shrinking violets and it's unlikely that people will pro-actively seek you out to unearth your inner brilliance.

Without magnetism, that all-important presence that gets you attention when you need it, you can't truly thrive in the work-place. You could have all the expertise in the world, but if you can't articulate it or it isn't noticed, you may as well be living under a rock. Or be one. In the same way that an unmined, uncut and unpolished diamond is just a black rock, unless you take the time to identify your unique strengths – your star quality – and find ways for them to shine, you will be minimis-ing your potential. You'll still be a black rock, with your true intrinsic value and enormous brilliance hidden. And from a

"

IN TODAY'S FAST-PACED, COMPETITIVE WORLD, BEING GOOD ISN'T ENOUGH. YOU HAVE TO LET IT SHOW.

social perspective, if you don't shine your light, you'll miss out on a variety of interactions that make life worthwhile.

You've got to be comfortable with yourself to exude magnetism. The good news is that it can be learnt and that the other sources of power from the Power Up Model© will help you: *Intuition* and *Knowledge* will give you something magnetic to share, and *Resilience* will give you the strength to stay magnetic, even when the going gets tough. Magnetism will also magnify your other sources of power, making it easier for you to generate *Relationships* and communicate *Assertively*.

Why do we need it?

Knowing how to 'switch on' your magnetism can make a huge difference to your effectiveness at work and in life – and this chapter will show you how. When you switch on your magnetism:

■ **You make a memorable impact**: we all know people who hide their light under a bushel and find themselves walked over, talked over or passed over as a result. Having magnetism is the opposite: your presence, ideas and interjections are noticed and you make a difference.

■ **You stand out from the crowd**: having a magnetic quality means you develop a strong personal brand. People not only know who you are, but also what you represent and what makes you different, both in person and online.

- **You deliver a compelling message:** magnetism means people want to hear you speak because you communicate your vision, opinions and demands in ways that resonate with them. Result: your message is received loud and clear.

- **You draw people to you:** with magnetism, you entice people to want to be around you, whether that's working in your team or spending time with you socially.

- **You inspire people to take action:** your energy and passion galvanises others to buy into your vision and they want to deliver results for you. This quality is like gold dust for anyone in a management or leadership position and great for both engagement and motivation.

- **You influence people to say 'yes':** with the quality of magnetism, people will want to find ways to work with you, rather than against you. Through focusing on shared goals rather than entrenched positions, it's possible to overcome barriers, move through conflict and reach a resolution that everyone's happy with.

What gets in the way?

We have already explored how girls from a very young age are told to 'be quiet', 'don't show off', 'sit still' and not take up space, none of which is conducive to practising those magnetic behaviours which attract attention to you. Unfortunately, there are a number of other powerful factors that stop us from truly shining our light.

1. **Reluctance to put ourselves out there.** Women may feel nervous or uncomfortable about being the centre of attention, in real life or on social media. Some of us worry that we'll be seen as show-offs if we do. I have a client who, as part of her role, is required to travel around the world, visiting her company's local branches and sharing her expertise with people at different levels across the organisation. She has been told that she needs to increase her personal presence and although she now feels comfortable delivering her message from the stage and introducing herself at networking events, she draws the line at adapting her personal style to look more professional or attract attention, even though she knows this could be a quick win for her visibility. Unfortunately, if you're quietly doing your thing in a corner, people will not get to appreciate all the amazing qualities you bring, which means that they'll be missing out and so will you. Far from being a self-serving quality, magnetism is about sharing your gifts in order to enhance your impact on the world.

2. **Others shining brighter.** Although some of us are comfortable commanding attention when we need to, there is only so much room under the spotlight. What can sometimes get in the way of our magnetism is when someone else is shining their light so brightly that it ends up eclipsing ours. This is a shame because it's important that we all get the attention when we want or need to.

3. **Mood hoovers.** Motivational speaker Jim Rohn said that we are the average of the five people we spend the most time with. When it comes to relationships we are

hugely influenced by those closest to us, who have a big impact on our self-esteem, the way we think, the decisions we make and how we come across. Being around people with whom you have complex and difficult relationships can have a detrimental effect on how you come across. Whereas if you spend time with positive people who believe in you, cheer you on and are themselves doing great things, this will undoubtedly rub off and brings out the best in you. While it's really important to be surrounded by people who believe in us, it's also necessary to have those who will give honest, critical feedback when necessary, if we are to bring out the best in ourselves. But some influences are truly to be avoided, so be conscious of who you spend your time with.

4. **Competitiveness**. There are moments when it's hard not to feel envious of others' success, especially if we see them as our peers. It can be especially challenging if we feel they are storming ahead and 'owning' something that we see as our 'patch'. This kind of attitude will zap your magnetism faster than putting a bag over your head. It reroutes all the energy you could have been directing towards propelling yourself forward into a far more negative place.

It's important to realise that there's room for everyone to sparkle, rather than seeing everyone as a competitor. In his book, Become A Key Person of Influence, author and motivational speaker Daniel Priestley famously identified the fact that we are all standing on a mountain of value – all the unique experience, skills and knowledge we have accumulated. Your mountain of value is not the same as somebody else's because they are not you. And there's room for everyone to succeed. When you create a magnetic connection, you radiate your force out and receive energy back, which can be reciprocally brilliant for both. In other words, if you find a like-minded peer who you really connect with, support them and they'll support you back and you'll both benefit.

So how can we all find a way to exude the magnetism that other people want to see in us, even if we're not the most outgoing person in the world or we're not necessarily 'feeling it' on a given day? The answer lies in understanding what magnetism is and applying the tools and techniques I'm going to share in this chapter. You may not want to do everything I recommend – and in my opinion, it's completely OK to not be the most magnetic person in the room – but I strongly recommend that you find ways to step out of the shadows and claim your place in the sun because if you don't, the world will be a much duller place.

WHAT IS MAGNETISM?

Sometimes referred to as presence, magnetism is intangible, like a love potion or catnip. We don't know what it is when we meet someone imbued with it, we just know how powerful it is. Whether it's a face across a crowded room, the only person at an event we feel compelled to speak to, an Oscar-winning actor or a speaker at a conference, some people just ooze magnetism.

In a recent poll, I asked people to name women in the public eye who have personal magnetism and why. The results were an eye-opener, with celebrated qualities including women who are "unapologetically themselves", "comfortable in their own skin", "full of sparkle", "glowing from within" and "clever, with a sense of humour".

The diverse list included Joanna Lumley, Sandi Toksvig, Fearne Cotton, Courtney Love, Lauren Laverne and Sue Perkins. Comments included Michelle Obama: "she's real"; Olivia Colman: "no sudden diva behaviour"; Meryl Streep: "comfortable in her skin"; Judy Dench "unassuming, lady-like, fun". It was cheering to see a few businesswomen nominated too: Christine Lagarde, Karen Brady and Mary Portas. But notice how the same themes kept coming up – sparkle, authenticity, realness, fun.

These are the qualities we value when we meet new people, the ones that make us want more. Interestingly, when I ask delegates in my masterclasses to name people in the public eye who have magnetism, I find it fascinating that often, the people they name remind me of the individuals themselves. The same will apply to you. If you think of someone with magnetism, invariably, there will be something about them which mirrors how you speak, what you look like and the values you hold dear. This is because we tend to appreciate characteristics in others that we hold within ourselves, even if we don't recognise them.

As well as these personal qualities, magnetism is undoubtedly linked to attractiveness and allure. But this doesn't have to be about your physical attributes or sexuality. It could equally be something else you're drawn to, for example, their ability to make everyone laugh, or the care they show in making sure everyone's having a good time at a party.

Personal magnetism is also about influencing others through your interestingness and personal appeal. Although we may not all feel comfortable using our physical allure, the power of holding someone's attention because what we're offering is unusual, exciting or compelling is something we can all develop and will be amplified if we access our powers of *Intuition*, *Knowledge* and *Resilience*.

Where does it come from?

To understand the true meaning of magnetism, it's useful to turn to the world of science, which is where the word and concept originated. Magnetism is defined as: "Physical phenomena arising from the force caused by magnets, objects that produce fields that attract or repel other objects."[31]

Think of the science experiment from school, when a magnet was placed near a pile of iron filings on a table, causing them to all point in the magnet's direction. Every single one of them in unison. That's the power of magnetism, and if you have the right kind, you can inspire anyone to follow and say 'yes' to you.

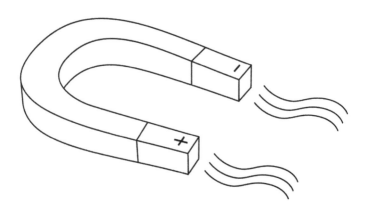

You probably also remember what happened when you try to push two of the same magnetic poles together – they repel each other. In the same way, personal magnetism can be so powerful that you end up putting people off. Shout too loudly and people cover their ears. Come on too strong and they run away.

From a leadership perspective, its impact can cause people to change direction and reconsider their true north, just like the needle in the compass. This may or may not be a 'good' thing, depending on the intention behind the force.

Although the diverse list of women I have identified in my research indicates that magnetism comes in many different forms, it also highlights the one thing that all magnetic people have in common: the ability to manage the energy between themselves and others in a compelling way, generating a mesmerising force that is mutually rejuvenating and self-perpetuating.

A great example of this is Helen Mirren. If you watch her being interviewed after she's won an award for her acting prowess, she manages to beautifully balance acknowledging the accolade and sharing the glory, drawing attention to herself and deflecting it away to her co-stars in a mesmerising dance of magnetism shared.

For lasting magnetism, you've got to realise that it's not all about you, it's just as much about other people. You can think of this like the ancient symbol for infinity (see illustration below).

This symbol, as it relates to magnetism, illustrates the eternal play between push and pull, where you give out an attractive aura, powered by warmth and generosity, and at the same time draw people in through your attractiveness and allure. This ongoing push and pull becomes even more powerful when you come into contact with other people who are doing the same thing: you push your energy out and they pull it towards them and vice versa.

Generating Magnetic Energy

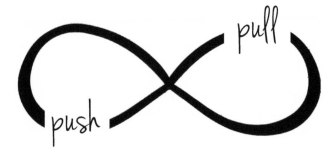

- **PUSH:** giving out an attractive aura powered by warmth and generosity

- **PULL:** drawing people towards you through your attractiveness and allure

HOW CAN YOU DEVELOP IT?

Now that we understand what magnetism is and why it's such a potent source of power, let's explore how you can define, enhance and utilise your own.

The good news is that we can all learn how to switch it on if we choose to. As a shortcut, I've developed the Triple A System© which will help you to Power Up your magnetism whenever you need to. Let's explore the three As one by one.

The Triple A© System

If you look at the table below comparing minimal and maximal magnetism, you'll see that it breaks magnetism down into three interconnected parts, all of which are within your control:

 Awareness: a deep appreciation of your impact on others and the value you bring

 Attitude: a sparkling mindset of warmth and generosity

 Allure: the ability to attract attention through using your authentic style

We're now going to explore each element of Magnetism in turn, starting with **Awareness.**

	Minimal Magnetism	Maximal Magnetism
Awareness	Limited appreciation of your strengths Limited understanding of the value you bring to others Low sense of self-worth or over-inflated sense of self-worth (arrogance)	Significant awareness and appreciation of your strengths Comprehensive understanding of the value you bring to others High sense of self-worth Ability to share your worth appropriately (without tipping over into arrogance)
Attitude	Closed-mindedness Pettiness, small mindedness Ingratitude Coldness, aloofness Fakeness Self-criticism Lack of confidence Apathy	Openness Generosity, abundance Gratitude Warmth Authenticity Self-acceptance Confidence Excitement
Allure	Closed body language Neutral/cold expression Minimal energy Dull, drab clothing Flat, monotone voice Over-complicated language Hackneyed phrases, jargon	Open body language Eye contact, smiling Energetic, movement Colourful, vibrant clothing Varied vocal tones Clear, simple language Unusual word choice, precision language

Awareness: A deep awareness of the value you bring

Take a moment to think of the most compelling people you know. As you imagine them talking, do they seem unsure of their message, do they ramble on? When they've stopped talking, are you hazy about what inspires them and their purpose in life, or are you crystal clear?

A key part of magnetism is being aware of your personal brand: how you're perceived, what you're known for, how people describe you to others, e.g. "She's the one who always sits in the corner and says nothing" versus "She always comes up with great ideas" or "She's the expert at..." Whether you like it or not, people are subconsciously or consciously making their mind up about you all the time, and so it makes sense to be in control of what they come away thinking.

Defining your personal brand is also about recognising your audience, identifying not only who you want to attract, why and how, but also who you want to keep at arms' length – you don't need to please all the people all the time.

In the workplace and on the job market, your reputation is everything. A friend told me that in the early days of her career she merrily filled her days with team drinks, gossip and banter with fellow colleagues, little realising that this would be frowned upon. As a result, no one seemed to notice all the hard work she was also putting in and she failed to get promoted. Until the day a frank line manager pointed out that she wasn't known for her commitment to the team or her brilliant ideas, but her 'bit of a giggle' persona – and wasn't seen as someone worth promoting. A short, sharp shock. But also an important lesson on how to maintain office relationships. Although it's possible to develop great

271

friendships at work, ultimately, the main reason we're there is to do a good job and progress, so it makes sense to balance having fun with your colleagues with making sure that your professional capabilities are seen.

Your personal brand

There are many definitions of the term 'brand' – here's one of my favourites, which can be applied just as much to personal branding as to traditional brands.

> "A brand is the set of expectations, memories, stories and relationships that, taken together, account for a consumer's decision to choose one product or service over another. If the consumer... doesn't pay a premium, make a selection or spread the word, then no brand value exists for that consumer."
>
> **–SETH GODIN**[32]

Your brand encapsulates your reputation. It represents who you are, what you're known for and how people experience you. Creating an authentic 'brand you' is about bringing more of you into what you do and how you do it. Delivering your brand clearly and consistently will create a memorable experience in the minds of those you interact with – your audiences – and open up new opportunities for you to deliver results.

To define your personal brand, it's useful to explore who you are now and how you would like to be seen at different levels.

This is a combination of what people see on the surface (brand attributes) as well as your personal qualities, your values, your passions and your inner purpose, as illustrated in the diagram I've created. When you identify your values, engage your passions and connect with your purpose, you will find it much easier to act authentically and therefore build a powerful, magnetic brand.

EXERCISE 1: AWARENESS OF YOUR PERSONAL BRAND

Defining your brand is a four-step process.

★ Personal Brand: Step 1

To find out what your authentic personal brand is, reflect on the following questions and get feedback from a mixture of colleagues, team members, managers, family and friends:

1. How would you describe my 'personal brand'? If this is too abstract a question, you could probe by asking: what professional and personal qualities am I known for in the organisation?

2. What do you see as my greatest strengths?

3. When thinking about how I present myself, how might I hold myself back?

4. What small changes could I make to the way I present myself that would make the biggest difference?

★ Personal Brand: Step 2

Now look at the brand pyramid above and note down what is characteristically 'you' at each level, as well as any qualities you would like to develop further to enhance your magnetism. You can use the descriptions of each level below to aid your thinking:

Brand attributes = the unique skills that make you stand out from the crowd, as evidenced through your most successful projects, roles and tasks that you perform well.

Personal qualities = personality traits that you bring to your role. Examples might include creativity, patience, energy, dynamism, clarity, logic, objectivity, motivation, etc.

Values = a set of words that encapsulate the core beliefs and philosophies that you hold about life. For example: respect, integrity, creativity, collaboration.

Passions = what you love about what you do; the drive that fuels your actions and inspires change. For example, you might be inspired to bring creativity into everything you do. Or you might be on a mission to bring the fun back into financial services.

Purpose = your internal vision of what you would like to achieve. This also sits at the heart of the Power Up Model©. For example, if your purpose is continuous improvement, you might be driven to streamline all processes so that your team operates more efficiently, or you might be inspired to explore how artificial intelligence will empower your organisation rather than take people's jobs, or you might be passionate about bringing diversity and inclusion into your sector.

Once you've got clarity on your personal brand, you can think about how to make the way you come across match your qualities, values, passions and inner purpose, so that you do yourself justice. A brand, like a diamond, is multi-layered and multi-faceted. What's important is revealing the most appropriate facet to suit the context you're in and the audience you're with; for example, you will reveal different aspects of your personality and explain your role differently depending on whether you're talking to a board member or a graduate recruit.

When marketing brands, it's all about knowing what your audiences are looking to buy, not what you are trying to sell. It's about knowing your audiences well enough to create an offering that's tailored to them but still feels authentic. The same applies to your personal brand. Although it's essential to know which values you represent and what you will not compromise on, it's also important to think about how you will tailor your approach depending on who you're talking to.

★ Personal Brand: Step 3

Now use the table below to identify and profile your top three audiences. This will ensure that you're presenting the most attractive version of yourself to each, in an authentic way. For example, if one of your target audiences is your company's MD (and why wouldn't it be?), find out what role they fulfil, their year's goals, as well as the opportunities and challenges they face. You can glean this by doing some research into your company's performance and the marketplace you're in, as well as asking colleagues or even the MD themselves. Having reflected on this, you will know which parts of your role they would be most interested in and, therefore, which projects you should be ready to discuss with them. Revealing your personal brand isn't just about what you say, but how you say it. If they have a reserved communication style and you're more outgoing, it would serve you to turn down your persona and instead, demonstrate to them how much care and attention you're devoting to your responsibilities.

★ Personal Brand: Step 4

Finally, consider how you can ensure your priority audiences get to know about your personal brand. This could include those chance 'elevator' encounters, although these are less likely to happen if you work remotely, plus you don't always get enough time in these kind of situations to present yourself in the best possible light. So you should also think about how you can proactively create opportunities to speak with the people you want to, whether that's by arranging a meeting to discuss a project you know will be of interest to them or asking a colleague to introduce you.

For more on how to raise your profile, take a look at the *Knowledge* and *Relationships* chapters.

Target audience			
Who are they? (Role, Responsibilities, Goals, Opportunities, Challenges)			
Why would they be interested in you?			
In which contexts would you be communicating with them?			
Which facet of your brand should you be revealing to them?			

Being real

While consistently demonstrating your brand is important, magnetism isn't always about putting on your A-game and making out everything's perfect. Expressing your own authentic feelings can help people to relate to you and engage more with your thinking. Think Andy Murray breaking down at the press conference when he announced his retirement – this enhanced his magnetism to the nth degree because we could relate to his emotional turmoil. There is, of course, the frustrating fact that when a man cries everyone applauds, but if a woman cries people say, 'She's lost it.' (What's that all about?) Nonetheless, this is a good example of how authenticity and occasional glimpses of what really matters to you can get more people on side. Another example is Marilyn Monroe. Yes, people loved her voluptuous and seductive beauty, but they were inexorably drawn to her fragility too. This made her just that bit more enthralling to her audience and gave her longevity – and fame that lingers to this day.

Being real can also get people to 'buy into' your unique approach and want to be part of your tribe. An example of this is Sheryl Sandberg. In her first book, *Lean In*, the message was 'Women you can have it all', which alienated some. By contrast, with her second book, *Option B: Facing Adversity, Building Resilience, and Finding Joy*, co-written with Adam Grant after she'd lost her husband, the subject was how to handle grief. It was very real and honest. In it, she admitted that life sends curveballs and she kind of fell apart. The book explores how she got herself back together again, which was really attractive because it was so real. Elizabeth Gilbert, the author of *Eat Pray Love*, lost her partner in 2017 and has been equally open about her grief, anger and survival. Her following is now off the scale, and it's her authentic voice that attracts such an enthusiastic response. People love real.

Flexibility and adaptability

As well as understanding how your brand can attract people to you, honing your self-awareness will also help you to appreciate that you could, through your magnetism, be putting people off.

I recently delivered a keynote about leading with gravitas at a conference and a slightly confrontational question came from a young woman at the back of the room: "I get told by my bosses that I'm too much, but why should I change? This is who I am." It was confrontational because I had been talking about the importance of adaptability, and although how she was being at work was clearly not working, she seemed reluctant to change. And so my response was: "It's entirely up to you, but if you go through your whole life like this, you run the risk of alienating 80 per cent of the people around you. Another option would be to learn flexibility and self-awareness and become more magnetic as a result." Sometimes it's a good time to turn up the dial and sometimes it pays to turn it down.

The fact is there are different types of magnetism – some people are in their element attracting attention by sheer force of their personality, which is great. However, the people with the loudest voices can sometimes have a dominating element which ends up putting others in a subordinate role. Have you ever been at a party or event when someone walks in and exudes so much star quality that they literally suck it all up for themselves? They're witty, charming and beautiful, but they don't hear a word you say. This is counter-productive as that person will soon be seen as a showboater – someone who likes the attention but you cannot make a great connection with. This is when magnetism starts repelling rather than attracting. And it's not always about being loud and showy – you can radiate magnetism without saying much at all. Someone just saying one word or looking at you in a particular way can make you want to start a conversation – it's an invitation to connect in an equal way.

Self-awareness will not only let you know when it's important to adapt and flex to your surroundings, it will also help you to realise that the Marmite effect is OK. Accepting that not everyone will 'get' or like us rather than tying ourselves in knots trying to please all the people all the time is an important lesson to learn as early as possible. However much we try, we won't get the whole world to love us. What's more important is to use our magnetism, combined with the other power sources explored in this book, to generate respect, which doesn't come from being everyone's friend, but instead, from standing in your power and using it for the greater good.

In time, you'll reach a level of self-acceptance where you'll be at ease with who you are and adopt a 'take it or leave it' attitude when it comes to your impact on others. And ironically, there's nothing more compelling than that!

Attitude: A sparkling mindset of openness and generosity

As well as increasing your **Awareness** of the unique qualities that will draw people to you, it's important to know how to adopt a magnetic **Attitude** so that you can project yourself outwards. For many of us, this involves liking ourselves enough to let our natural sparkle be seen and believing that we have something valuable to share. Although some people operate like this all the time, others find it quite draining to do so, which is why it's helpful to know that projecting a magnetic attitude is something you can Power Up when you need to and power down when you don't. A great example of this is Beyoncé, who created her alter ego, 'Sasha Fierce', who she's said is nothing like her in real life, to get herself into the most magnetic state to smash it on stage. Although I'm not saying you need to go to that extreme, imagine how powerful you could be if you channelled just a tiny bit of this energy when you need to. So how about creating your own version?

Switch on

The ability to 'flick that switch', is harnessed by actors, performers and public speakers to command attention, rally a crowd and perform at their best. The concept is beautifully illustrated in a story about Marilyn Monroe, who was out shopping one day with Norman Mailer. Norman expressed surprise that Marilyn wasn't getting her usual attention and she replied that she was not 'being Marilyn' at that moment. To demonstrate the difference, she flicked a switch and 'became' Marilyn, at which point she was instantly mobbed. So what can you do to switch on your magnetism?

CASE STUDY

Natalie Haverstock, AKA Miss Ballooniverse, runs a company that goes to events and delights people of all ages with their balloon creations. She's the most magnetic person I know. But when I interviewed her, I was surprised to hear that she hasn't always been that way. She explains:

"When I was a child, I went through a phase of crippling shyness. It really was the most awful feeling, that I was being negatively scrutinised by the whole world. Then one day, I was in a room where I saw someone else who looked extremely shy. It was a revelation to me that other people could have that same feeling, and I realised that I could put other people at ease, so they wouldn't feel so shy. To this day, I try to turn the attention outwards, to engage with others and be a welcoming face. If ever I find a social situation a little daunting, I just say to myself, I surely can't be the only one, let's get the ice broken."

So how does she do it? For a start, it's not just about the balloons. Natalie and her team of Balloonistas all dress in bright, 50s-style dresses with waspish waists and big skirts that powerfully attract attention. But it's not about the dresses either. Natalie does something else. When I probed her about how she can have a whole room of people in the palm of her hand from the moment she walks in, she advises: "A smile is a must. Coupled with plenty of eye contact, which makes you approachable. Try to find the common denominator with them: you might have been invited by the same person or have a shared interest. Ask questions. If it's a networking event, it can be about their business. Be genuinely interested in the other person. Don't be too serious. If you trip over your words or stutter, just laugh about it. Don't be afraid to bring people into your conversation. Introduce people. Work the room so you don't get stuck with one group. Every gathering is an opportunity to make new friends and network, so make the most of it!"

Flicking that switch will come more naturally for extroverts because they get their energy from being around people and are used to performing on a stage of their own making. This doesn't necessarily mean they always get the best results, however, because they can sometimes go too far and end up overwhelming everyone else. On the other hand, introverts may struggle more with switching on because they are more comfortable in their own company and don't need validation from others for any feeling of self-worth. They need to remember that if they want their value to be appreciated, they will need to actively demonstrate it.

EXERCISE 2:
FIVE STEPS TO A MAGNETIC ATTITUDE

The best way to adopt a magnetic attitude is to plan in advance how you'd like to come across and then, on the day, focus on maintaining a magnetic mindset.

1. **Identify.** Start by identifying an opportunity to Power Up your magnetism, for example, meeting your new CEO, going to an interview, inspiring a new team member, attracting attention from the stage or going to a networking event.

2. **Switch on.** Decide that, for that time period, you are going to bring 10 per cent of your energy and attention to the present moment. A key part of this is eliminating distractions, so remove all technological devices from sight or earshot, and decide when you will next check in, as this will stop your mind from wandering.

3. **Get excited.** Choose to be excited about what you have to share – your message is a gift. When you're having the best time energising people and, in turn, being energised by them, the atmosphere is electric. To do

this fully, it helps to identify in advance who will be there, visualise the warm, sparkling conversations you'll have together, the exciting news you'd like to share and what you want to find out from them.

4. **Pay attention.** Look to your surroundings, it will help to keep you present, minimise your self-consciousness and take attention away from any nerves or negative thoughts going on in your head. Carefully observe the people around you – their expressions, their gestures, their points of view. Give people the gift of your undivided attention, *decide* to be fascinated by what they say rather than disengaged, because you truly want to find out more. As you communicate with people, allow yourself to look into their eyes, listen deeply and respond with your own thoughts.

5. **Notice the energy and warmth.** This is created when you decide to connect with other people. Observe the balance of airtime – you should be aiming for an equal amount of time unless you're on stage – and how, by paying attention to them, they then respond with their attention and focus.

Igniting a spark

Of course, there are some people you naturally connect with more than others, but it is possible to find a spark with almost everyone, if you choose to. This summer, I was lucky enough to attend a concert at the O2 Arena in London. From where I sat, I could see the performers preparing to go on stage. There was one group that particularly caught my eye. In the fifteen minutes before going out, having done their warm-up, they gathered together in a circle and performed a dance that reminded me of a graceful version of a rugby huddle, where the players gather together to agree their match tactics. They may not all have been best buddies, who knows, there may have been some professional rivalries, but for that moment, they were collectively flicking a switch to spark the best in one another. And they duly went on to deliver an amazing performance.

A spark only ignites when two objects are rubbed together and magnetism is only generated in vast quantities when two people have chemistry, that amazing synchronicity and magic that can be generated by a dynamic pairing. Think of Ally, the young singer played by Lady Gaga, and Bradley Cooper's Jackson 'Jack' Maine, the famous hard-drinking country star in *A Star is Born*. Think Ginger Rogers and Fred Astaire. Or Mia and Sebastian in *La La Land*.

A real-world example is Hela Wozniak-Kay and Annie Brooks, the yin and yang duo who founded women's networking group, Sister Snog. Although they are complete chalk and cheese, they have a chemistry which makes them fizz and sparkle with electricity when they interact and manage to be funny, deep, professional, irreverent and super-stylish all at the same time, through the way they bounce off each other.

Individually they're dynamic, but together they're dynamite. What is it and how can we bottle it?

To create that all-important spark you need to start by finding something in common that fires you both up. To do that you will need to hone your questioning skills – more on that in the Relationship chapter – but more importantly, be willing to invest energy in connecting with the other person.

For this you need to have an attitude of warmth, generosity and openness – i.e. your attention isn't purely on 'pushing out' your own energy, but rather pulling people in by putting them at ease and making them feel good about themselves. People can only take so much of a big personality or charm offensive before it starts undermining that person's power. Come on too strong and, in the end, the person on the receiving end switches off.

Bill Clinton was reported to be extremely good at making each individual in a room feel like they were the most important person there. He did this through eye contact, physical proximity and truly looking the other person in the face, as though he wanted to inhabit their world. As copywriting expert Jackie Barrie puts it: "Everyone's second favourite word is 'I', but their number one favourite is their own name, so focus on the word 'you' rather than 'me' or 'I' when talking or writing to people". You can also pay attention to their names, their lives and identities which will inevitably draw them in, because everyone likes to talk about themselves and everyone wants to feel interesting and special.

Affirmations

Another powerful way to become more magnetic is through affirmations. Science tells us that our brains are malleable and can be rewired by our thoughts. Fortunately for us, with practice, we can control our thinking. If you see yourself as a little kitten instead of a mighty lion you'll never communicate in a magnetic way. If your self-talk is negative, your brain will respond in kind and those thoughts become a self-fulfilling prophecy. Although some people may write them off as wishy-washy, positive affirmations are a quick and effective way to change your thought patterns and subsequently, your brain activity, to achieve our outcomes.

EXERCISE 3: USING AFFIRMATIONS

Getting yourself into the most empowered, magnetic state is about preparing a series of statements that reinforce your right to be yourself, a powerful pep-talk that celebrates the authentic you.

To do this, think about those situations when you want to be your best and when you feel most challenged, for example, going up on stage to receive an award or being the most inexperienced person in a meeting. Think about how your least powerful self might respond in these situations (for example, "I feel self-conscious", "I have no right to be here", "All eyes are on me, what pressure").

Now think about how you would like to feel in these situations, which is usually the opposite of the above and create your affirmation to describe this. One client concocted this fabulous mantra, which she repeats whenever she is going into a situation where she wants to present her best self: "I belong in this room. I'm absolutely prepared. What I'm about to say is incredibly valuable." This will Power Up your confidence and give energy to what you say. You can create a series of affirmations to go with each challenging situation you face or create a one-size-fits-all. Write down your affirmation and put it somewhere where you'll regularly see it for example, as a screensaver on your phone, on your laptop or desk. Make sure that each time you go into a challenging situation, you remind yourself of your affirmation.

Allure: The ability to attract attention through using your authentic style

What do people see when you walk into a room? Do you light it up with your smile? Or do you slink in and avoid eye contact? Think about what people see, hear and feel when they're around you. Do you greet people, accept compliments and give them out, radiating verve and va va voom? If not, now would be a good time to start. Knowing how to sparkle and ignite sparks with those around you is key to magnetism; having that energy and letting it be felt.

There are many factors that contribute to our allure, that quality of being powerfully and mysteriously attractive or fascinating. People who are memorable are those who are excited and passionate. They are the people who fizz with life and energy as they chat about their life, your jacket, the venue… whatever. They are not standing there moaning or being closed off, but exuding positivity. When you compliment their dress, they don't say, "Oh this is ancient," and when you say their hair looks different, they don't reply, "Yes, but I haven't washed it all week."

People who put themselves down, even humorously, are not putting out the right message about themselves. They are not saying, "Talk to me, I'm interesting," but, "Who me? I wouldn't bother." And so our allure can be turned on or off, depending on what people see, hear and feel in our presence. And we are in control of that.

What gives us Allure?

We all have our own unique allure, whether it's your captivating smile, bewitching eyes, the fall of your hair, your sense of style, your mesmerising voice, your signature scent, your distinctive laughter, your curiosity about the world, your passion for your subject, your unshakeable drive, the list is infinite. And what one person finds alluring, another person might not, for example, our use of humour and sense of fun can be enormously attractive to some while equally others can find it too much.

Allure can be transmitted actively, for example, when someone speaks in a compelling voice, or it can be conveyed passively: your humility when praising the role of your team can be a breath of fresh air compared to a colleague who takes all the glory; we can be extremely powerful by being humble and keeping schtum so that others can speak.

"There's nothing more powerful than a woman who knows how to contain her power and not let it leak, standing firmly within it in mystery and silence. A woman who talks too much sheds her allure."

–MARIANNE WILLIAMSON

Dressing attractively

Your sense of style will also contribute to your allure. In a garden of flowers, we notice the tall poppies and the brightest petals. Really beautiful people will have an advantage because we're drawn to them anyway, but we can all choose how to dress. Do you want to go for greige or black and float unnoticed into a room, or turn up the heat a little in bright colours and stride into a room with a smile?

A series of experiments by Princeton psychologists Janine Willis and Alexander Todorov revealed that it only takes a tenth of a second to form an impression of a stranger from their face, and that longer exposure doesn't significantly alter those impressions[33]. It follows that it takes nanoseconds to make a strong first impression, which means our personal appearance matters enormously. In her book, *Look Like The Leader You Are*, executive image consultant Lizzie Edwards recommends taking a good look at what your clothes are saying about you. "What you wear not only affects how you feel about yourself, how you perform and how you behave, but also affects how others perceive you... The choice you make every morning while standing in front of your wardrobe has an impact both on yourself and others and can, therefore, be a career game-changer."

What's more, studies reveal that psychological changes occur when we wear certain clothes. As Lizzie puts it: "When you put on clothes you associate with power, you feel powerful, which in turn enables you to be powerful. The clothes you wear can also affect your body language and how you communicate." If deciding what to wear is a daily struggle, Lizzie's book gives excellent advice on creating an easy wardrobe that projects all the right qualities.

Lighting people up

Generosity in conversation is very attractive, as is choosing when to let other people have the limelight, asking a question to let other people into the conversation, really taking an interest in their reply, remembering their name, and inviting further connection. Being a good listener is a big part of the allure.

It's not only about listening but also about making people feel amazing and being genuinely happy to be in their presence. Paying compliments lights people up, as does making them feel special, by saying in a heartfelt way, "You look great today," and "I'm so happy to see you."

A can-do attitude is way more attractive than a mood hoover, or someone who is negative, bitchy or a bit of a peeve. While a certain cynicism can be funny in the right situations, negativity either turns people off or scares them; because if a person's being that negative about someone or something else, what might they be saying about you?

And it's not only what happens in that moment but afterwards, that makes you attractive. Because if we're all show and no go, that attractiveness is only skin-deep. It's also about having a certain memorability: being 'sticky' (i.e. so memorable that things you've said or done stick in the mind); standing out in people's memories is what gives you true allure, rather than show-offs who are all sizzle and no steak. What you want is for people to fall in love with you and what you're saying, so they'll buy into you as well as your message.

Using body language

The way you position your body is directly linked to radiating an alluring and confident presence. Research conducted by social psychologist, author and speaker Amy Cuddy, a social psychologist and researcher at Harvard University, found that adopting strong and powerful postures – think Wonder Woman or Superman at their strongest – for just two minutes, has a fundamental effect on your confidence levels, at least for the time it takes to deliver a presentation or be interviewed for a new role.

EXERCISE 4:
POWERING UP
YOUR MAGNETISM

A great tip for switching on your magnetism is paying attention to your posture. You can use this whether you're at the front of a room delivering a presentation or in a networking meeting, and the same tips apply whether you're standing or sitting down. The best way to practice this is with a partner who will give you an honest appraisal of how you look, or in front of a mirror.

1.   Start by planting your feet on the ground, placing them directly underneath your hips and shoulders, with your weight evenly distributed. Feel the solidity of the ground beneath you, the gravity of the earth drawing you down.

2.   Now imagine that you have a string running all the way through the middle of your body up to your head; imagine the string at the top of your head is pulled up gently. Notice how this aligns each vertebra along your spine, making you stand taller. Bring your shoulders back and down, draw your belly in and tuck your bottom under.

The equivalent to this if you're sitting in a chair, is to sit up, positioning your backside squarely in your chair and lean forward slightly. This will keep you energised and in the room while keeping the attention on you.

Next time you walk into a room, walk with purpose and intent. Before you cross the threshold, put your shoulders down and back, open up your chest, look up at the ceiling for a short moment, smile, and then stride into the room, imagining the air parting before you as you enter.

You can also modify your body language to communicate different messages. For example, body language can be used to convey approachability and credibility – both crucial for magnetism. Michael Grinder, a non-verbal communication expert, refers to these styles as 'approachable dog' and 'credible cat'.

- **The approachable dog style** is useful when you want to build rapport, open up a conversation, elicit people's views or lighten a mood. In this mode, you will choose open, expansive gestures with palms turned up, your posture will be asymmetrical with plenty of movement, lots of eye contact and smiles, and a friendly tone with a voice that goes up at the end of sentences.

- **The credible cat style** is appropriate when you want to assert your views, convey serious information, or share opinions without being interrupted, shut down conversations or bring the meeting to a close. In this mode, you will have a symmetrical posture, minimise your movement and gestures, keep your palms down rather than up, adopt a serious tone with plenty of pauses and use a voice that goes down at the end of your sentences.

Magnetic phrases

- Don't say: "How are you?" because the only option open to them is to say "Fine!" That is the biggest conversation killer. Instead, say: "What's the best thing that's happened to you this week?"

- In response to "How are you?", don't say: "Fine, thanks." Because that's boring! Instead, create your own version of: "I'm feeling fabulous, thank you for asking. One thing I'm excited about is... And how about you, what's the best thing...?" (see above).

- Don't say: "You look nice." It may be well-intentioned but it's so bland that its impact will be minimal. Instead, say: "I love your blouse, it really brings out the colour of your eyes." Or: "You look incredible today, those shoes are spectacular."

- By using words like "fabulous", "incredible", "majestic" and "spectacular", you will be cementing your own brand with these words, so that when people think or talk about you, these are the descriptors that will come up. Of course, these exact words may not reflect your authentic brand, which is why creating your own version of the phrases above is so important.

Magnetism online

Allure is also linked to visibility – it's undeniable that when someone comes in who looks fantastic you're instantly drawn to them and compelled to find out more. Of course, as we know, there's so much more to it than how someone looks. And it's not only offline but online too – notice how you are drawn to attractive personalities on social media and why.

A good example of an attractive social media personality is Dr Lynda Shaw, neuroscientist and author of *Your Brain Is Boss*. Lynda is very clever at engaging with people in a way that's charismatic. On Facebook, she generously comments on other people's posts and activities and is always positive and encouraging as she adds a little twist to the interaction. As a result of this, Lynda is continually visible because she's always uppermost in my social media feed and my thoughts – and for good reasons.

Passionate, positive, supportive social media profiles are alluring because you feel drawn to them. When something comes across as genuine it really stands out from the fakery. These are the people who stick in the mind, who become your cheerleaders. These people are actually building relationships rather than being obsessed with numbers without any real interaction or engagement with each other's content. Your personal magnetism online is a big part of how you interact with other people – and it needs to be real, not mercenary.

EXERCISE 5:
INCREASING YOUR MAGNETISM ONLINE

If you want to increase your magnetism and raise your profile online, a great first step is looking at how other people do it for inspiration.

Start by identifying people who you think have a strong and compelling social media presence. These can be people in the public eye, as well as your friends and followers. Examine how they communicate with their followers online. What do they say, how do they say it, what kinds of pictures do they use to illustrate their feeds? Look at who follows them, the kinds of comments they receive and to what extent they engage.

The most powerful social media presences are those that are authentic, so think about how your brand will reflect your professional and personal qualities online. As I've stated before, cultivating an online presence should be only a percentage of what you do to Power Up your magnetism and it's important to make sure you're also applying the Triple A© approach offline too.

Magnetism when networking

Now that we've explored the Triple A© approach to switching on your magnetism, here's some specific advice on how to channel and amplify it when all eyes are on you: networking.

Magnetism is a big part of successful networking. Looking good, dressing attractively and presenting your best self are important. But what makes us attractive to others when we connect with them is our honesty, our ability to open up and be real, as well as share our passion for what we do. One of the biggest passion-killers in networking terms is the elevator pitch. We've all been in those situations when you're clinging onto the wall for dear life, balancing a glass and an oozing canapé, while someone delivers their formulaic 'one minute' at you without pausing for breath or checking you're still listening.

To avoid being that person, it pays dividends to have a set of phrases ready to answer the dreaded 'What do you do?' question. You can equally use this tactic for when someone asks, 'How are you?' especially if your answer tends to be, "Really busy and stressed", which isn't going to reflect you at your most magnetic.

The Rocket Pitch

I was at an event once when someone asked, "What do you do?" and when I said, "I'm a coach," he looked down his nose and said, "Oh, I know thousands of coaches," in a really disparaging way. Although I wondered what gave him the right to be so patronising, especially as he then said he was an Independent Financial Advisor, hardly the most distinguishing title, but he had a point. The need to have something ready

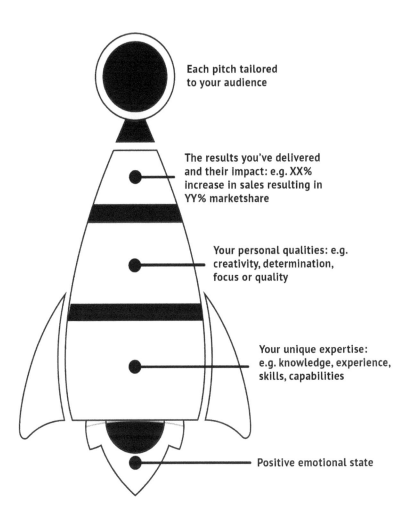

Each pitch tailored to your audience

The results you've delivered and their impact: e.g. XX% increase in sales resulting in YY% marketshare

Your personal qualities: e.g. creativity, determination, focus or quality

Your unique expertise: e.g. knowledge, experience, skills, capabilities

Positive emotional state

to make people sit up and listen was what inspired me to create The Rocket Pitch.

As you can see from the diagram, a successful Rocket Pitch is made up of a series of sentences that illustrate your professional skills and capabilities, convey your sparkling personality and highlight the results you've delivered and their impact, all powered up through your positive emotional state. The best way to stop this from coming across as too robotic or formulaic is to tell a story that illustrates all the above in action. And this is best done when you talk about a recent project that you've been particularly proud of because it's at that point that you let go of the script, your eyes light up and we can see your personality.

When putting together your Rocket Pitch you want to show evidence of the expertise you have that others don't. Combine that with what you uniquely bring to your role – your passion, enthusiasms and inspiration. Another memorable way to talk about the results you deliver and their impact is through simple statistics, but remember to put them into context (an increase of 15 per cent sounds small unless you know that last year, it was only two per cent) and don't overdo it.

EXERCISE 6:

CREATING A MAGNETIC ROCKET PITCH

For maximum impact, you need to create a selection of rocket pitches appropriate to the different types of people you meet.

1. Identify three scenarios where you would like to have a magnetic presence (for example, an event coming up, a meeting or presentation).

2. For each scenario, ask yourself who your audience is and what will they be most interested in hearing about you. Remember different audiences will need different pitches.

3. Then, think about a project you've worked on recently which will be relevant to them and reflect you in the best possible light.

4. Then create a Rocket Pitch for each audience which illustrates your skills and capabilities, conveys your personality, highlights the results you delivered and their impact. For example, when meeting someone for the first time:

"I'm Jane, a manager in a retail store. I have a team which helps customers find the most glamorous outfits for special occasions, so they come away feeling confident and fabulous. I make sure my team works together to convey our unique brand, but I'm passionate about ensuring that each individual showcases the clothes in their own unique way. Over the past year, our turnover has increased from £X to £Y and that's in part due to the freedom my team has to interact with customers in their own way, which I'm really proud of. This contains all the Rocket Pitch elements while conveying your energy and personal qualities.

5. Having worked out what you're going to say to each audience, you now need to practice until you sound and feel natural. Think about the order in which you convey the information – although the example above talks about the results last, it can be even more impactful to do this first, i.e. tell them about the great results you've delivered and then talk about how you did it.

6. Although it's good to give credit where it's due, there are times when you need to make sure you are linked to the results you're talking about. Make sure you don't over-use 'we' and identify what you can say 'I' have done, so it's you that's memorable, not just your team.

7. Once you're happy with the words, rehearse out loud, either with a friend (remember to ask them to feed-back on what you did well and what you need to improve) or by videoing and then critiquing yourself.

8. Record what you said and how you said it, either virtually or on paper, or video yourself as an aide-memoire ready for when you need it.

Having a selection of Rocket Pitches up your sleeve will ensure you have a magnetic presence when networking and leave a memorable impression long after the event is over. Ongoing magnetism leads to the building of a real relationship. So it's really important to follow up and keep that connection going. If you make a new contact or 'click' with someone, follow up on social media, connect with them on LinkedIn, comment on their blog and – if it seems appropriate – arrange to meet for coffee and deepen that common bond.

Magnetic influence

As well as making networking a more enjoyable and productive experience, developing your personal magnetism makes it easier for you to influence people and persuade them to say 'yes'. If you have an open attitude and an attractive personality, they will be more likely to want to be around you, which will make it easier to find ways of working with one another, rather than against one another.

If you think about times when individuals, teams or groups disagree or clash, whether that's arguing about who has access to a meeting room, which department should receive the most funding or which driver has the right of way in a busy street, conflict occurs when each party is firmly fixed on their own self-interest.

If you want to influence people, what's important is moving beyond thinking about what's best for you and instead, what would be best for all concerned. You can think of this as the difference between each party being stuck on their own 'position' versus both parties looking at their 'shared interests'.

Using the example above about which department should get the most funding, both parties will be locked in a stalemate until one of them initiates a conversation about what would be better for the company as a whole: something that everyone can agree on. For example, a discussion might reveal that each department's 'Position' is that they want to invest in a new member of staff, but by having an open-minded conversation they may discover that if they pooled resources they could upskill their existing staff and no longer need to recruit. This would not only save money all round, but also meet their 'Shared Interests' of more capable staff, greater staff engagement and collaboration between teams.

Of course, in these circumstances, someone has to go first. Although pride or bloody-mindedness may get in the way, it's worth remembering that the person who initiates a move towards resolution is often the one with the most influence. And if you use your magnetic powers, you will be more likely to bring people around to your way of thinking.

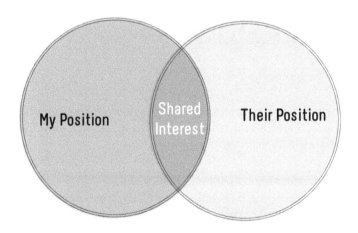

EXERCISE 7: POSITIONS VERSUS INTERESTS

If you would like to use your magnetism to influence or persuade, identify a situation coming up, or one from the past where you would like people to say 'yes'.

1. In the Venn diagram opposite, start by listing all the factors that are important to you in the left-hand circle (My Position).

2. Then, put yourself in the other person's shoes and list all the factors that are important to them in the right-hand circle (Their Position).

3. Now, in the Shared Interests segment where both circles overlap, write down all the factors which you and the other person have in common: things you both want, areas you can agree on.

Having done this preparation, it will be down to you to initiate a conversation or meeting with the other person.

1. Start by stating what you see as the common goal – i.e. reaching a resolution and what that might look like.

2. Then invite them to share their Position (and compare what they say with what you had written down). It will then be down to you to share your Position (which you may have adapted after having heard theirs).

3. You can then initiate a conversation about how you can reach a resolution based on your Shared Interests.

4. To arrive at a resolution, it is likely that both parties will have to be open-minded about their positions. Again, if you go first, they will be more likely to follow suit.

5. Throughout the meeting, make sure you maintain an open body language: arms folded indicates low trust and defensiveness so keep your arms open, ensure steady eye contact, avoid covering your mouth or frowning, and keep your voice steady and calm.

Of course, you may not reach the outcome you're looking for, but at least, by adopting a magnetic approach you will have conveyed your views in a rational way and drawn them towards a deeper level of mutual understanding. For more on communicating with confidence and credibility, turn to the *Assertiveness* chapter.

MAGNETISM CONCLUSION

Having explored the variety of ways you can harness your magnetism, you should have realised that being magnetic isn't only about being the brightest star in the galaxy, but is also about knowing how to switch on a subtle compelling glow that people just want to be around.

Being magnetic is about finding your own way to sparkle. In taking the time to appreciate the impact your personal magnetism can have on the world, I hope that you will find a way to shine your light more often, and in this way, ignite the potential in others.

IN SUMMARY

★ Magnetism is the ability to attract attention to yourself and make a powerful impact, which is essential in a world that remembers the shiny and forgets the dull.

★ Developing the power of magnetism is about understanding the unique qualities that represent your authentic personal brand and knowing how to 'switch on' your most magnetic self through using your attitude, body language, voice and word choice.

★ Magnetic influence is moving beyond thinking about what's best for you to what would be best for all concerned, drawing the other person towards a deeper level of mutual understanding.

★ Magnetism doesn't have to be about your physical attributes. It could equally be something else you're drawn to; for example, their ability to make everyone laugh, or the care they show in making sure that everyone's having a good time at a party.

★ The good news is that we can all learn how to switch it on if we choose to by using the Triple A© system. Just remember, the three interconnected parts:

- **A**wareness: a deep appreciation of your impact on others and the value you bring

- **A**ttitude: a sparkling mindset of warmth and generosity

- **A**llure: the ability to attract attention through using your authentic style.

Chapter 8

RELATIONSHIPS

"Each friend represents a world in us, a world possibly not born until they arrive, and it is only by this meeting that a new world is born."

-ANAÏS NIN

THE POWER OF RELATIONSHIPS

The ability to instigate and sustain relationships is vital for anyone to survive and thrive and one of the most enriching expressions of female power. Prioritising relationships – not the romantic kind but the human kind – is a way of tapping into a more collective power that is incredibly valuable. And it's something that women tend to be naturally good at.

315

"

TAKING THE TIME TO
BUILD STRONG AND
WIDE-REACHING
NETWORKS AT WORK
MEANS YOU'LL FIND
IT EASIER TO ACCESS
PRACTICAL SUPPORT
AND ADVICE WHEN
YOU NEED IT.

Successful women know the power of relationships. And in many cases, it's other women, friends and colleagues who are central to their success. Think Michelle Obama, who in her memoir *Becoming* writes of the huge impact on her of friends like Suzanne ("Screwzy"), who sadly passed away aged 26 and Valerie Jarett, who started out as her boss and went on to become her close confidante.

Relationships in action

Ten years ago, I was on my way to a conference at Wembley Stadium. It was an important event and so I was feeling particularly stressed when I realised the road I was meant to walk down was blocked. Glancing around in despair, I spotted a woman across the street with the same exasperated expression on her face as me, blonde hair billowing about in the breeze. She was wearing red shoes just like mine, and at that moment, I knew we would become friends.

As I look back over my life, I can pinpoint specific relationships that emerged at significant points in my life; people who were highly influential in my development. From my RS teacher, Miss Wilson, who opened my eyes to multiculturalism, to my favourite manager, Noreen, who gave me my first personal development book. From friends who at times were brave enough to hold up a mirror when I'd lost sight of myself, to strangers on trains who saw into the heart of me and with whom I've shared experiences I have never had with anyone else.

The benefits of relationships are huge, both for your career and life in general. Taking the time to build strong and wide-reaching networks at work means you'll find it easier to access practical support and advice when you need it.

As a leader, manager or business owner, you'll be able to influence and persuade far more effectively if you've built up a meaningful connection with people, than if you try and 'tell' them what to do. Not only that, forging female relationships makes business sense. If you run your own business, collaborating with like-minded sisters leads to innovation and ensures you achieve your goals far more quickly than going it alone.

Equally, climbing the career ladder can be tough and once you get there, it can be lonely, especially if you're the only woman on the board. And so it's essential to find women who can be your cheerleaders and have your back while you're smashing the glass ceiling.

In addition, making time for relationships outside of work is essential for balance. Friends love you for who you are, they define and bring out the best in you. Family members are usually the ones who will stand by you, regardless. Not only is life more fun with friends and family, they also act as your safety net when the going gets tough.

For me, true friendship has always come from my best pal, Heather. We met as teens and bonded through many escapades that included travelling Europe on a wafer-thin budget. We looked out for each other then and we still have each other's backs now. Even though she lives in the US and we only speak once every couple of months, the bond is still strong because we know each other inside out and would drop everything for one another if needed.

How do Relationships relate to Power Up?

If you think back over the past week, how many roles have you performed? Colleague, carer, friend, mother, manager, partner, sister, boss, cleaner, chef, holiday organiser, present buyer, form filler, grocery buyer...? Some even seem to achieve all that by lunchtime!

Although the world is changing, women have been expected – or have put pressure on themselves – to juggle a multitude of roles, far more than men, who have traditionally focused on being the breadwinner.

All that juggling can compromise our ability to prioritise our own goals and make our day-to-day existence harder, particularly when one of the balls drops. Life can sometimes feel like a battle, which we need to Power Up to fight, making it all the more important to have an army of people who can fight our corner and help us to win.

The power of the collective is awesome: we are often more effective when working in a group and get things done quicker and better. If you feel part of a tribe, for example, a club, society or group, and invest time in building relationships within it, you will undoubtedly accelerate your potential and gain satisfaction from doing the same for others. If you're faced with an opportunity but are scared to act, you will be more likely to do so if you have people behind you who are willing you on. Likewise, if you feel under threat, the support of your network can help you to power through and give you the confidence and support to handle it.

Relationships are a great way of galvanising people into action, and digital relationships are becoming increasingly powerful. If you feel strongly about something, the fastest and loudest expression of this is often social media because it unites opinion and creates a unified voice. You can create a whole groundswell of support via social media if you know what you're doing. The most potent recent example of this was #MeToo, popularised in 2017 by the American actress Alyssa Milano, who encouraged victims of sexual harassment to tweet about it and "give people a sense of the magnitude of the problem"[34]. This has since evolved into a global movement. It takes a village to raise a child: it takes a sisterhood to call #TimesUp and move beyond it.

The power of Relationships is directly connected to the other elements on the Power Up Model©: you use your *Intuition* to identify people you like to form relationships with and your

Magnetism to form that mutual attraction between you. The ability to be *Resilient* will be largely dependent on your relationships and you will find it easier to be *Assertive* if you have people behind you to power bolster you up.

> "Women understand. We may share experiences, make jokes, paint pictures, and describe humiliations that mean nothing to men, but women understand. The odd thing about these deep and personal connections of women is that they often ignore barriers of age, economics, worldly experience, race, culture — all the barriers that, in male or mixed society, had seemed so difficult to cross."
>
> —GLORIA STEINEM

Why do we need them?

History indicates that relationships are more important to women than to men. Since the beginning of time, female friendships have been the bedrock of many women's lives. Back when marriages were entered into purely for economic reasons, female friends took on the emotional support that many marriages lacked.

As the saying goes, it's not what you know but who you know, and this works on both an emotional and practical level. We need strong relationships with people we can trust. With powerful support, it's far more likely you'll believe you can do anything, whereas if you feel like you're all alone, it's too easy to give up.

Building relationships is not only important for advancing your career, but also vital to doing your day job effectively and generally surviving life's challenges, because the more people you know, the more people know you. So the day you want information, a favour, something done quickly, or you need to draw a team together, doing it from a standing start will be much easier if the people you're asking know and like you.

There is an extra benefit to having a network of relationships. If you have challenging relationships in one area of life, for example, a patronising boss or petty-minded colleague, having people outside who are on your side means you get the benefit of their perspective, and even help with finding a solution, if need be. Sometimes work relationships can be uncomfortable. You may be 'friendly' with everyone but not friends because you're in competition, so it's important to have access to the camaraderie that comes from belonging to a wider tribe elsewhere.

What gets in the way?

Although it's easy to see the benefits of relationships, there are a number of factors that get in the way. Some people find it difficult to be sociable, whether due to their personality type or previous experiences. As with all challenges, it helps to understand the barriers before looking at how to overcome them. Here are some common ones that many of my clients have faced – and conquered – through the techniques in this book:

■ **Introversion**: if you're an introvert or have been allocated (or even put yourself) in the 'shy' box, it's not always easy to come out of your shell. Whereas people who are more extroverted find it easier to form light, easy connections, those on the introverted end of the spectrum are happier forming deeper relationships. To be truly successful you need to be able to be flexible and do both – to stay shallow and deep dive as required – which is easier said than done.

■ **Comfort zone**: building authentic relationships requires us to be open, honest and vulnerable; to let down our guard and ask for help when we need it. This level of trust is not in everyone's comfort zone. Forming good relationships means being brave and being prepared to make the first move, initiating contact. This means being prepared for knockbacks, for your invitation to 'make friends' to not be reciprocated, or for relationships to not go how you'd planned them to.

■ **Childhood experiences**: these can go a long way to influencing our ability to form fruitful relationships. We may get powerful messages from an early age that people can't be trusted – they can be dangerous, they break promises or let us down – and conclude, subconsciously or not, that we're safer and better off alone. If this is the case, when we find ourselves in new situations where we don't know the territory, we retreat into our cave and become quieter, less communicative. People falsely mistake this for aloofness, coldness or arrogance, and respond by leaving us alone, making it even more difficult for us to form relationships. Which makes our sense of isolation self-perpetuating.

■ **Queen Bee Syndrome**: the grim truth is that some women can be really poisonous to one another: they can be super competitive, territorial and behave jealously. At its worst, this can manifest as Queen Bee Syndrome, a term first coined by Staines, Jayaratne and Tavris in 1973[35], describing a woman in a position of authority who views or treats subordinates more critically if they are female. The term's meaning has since been widened to encompass female colleagues who are intentionally obstructive and snide towards other female colleagues.

Although most of us have been on the receiving end of this, some doubt its existence. Sheryl Sandberg observed that, "Women aren't any meaner to women than men are to one another. Women are just expected to be nicer." And Roxane Gay, author of *Bad Feminist: Essays*, urges us to: "Abandon the cultural myth that all female friendships must be bitchy, toxic, or competitive. This myth is like heels and purses — pretty but designed to SLOW women down."[36]

■ **Competitiveness**: another barrier is competitiveness, where we compare ourselves to others – usually unfavourably – and begin to see them as a threat. Although competition can be healthy between teams, it can often be detrimental between individuals. As we look over our shoulder at how other people are doing, we can come across as self-centred, insecure and petty-minded, and so lose focus on our own purpose or the job in hand.

Pearl Jordan coaches dancers on how to perform at their best in auditions, where people are sometimes 'greeted' with, "Thank you, next" before they've even danced a step. Imagine what that can do to your self-esteem! She recommends that instead of going down the usual competitive route of thinking that everyone else is better than you, the most empowering approach is choosing to be inspired by what they're good at. And with people who are more advanced than you, instead of being jealous of their success, imagining what it will be like when you reach their level yourself, and how you will shine in your own way.

■ **Cliques**: many of us have experienced the prickly sensation of being deliberately excluded from a female group. Cliques are often difficult to break into, as people feel threatened by a new kid on the block and so resist their advances. Alternatively, the new kid may get chosen over everyone else by a key player in the group, leaving everyone else feeling marginalised. Neither scenario fosters good relationships.

■ **Time**: relationships also require time. Women especially, with multiple priorities, spend their time rushing to get everything done, and don't necessarily make time for those coffees, one to ones, lunches and drinks after work that nurture relationships. It's very easy to be stuck behind your desk, being a diligent keyboard warrior and getting loads done, but not talking to people or seeking out new relationships. Prioritising getting to know people and putting the legwork into maintaining contacts over other activities that may feel more comfortable for you can be a stretch, especially when we have limited time for even the most important relationships in our lives.

Unfortunately, failure to build relationships can be the difference between unleashing your potential or not. Not making time to meet new people can mean we don't get to hear about brilliant opportunities, and we all know how much we hate FOMO (Fear Of Missing Out). So it's important to prioritise relationships and learn how to do so effectively so that you can make them work for you, in a way that will benefit you both.

WHAT ARE RELATIONSHIPS?

Now that we understand the importance of relationships and what can get in the way of them, let's examine the different types of relationships, so that you can prioritise those that are going to be of the most value.

The dictionary definition of 'relationship' is the way in which two or more people or things are connected, or the state of being connected. Writer and author Gideon Rosenblatt[37] makes an interesting distinction between relationships and connection, with *connection* being the act of joining two people together and *relationships* being the manner in which two things may be associated. For maximum power, you don't want to just connect, you want to form a relationship. For example, if your boss tells you that they've volunteered you for some sort of committee you have no interest in, you will be 'connected' to that group but gain minimal value from it because you won't bother building 'relationships' within it.

Relationships throughout life

The way we access relationships changes as we move through life. When we're very young, our relationships are confined to family and friends, people who are there to care for and entertain us. Throughout education, friendships become hugely significant as we learn how to initiate and maintain them and deal with the fallout when they break down.

When we're new to the workplace, we start by relying on the relationship-building skills we learnt at school, which were largely based around friendship. This can be challenging when we realise that those people you're making friends with may be competing with you for the next level, and this can be even more difficult to navigate when you're promoted and are expected to manage the people who were once your peers, or the other way round. Succeeding at work is not about hierarchy but the ability to influence people, and that relies on your ability to form real relationships.

"The new kind of business hero must learn to operate without the might of the hierarchy behind him. The crutch of authority must be thrown away and replaced by their own ability to make relationships, use influence and work with others to achieve results. Influencing is an important leadership skill for now and in the future."

–'WHEN GIANTS LEARN TO DANCE',
ROSABETH MOSS KANTER

As we get older, people become more dependent on us and vice versa. With more time spent at work and looking after others, we have less time to nurture our own relationships and can even get out of the habit of being sociable. This is a shame because being around people who bring out the best in us is a great way to let off steam, keep things in perspective or shake us up if we're in a rut.

A strategic approach to relationships

To explore how to create the most valuable relationships, it helps to understand the different categories of people you will encounter throughout life. Although this might sound calculating, the fact is, you can't be everyone's friend, nor can you please all the people all the time. So it makes sense to adopt a strategic approach, which includes knowing how to manage those people who may not have our best interests at heart.

Take a look at the following relationship categories and complete the steps in the exercise below.

■ **Inner circle:** these are the close friends, colleagues and family who will be with you through thick and thin, have your best interests at heart and have often been with you over a long period of time. It's possible to take these people for granted and we often underestimate the value they bring.

■ **Tribe:** this term has been coined recently to describe people with whom you share a common interest and identity. These might be people who work in the same industry as you or those who share the same beliefs and lifestyle. Examples might be the running club or debating society you meet up with once a week or a religious or community group you are part of.

■ **Network:** this is a collection of people who you've met throughout your life and career. They can be classified vertically (for example, people you know at work who are above and below you in the hierarchy and with whom you're in regular contact) and horizontally (a wider and looser collection of people who you may not be regularly in contact with). Unlike a tribe, there is no unifying identity to bond you to your network and so it's important to dedicate time to fostering the most valuable relationships within it.

■ **Stakeholders:** these are people in a position of authority who could have a powerful influence over your success. They will either know or have access to information or resources that could support you in your goals and will include decision-makers, gatekeepers and specialists in your field.

■ **Guardians:** these are seasoned and trusted advisors who could provide you with expert counsel and support you in achieving your goals. They could be mentors, sponsors, advocates and leaders, as well as experts in your field.

■ **Helpers:** these include managers and leaders whose responsibility it is to support you in reaching your goals and whose opinion you value and trust. There may be times when the people who have been allocated these roles do not fulfil their responsibilities effectively, in which case it will be down to you to find support from another source.

■ **Enemies:** the phrase 'keep your friends close but keep your enemies even closer', is often attributed to the Chinese philosopher Sun Tzu, and is just as relevant now as it was in the 6th century BC. Although we would ideally avoid making enemies, it's worth being aware of people who, for whatever reason, might actively block or harm you, perhaps because they're jealous or see you as a threat, and having a strategy for dealing with this.

EXERCISE 1: PRIORITISING RELATIONSHIPS

Having explored the different relationship categories, we're now going to apply them to your own relationships so that you can make sure that you're prioritising your time with the people who are most likely to support you in achieving your goals.

1. Think of a goal that you'd like to accomplish over the next year – you might like to look back on the goals you identified in Chapter 1.

2. Take a look at the relationship categories above and consider where you have developed strong relationships and where you have gaps. For example, you might find that you have strong relationships in the Tribe and Helper categories, but don't currently have any appointed Guardians.

3. Now think about which categories are going to be most important to achieving your goals. For example, if you're planning on moving into a different sector, you will need to build relationships with Stakeholders in that area. If you know there are a number of people in your field who are competing for the same role as you, you will need to use your full range of power sources to differentiate yourself from the others.

4. Finally, consider how you will prioritise your time for the most important relationships in your life.

The power of interdependence

Another way of assessing your relationships is to consider the balance of power within them so that you can ensure that as much as possible, you're both getting equal value. Although there are times when it's OK for us to give more than we get, if this becomes a regular occurrence we are essentially giving away our power and end up being taken for granted.

In his book, *The Seven Habits of Highly Effective People,* Stephen R. Covey talked about the difference between dependence, independence and interdependence. As you think about your own approach to relationships, it can be beneficial to remember that greater success is achieved for all through interdependence.

- **Dependence:** 'a paradigm of you' – i.e. 'you should take care of me', 'you should do that', 'you are responsible'

- **Independence:** 'a paradigm of I' – 'I am self-sufficient', 'I am capable', 'I am responsible'

- **Interdependence:** 'a paradigm of we', where individuals, groups and organisations come together and combine talents for the greater good – 'together we all succeed'

For interdependence to take place, Covey advised that people have to stop focusing solely on themselves and appreciate the value of cooperation and connection.

EXERCISE 2:
MOVING TOWARDS INTERDEPENDENCE

- Take a look at the relationship categories you identified earlier in this chapter and consider the balance of power within each of them.

- Consider whether your role across all relationship categories is mostly dependent (i.e. they are dependent on you or vice versa), independent (i.e. there is no dependency) or interdependent (where you combine individual strengths for the benefit of both)?

- Are there any patterns? Do you find yourself occupying one of the roles more than the others? Or maybe you're giving as much as you take in one category but not in another.

- Finally, consider what you can do to create greater interdependency in your relationships and what will be different when you do.

Where do relationships come from?

Now that we've profiled the different types of relationships, let's explore where they come from. Relationships come in many forms, whether transient – people you have an amazing time with on holiday or at an event, swear you'll stay in touch with but never see again – transactional – people you're working with on a project or deal – or transformational – people who appear in your life at a particular time and set you on a different trajectory.

Relationships can be developed at an individual level or collectively. One-to-one relationships are deeper and take longer to cultivate, whereas relationships with groups – the profile you develop and what you can get from that – can be quicker to establish. Occasionally, you can develop individual and collective relationships at the same time. The business club I belong to, Sister Snog, is an example of this – the group is 'like blood' – you'd do all you can to help a fellow sister and the sisterhood will always flex and open up to welcome new members. Equally, when it comes to developing one-to-one relationships within the group, you have a head start because you already share a common bond and a common interest.

The phrase 'The whole is greater than the sum of its parts' was first coined by the philosopher Aristotle, and aptly describes the power of relationships. For anyone who's played team sports, it echoes the T.E.A.M. acronym—Together Everyone Achieves More.

A great example of collaboration is the girls empowerment charity BelEve, (beleveuk.org), which I chair. Founded by sisters, Marsha and Chyloe Powell, after the untimely death of their mother, they deliver programmes in schools and community groups which teach girls how to become

335

leaders of their own world. Although the charity relies on grants to survive, a large percentage of their success has been achieved through partnering with other organisations, powered through the relationships the sisters are continually forging with supportive stakeholders.

> "The way power works at every level, at the United Nations or in your neighbourhood is, do you have a community that stands behind what you stand for. And if you do, you'll have more power. And if you don't, you won't."
>
> **–BARACK OBAMA**

For a relationship to deepen, it needs to move through a series of stages and this often happens when we have an interest in common. As Dr Robert B. Cialdini explained in his book *Influence*, we are most likely to say 'yes' to people who we like or people who are like us. This commonality might not be immediately apparent, and so it pays to spend time delving into what makes the other person tick and the values you share. You'll be surprised how quickly this can happen. As part of my confident communication classes, I challenge groups of four to find something in common in a game I call Sherlock Holmes. Last week, one group realised they'd all grown up abroad and another discovered they all had a passion for board games, all within two minutes of playing.

For the initial buzz of a new friendship to develop into a long-lasting relationship, there will need to be an incentive and this often comes when you support one another. For many, there is nothing more enriching than making a difference to someone's life, from little things like bringing them their favourite coffee, to coaching them to achieve the next goal, to recommending them for a promotion. If you're nurturing a relationship with a manager, it's worth bearing in mind that they will often get as much out of the relationship as you do.

Relationships will only survive if both of you make the effort. Some relationships are easier to cultivate than others, for example, building a strong working relationship with the team of people who sit around you is much easier than initiating a conversation at a networking event with someone who could be instrumental to your career. It's even more challenging to make contact with someone who you've fallen out with or you believe may have behaved obstructively towards you. But being brave in this way pays dividends. So rather than waiting for the other person to take the initiative, if the relationship is worth maintaining, it's down to us to make it happen.

HOW CAN YOU DEVELOP THEM?

We're now going to explore how you can create powerful relationships, breaking it down into:

1. Remembering your purpose

2. Making a plan

3. Creating the right mindset

4. Networking with ease

5. Relationship-building skills

6. Maintaining relationships over time

★ Step 1: Remembering your purpose

To make the most of the time you have for forging relationships, the first step is to remind yourself of your overall purpose, as explored in Chapter 1. A common mistake that many people make when relationship building is saying 'yes' to every event they're invited to, collecting stacks of business cards and having endless coffees with people who may be great company but bear no relevance to their goals.

Focusing on your *life* goals will mean that you will be naturally drawn to and attract people who will help you get there. Likewise, honing in on your *work* objectives will influence every interaction and ensure you create a mutually supportive network of people who will power you forward.

A few years ago, I decided to reach larger audiences through speaking on global stages. Rather than tackling this goal alone, I joined an organisation called the Professional Speaking Association and, as a result, have built up a valuable network of speakers who not only inspire, support and recommend me, but also 'get' the highs and lows of being in front of a large audience.

With the best will in the world, you can't connect with everyone and so it pays to prioritise your time with people who can relate to your purpose in some way, and instead of only thinking about your own fulfilment, think win-win. For example, if you want to increase your social media presence, find someone who wants to do the same thing so you can hold one another to account. If you want to get fitter but hate the gym, pair up with a friend for some private training sessions, and if you want to set up a 'side-hustle' business, find a like-minded partner to share the load.

★ Step 2: Making a plan

Having understood your purpose for relationship building, the next step is to create a strategic plan. Whether you're climbing the corporate ladder, running your own business or simply want to widen your circle of friends, the main thing is to get out there and meet people outside your everyday context who will relate to your purpose in some way; but again, this should be planned, not random. This is a combination of finding your tribe and going beyond its confines. Birds of a feather flock together, but make sure that the 'birds' you surround yourself with have a variety of plumage.

Finding people who are like you, who you feel comfortable with and share a similar mindset gives you a sense of support and comfort. Your tribe can be found in many ways – through joining networking groups, signing up for courses and connecting on social media. You need to invest a fair amount of time on this in order to deepen your relationships. After you've met interesting people, you need to follow-up and stay in touch, find ways to meet up again and see how you can help each other out.

But stepping out of your comfort zone is vital too. Going where you're in the minority allows you to explore aspects of your career and market that are unfamiliar and to understand different people's perspectives. For example, networking in male-dominated environments, or in locations far away from your home turf, or going where delegates are of a different age group or ethnic background from you can be eye-opening and often very rewarding.

If you're only having your own thoughts reflected back, you're never going to grow. If you're in a room full of people who are less experienced or knowledgeable than you, you're in the wrong room. To Power Up, you need to be around people you can learn from. Push yourself to speak to people who are not like you. Be brave.

Some people are really comfortable with this, while others are most definitely not. If you find yourself making excuses, like "I'm too busy" or "I'm really happy at the level I'm at" and "I like it as it is," you need to ask yourself if you're scared of putting yourself out there – or too lazy.

"Your network is your net worth."

–TIM SANDERS

EXERCISE 2: PLANNING YOUR NETWORKING STRATEGY

Planning your networking strategy is about following a series of steps, from mapping your current and ideal connections, targeting relevant organisations, developing a system to track your connections and making sure you nurture your priority relationships.

1. Mapping your connections

A useful metaphor for planning your networking strategy is a map, with **global** connections being world-class leaders who you aspire to meet but might be currently beyond your reach, **national** connections being those outside your immediate circle and **local** connections representing people in your everyday network.

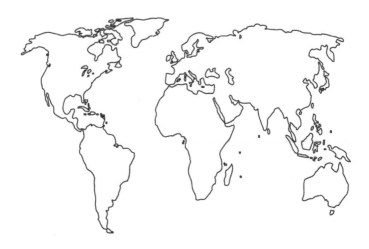

Although the easiest tactic might be to make connections at a local level, the most effective route to success is to extend your reach. It is by connecting with people on the outskirts of your world – both vertically upwards towards leaders in your field and horizontally outwards to extend your reach – that you will succeed in making your current world bigger, thereby increasing your influence and fulfilling your true potential.

As you think about your short, medium and long-term goals, think about what you need to do to create and strengthen relationships at each level. Take a look at the questions below and make a note of your answers:

■ On a **global** scale, who are the people you would like to be connecting with and why? Think BIG – the world's leading expert, the most successful entrepreneur, the most respected thought-leader in your field. The aim here is to expand your world and open up opportunities for the most enriching connections.

- On a **national** scale, who are the people currently outside of your immediate circle who could have a positive impact on your goals. For example, if you're planning on moving your business into another sector, who are the key influencers and opinion-formers who are operating there already? If you are looking to move into another department within your organisation, who are the key decision-makers who you will need to convince?

- On a more **local** scale, think about the people within your existing network – or those connected to the people in your network – who might relate to your purpose and be inclined to support you. Rather than limiting your thinking to your current colleagues, think about all the people you have had positive connections with along the way, even if you've fallen out of touch. Rather than purely focusing on business connections, think about people you know personally who may also relate to your goals and purpose.

2. Networking through organisations

As well as thinking about individuals you would like to connect with, think about the organisations that operate in your sphere of interest, which may have like-minded members who you could develop relationships with.

- Jot down a list of the organisations that you would like to be associated with, for example, networking groups, special interest organisations, professional bodies and social groups.

- Conduct some research into their remit and membership: who is involved, where and when do they meet?

- If appropriate, decide how you would like to become involved, whether attending events, or even signing up to their membership.

3. Tracking relationships

Now that you have begun to identify people you'd like to build relationships with, the next step is to create a clear strategy for profiling and tracking them. The grid below is a useful tool for categorising the people you come into contact with and those you would like to have in your network. As you meet new people, take the time to create a record of who they are, how you met and your common interests. You can also use LinkedIn as a virtual little black book, because it captures all your contacts in the same place.

Taking all the names you have listed in task 1 above as your starting point, create your own version of the grid below, using the four quadrants as your guide to segment people who have comparatively low and high levels of interest in you and your purpose and goals, and comparatively low and high levels of power in helping you to achieve them.

High

POWER

High Power/Low Interest, eg:

Key opinion leaders operating in your field

Authors and public speakers

Key decision makers

Board and shareholders of your company

Senior leaders in other departments

Potential purchasers of your products/services

Organisations related to your purpose in some way

High Power/High Interest, eg:

Existing or prospective clients, customers or buyers of your services

Key competitors

Your line manager

Senior colleagues and stakeholders in your department and related departments

Mentors and previous senior colleagues who remain current contacts

Low Power/Low Interest, eg:

Past/current colleagues with whom you have little common interest

People who seem to be connecting with you only for what they can get

Low Power/High Interest, eg:

Colleagues, team members and associates who value your support but have little influence over your success

Friends and family who want the best for you

Low

High

INTEREST

4. Nurturing priority relationships

Once you've plotted names in each of the four quadrants, you can then think about how to prioritise the time you spend communicating with each group, focusing on people who are likely to have the greatest influence on your success. Depending on whether their levels of Power and Interest are High or Low, your contacts can be divided into Minimum Effort, Keep On Side, Keep Informed and Nurture groups, as illustrated in the grid below:

5. Consider how you might support one another.

As you think about the people you would like to connect with and nurture, also consider how you might support one another.

It's important to note that as people become more senior or as your relationships deepen with them, their Power and Interest may move from Low to High, in which case you will want to move them to another box in the grid. Take a look at the grid above and complete the following steps:

■ Make a note of the key people in your top right-hand **NURTURE** quadrant and how you can create opportunities to connect with them.

■ Then look at the key people in the top left-hand **KEEP ON SIDE** quadrant and think about how you can increase their interest in you, and move them into the **NURTURE** quadrant.

High

POWER

High Power/Low Interest, eg:	High Power/High Interest, eg:
KEEP ON SIDE	**NURTURE**
Keep informed of their activities and areas of interest	Maximise opportunities to meet with them face to face
Identify areas of common interest/ potential partnership	Discuss areas of common interest and opportunities for partnership
Create opportunities to network and get to know them better	Look for opportunities where you can support them, both formally and informally (eg: collaboration on projects, sharing information or ideas, introductions)
For people you don't know personally, identify people you know in common and consider asking for an introduction	
Low Power/Low Interest, eg:	**Low Power/High Interest, eg:**
MINIMUM EFFORT	**KEEP INFORMED**
Maintain polite contact	Become a mentor for them
Refer them to other people/ resources they might find useful	Support them in their career

Low ——————————————————→ High

INTEREST

■ Now look at the key people in the bottom right-hand **KEEP INFORMED** quadrant. Identify those whose influence is likely to increase and identify what you can do to keep them close.

■ Although the people in the **MINIMUM EFFORT** may not require proactive effort from you, you might like to identify what you can do within a minimal timeframe to keep them on side.

6. Create a strategic approach for building relationships

Once you have identified who you want to connect with, you can then create a strategic approach for building relationships with them. The most successful people think end-game versus quick win, career path versus job interview, so take the time to plan your connection strategy over the short, medium and long-term.

Although some of the best connections are completely spontaneous, spend a bit of time thinking about the people you would like to meet and what you would like them to know about, as it can be the difference between a lasting relationship and a missed opportunity. For a systematic approach, complete the following planner:

❝

IT IS BY CONNECTING WITH PEOPLE ON THE OUTSKIRTS OF YOUR WORLD THAT YOU WILL SUCCEED IN MAKING YOUR CURRENT WORLD BIGGER, THEREBY INCREASING YOUR INFLUENCE.

PEOPLE	NURTURE GROUP	KEEP ON SIDE GROUP	KEEP INFORMED GROUP	MINIMAL EFFORT GROUP
What is my overall goal in connecting with this person?				
What do I have in common with them?				
What can I do for this person?				
What can this person do for me?				
What organisations does this person belong to?				

PEOPLE	NURTURE GROUP	KEEP ON SIDE GROUP	KEEP INFORMED GROUP	MINIMAL EFFORT GROUP
What are their key areas of interest?				
When can I meet this person?				
How can we create opportunities for win/ win?				
Action				
Deadline				

★ Step 3: Creating the right mindset

As well as having a strategic approach to relationship building, it's important to have the right mindset. This is about:

- Prioritising relationships, not just because you should, but because you want to

- Deciding people are fascinating and the world is full of good people who are there to support you

- Choosing to believe we're all part of a bigger interconnected system where if you succeed, I succeed

- Remaining open-minded and curious about the people around you

It's also about believing in the power of humanity. On a train to Chester recently, I struck up a conversation with the girl opposite and was so distracted that I left my case in the luggage hold when I got off: *ARGHHH!* Rather than panicking, I reported it and to my delight and relief, the railway staff texted me to say they'd located it and sent it to another station where I could collect it later. We've all got stories like this. If we believe that the world is full of people who have our back, we notice them more and become more like them – and everyone benefits.

Such empowering beliefs open everything up. What closes things down is connecting with people just for what they can do for you, restricting your relationships only to your 'backyard' and avoiding those who are 'not like me'. So decide to commit to relationship building, and be open to the growth, richness and joy that occur as a result.

EXERCISE 3:

CREATING A RELATIONSHIP BUILDING MINDSET

Go back to the life and work goals you identified in Chapter 1. Complete these sentences:

1. I am building relationships at work so that...

2. I am building relationships in life so that...

3. Relationships are precious to me because...

Having reflected on your answers to the questions above, create your relationship mantra, a single sentence that encapsulates your thoughts on the power of relationships. This will help you to transcend any barriers to relationship building (for example, shyness, lack of time, not knowing where to start). An example is: 'Taking the time to form meaningful relationships is enriching for me and the people I meet. As I open up to the people around me and see them respond, I become more aware of the gifts I bring and learn to appreciate the gifts in others'.

★ Step 4: Networking with ease

Now that you've thought about how to proactively manage your relationships, the next step is to hone your networking skills, which I've found the majority of people dislike intensely!

Part of the issue is with the word itself, which can sound overly calculating and make it all seem so much more of a big deal than it needs to be. I remember my first boss used to send us out to events with a box of business cards and tell us that we needed to come back with the box empty, thereby condemning us to an evening of networking by numbers which used to terrify the living daylights out of us!

For me, learning to enjoy the whole networking process has been about reframing it as an opportunity to have real, authentic conversations with a variety of amazing people I wouldn't otherwise have met.

Although it's likely we will be going to networking events for business reasons, it pays to put aside thoughts of 'I must go and sell'. Avoid being transactional – these are human beings and you need to find a way of bonding in a natural way instead of by rote. It's more valuable to have made one or two really good contacts than to have flitted around a room and collected 20 business cards, because a lot of them are not going to be relevant to you, nor you to them. That said, try to keep an open mind. Even if there might not immediately be an opportunity, it doesn't mean that you won't have an enriching conversation and you never know, they could introduce you to people who could, as the founder of Sister-

Snog Hela Wozniak-Kaye puts it, "be your fairy godmother" and help make your dreams come true.

An amazing example of this happened to me just yesterday when I was discussing the launch of this book with another author. Once she'd heard about the concept of powering up, she offered to introduce me to the producer of a well-known radio show, which she had been on recently and I would LOVE to be on! Of course, nothing is guaranteed, but if we hadn't struck up a conversation about feminist literature, the opportunity would never have come up.

So decide to be interested in other people. Listen to their hopes, dreams and fears and consider how you might help them. This opens us up and makes us more interesting, memorable and attractive to others as well.

Sending out the right signals

As well as opening up to the people around us, it's important to send out signals that invite other people to approach you. What often happens is we arrive at an event, look around and think, "Everyone's having an amazing time, they all know each other, why would they want to talk to me?" so we scuttle off to the nearest corner and shut down. But this is not necessarily the case. What those people are doing is non-verbally sending off messages of fun, energy or inspiration, and you too can learn how to use body language and your voice to do that.

If you want to be one of those people who looks like they're having fun, try these tips:

- Make sure you walk into the room smiling – it will put you at ease, and people will be more likely to invite you into their conversations than if your face is neutral.

- When you're in a conversation, have an open, relaxed posture, with arms and hands open rather than folded in, as this will make you more approachable.

- Be careful not to face the person you're speaking to square-on, which can be quite confrontational and intimidating. Having your feet in a V – one pointing to the person talking, and another slightly open, will invite other people to come and join you as well; by contrast, keeping both feet facing the person you're talking to will indicate that you're having a closed, conversation which others are not welcome to join.

Knowing what to say

A lot of people are genuinely scared of initiating conversations and think they have to come up with loads of scintillating topics, so much so that they end up talking too much and scaring off or boring the person they're talking to. So choose to listen more than you talk. The balance between asking questions and speaking should be approximately 80/20, so if you're not a natural talker, become a really good listener, but don't do what a lot of coaches do and end up asking so many amazing questions that you don't get the chance to share anything about yourself, leaving people none the wiser about how brilliant you are.

It also makes a big difference if you do some research before attending events, so you know who to look out for and what they are likely to be interested in. Have some questions prepared in advance to keep things interesting and some unusual conversational subjects up your sleeve.

Create different themes, whether that's the focus of the event you're at, or something relevant in the news; the fact you're at the same event means there are so many potential conversation openers because you have that shared interest. For example, if the conference theme is diversity you could ask, "How is your company addressing diversity issues? What's your view?" etc. And get good at remembering people's names. Firstly, ask them! It's such a disarming question, particularly if you pay attention to the response. If you don't have their business card and haven't heard their name or can't remember it, ask them to say it again and repeat it back to them. It shows that you care enough to get it right – especially if it's an unusual name.

Of course, some are better at this than others and so a great tactic is to observe how great networkers operate and try to emulate it.

CASE STUDY

Jackie Handy is a professional speaker, training consultant and diversity and inclusion advocate. I met her at PSA Inspire, a huge networking event for professional speakers. I remember chatting with her on the first day when she knew no one. We had a brilliant conversation and have remained friends ever since. What's unique about Jackie is her ability to build relationships with lots of people by having short but meaningful conversations with them all. But she doesn't just do this with the people at the event, she'll do it with everyone, from the restaurant staff to the organisers to the taxi drivers. She is genuinely interested in, and cares about, everyone.

I was curious about how she does this, but in the same way that Natalie Haverstock's magnetism story surprised me, Jackie also confessed that she hasn't always been the most outgoing person. Speaking about her upbringing, she said:

"When I was growing up there were a lot of things I was conscious of that made me different; many of which I found myself hiding as a protection mechanism. At the age of four, I had a squint which meant my left eye turned inwards, so I looked quite different to the other children in my street. I was called names and laughed at because of it, which left me feeling incredibly isolated. In addition, it turned out that I was also the only child in the street with Catholic parents, which meant I'd also be going to a different school to the other children. At 15, I came out as a lesbian to my family and friends, made all the more difficult with the religious pressure surrounding me. Thankfully, my parents were amazing in how they responded, using conversations to help their understanding. But once again I felt the impact of name-calling and bullying from some of my so-called school friends, just because I was different to them. Thereafter, for many years in the corporate world, I felt safer hiding my sexuality for fear of being treated differently or passed over for promotion and it wasn't until my late thirties that I felt comfortable enough to be my 'true self' at work. I genuinely believe those early life experiences had a profound effect on how I relate to people and especially my empathy with people in minority groups".

I wondered how Jackie's experiences growing up have impacted on her relationship-building skills. She said, "When I think about relationships and relationship building, I don't over-analyse. But I do see conversations as needing to be genuine and authentic. This comes from my own experiences of just wanting to be heard and accepted for who I was. I am genuinely interested in other people and don't try to be someone I'm not when I engage. I also feel that networking should be more 'you' than 'I'. In other words, I ask questions of people I meet to understand more about them and their story/background/

purpose, rather than rushing in to talk about myself. There's an age-old saying, 'You have two ears and one mouth and they should be used in proportion'. And I feel there's still a lot of truth in that statement. Whether as a networker, salesperson, leader or simply one human being to another, the art of being able to listen – truly listen – to the other person in conversation is extremely powerful.

"Going back to my earlier point, conversations have to be authentic. We humans are extremely perceptive by nature and know when there is a hidden, selfish agenda at play. So to truly connect with others, give yourself wholeheartedly to the conversation, seek to understand and do so without judgement. Because when we do, the results can be magical and the possibilities endless."

Another question people often ask is how to move on from a conversation politely. Although there's no need to be stuck with someone for half an hour, you need to be tactful in moving on. Options include saying, "It's lovely to meet you but I need the bathroom/to find my colleagues/ get a drink/ find someone I arranged to meet". Or say, "I'd love to connect on LinkedIn and continue this conversation later, but for now can we exchange cards?" And then move on. Because it's OK to be open about the fact that you're there to network – you both are. You don't need to make a big deal of it.

Using business cards

Business cards play a really important role in networking because they give someone a reminder of who you are and why they wanted to connect with you – a photo on your card can help that. But there's an etiquette to it. It's really tacky, two minutes after meeting someone to flip a business card out of your back pocket or ask them for theirs, as though you were collecting them. Instead, after taking the time to establish a rapport, ask them for their card first and actually look at it rather than just sticking it in your pocket and use it as an aide-memoire – a way of cementing their name in your brain.

★ Step 5: Relationship-building skills

So, what needs to happen for an acquaintance to evolve into a relationship? Swiss psychologist, Eric Berne, identified that relationships can be built up or knocked down through positive or negative 'strokes', which he described as fundamental units of physical, verbal or non-verbal social action; for example, a handshake, a "good morning" or a smile. Berne's theory was based on the work of Rene Spitz, a researcher who did pioneering work in the area of child development and observed that infants deprived of cuddling, touching and handling (in other words, an absence of physical strokes) were more likely to experience emotional and physical difficulties. Berne suggested that adults need physical contact just like infants but have learned to substitute other types of recognition for physical stimulation. So while an infant needs cuddling, an adult craves a smile, a hand gesture, or some other form of recognition. Strokes can be simple to give, for example, a wave, a compliment or a nod of the head and just as easy to unwittingly take away, for example, a sarcastic remark, a dismissive gesture, or not returning someone's smile. As you get to know someone, you can build up the strokes, for example, a subtle nod to the new receptionist can evolve into a 'good morning', which can turn into a conversation, which can blossom into a friendship over time.

Trust

> **"The best way to find out if you can trust somebody is to trust them."**
>
> **–ERNEST HEMINGWAY**

As well as positive 'strokes', all the best relationships are founded on trust, which comes from the certainty that you have each other's best interests at heart. Although it may feel like trust is elusive and arbitrary, Charles H. Green, author of *The Trusted Advisor*, found that trust can be built by the presence or absence of certain factors. Of course, you could be the most trustworthy person in the world, but unless people can see evidence of this, they won't know that to be the case, and so it makes sense to not only ensure you possess these factors but that you are also actively demonstrating them.

- Factors that build trust: your apparent **credibility** and **reliability** combined with your **intimacy** (i.e. level of emotional connection with the other person)

- Factors that reduce trust: your apparent **self-orientation** (i.e. where you appear to have only your best interests at heart).

Of course, you can't always choose the people you interact with, either at work or at home. Sometimes, we feel a subtle sense of threat from someone who's hard to read, which we may interpret negatively. Ambiguous or passive-aggressive behaviour can be particularly hard to fathom, and these relationships are tricky to pin down. Are they friend or foe? Are they just shy or awkward or do they have something against you? This is when you need to tune into your power of *Intuition* and sense when someone's not being true. For example, if they're saying they're really excited about something but their voice and demeanour are flat, these will be signs that something isn't quite right.

This works in reverse as well. If you believe that 'you can't trust anyone nowadays' or 'that everyone's out to get you', you will approach every interaction with suspicion, which will show up in your words and closed, defensive and guarded body language. They will, in turn, see you as having something to hide and will treat you the same way back, thereby creating a vicious cycle of mistrust that will be difficult to break.

Trust building tips

The following simple actions can rapidly improve how trustworthy people think you are and form a solid foundation for any relationship.

- Illustrate your credibility by demonstrating your expertise and showcasing your results.

- Demonstrate your reliability by delivering on your promises.

- Enhance your emotional connection by prioritising the relationship.

- Minimise your self-orientation through giving without expectation of return and valuing their opinions, needs and wants.

- Demonstrate your openness through your body language and welcoming, supportive and inclusive language.

Initiating and maintaining conversations

Although some people are natural conversationalists, not all of us have the confidence or skills to just dive into a conversation with a stranger. But you have opinions and lots to say, right? A great way to approach any situation where you're going to have to share your thoughts is using the OPRAHS© method which I've created to help you prepare for success. People have found it an extremely valuable tool to prepare for formal interviews, meetings and presentations, as well as informal networking situations where it's important they deliver their best. Run through these questions in your head:

OPRAHS©: Powering up your potential

 Objective: what are you there to achieve?

 People: who are the other people and what's their reason for being there?

 Role: what role will you choose to adopt to suit the circumstances? For example, based on your objectives and the people there, will it serve you best to be facilitator, connector, strategist?

 Attitude: what attitude will it be most helpful for you to adopt, given the above? For example, excited, curious, concerned, playful or challenging?

 Hear: rather than focusing solely on what you're going to say, pay attention instead to how you're going to listen to other people's points of view.

 Say: you will now be in a strong position to consider how you can make the most valuable contribution to the conversation and get the most out of it.

This approach is the opposite of what most people do to prepare, which will be to solely think about what they're going to say, which may not bear any relevance to the situation or people.

When it comes to initiating a conversation with someone new, start with a shallow dive into the conversation, an opening

365

gambit that won't scare them off, like a comment about the weather or a genuine compliment. You can then move onto what I call a 'fishing expedition' to find out more about them and, hopefully, discover touchpoints and common areas of interest. This could include latest developments at work, either person's subject matter expertise, global or national business news, your respective backgrounds etc.

It's important to remember that enriching conversations are dialogues, not monologues, and will happen when you've identified topics you're both interested in. Because every person is different, it's important to have a flexible approach, with 'scene-setting' topics that will move at their pace to deeper conversations, where inner thoughts, values and vulnerabilities can be shared. Little things that will draw people to you include the stories you tell and how personable you are – people always remember stories if they are well told and relatable. From here, moving to a deeper level of conversation should be initiated with care, so take your lead from the other person.

Showing your softer side leads to trust and makes people want to spend time with and support you. But don't over-share the bad stuff.

If you wear your heart on your sleeve 24/7, you run the risk of being perceived as a victim and compromising your credibility. So choose which elements of yourself you're happy to be vulnerable and self-deprecating about and what it will serve you best to keep hidden.

Areas that you could explore include your respective purpose, identity, values and beliefs as they relate to the topic under discussion, your unique point of view, your challenges and how you've overcome them.

As part of the discussion, be aware of your tone. Being keen and enthusiastic is fine, but overdoing it can put people off. Also, be careful with humour: what you see as harmless banter may be offensive to others. And it's important to respect that some people just don't want to connect or are simply having a bad day and so won't appreciate your approach, however hard you try.

Building relationships online

While it has many positive benefits, relying on technology and social media for so much of our communication can make it more difficult for people to form genuine relationships. For all its convenience, you can't fully 'read' people via an email/text/instant messaging. Plus it is much harder to convey real emotions and nuances across a screen, as messages are often truncated and devoid of personality – and emojis hardly fill the gap!

What's more, with social media communication, nothing is natural and immediate and many posts are perfected, polished and curated content as opposed to spur-of-the-moment speech. The danger of the emphasis being on online communication is that we might lose the ability to make conversation in the real world and find it more difficult to relate to one another as a result. And we have less patience for people when it's so easy to swipe right if we don't get instant gratification.

There will be times when we find ourselves at crossroads, maybe a lifestyle change, a time where we need to prove ourselves, be selected over others or when we need to articulate our opinion or defend our views, where the only option is real-world communication. When this is the case, we have to be

"

WHETHER REAL-
LIFE OR ONLINE
RELATIONSHIPS
SUIT US BETTER, WE
NEED TO BE ADEPT
AT BOTH, AS THIS IS
THE WAY OF THE
FUTURE.

able to speak fluently and adapt and flex our communication style according to what or who is in front of us.

It's then that we need real-life relationship skills and when all those hours of online communication are useless. If your main interactions are comments on social media, where you can take all the time you want to hone and edit your words, you may come unstuck face to face. It's therefore crucial to maintain those skills so that you can make your point persuasively in the moment.

Whether real-life or online relationships suit us better, we need to be adept at both, as this is the way of the future.

Social media works extremely well for many of us when it comes to finding our tribe. This is especially true of the home-based business owner, or women who live in an isolated way, far from friends and who thrive on making connections with like-minded people on social media. These women feel buoyed up by their online network and can form solid friendships that sometimes translate into real-life relationships.

Julie Creffield, social entrepreneur, speaker and founder of global brand Too Fat to Run, which is made up of women who primarily communicate online, says: "When we allow ourselves to be visible and vulnerable online, we attract people to the things we care about, we enable people to feel like they are part of our world, no matter how far away they are. That is the basis of any successful business, or any other kind of relationship really. Show people who you really are. Create a real connection. Allow for some give and take. With all the talk of social media taking over our lives, it has done nothing but enrich my life, and I now have an army of women all over the world that I am lucky enough to call my friends."

EXERCISE 4:
BUILDING RELATIONSHIPS ONLINE

If you want to develop relationships via social media, it's important to prioritise those channels where the people you want to reach spend their time.

1. Start by considering your overall goals and why you want to build relationships online as well as in real life.

2. Then conduct some research into the most appropriate channels for you.

   - If you want to raise your profile in a professional context, the most appropriate channel is LinkedIn, so make sure your profile is up to date, that your photograph looks like you and is in a suitable setting, rather than in a bar or bungee jumping, and make a note to post regular opinions and updates that build your brand.

- If you run a business that targets consumers, it may be more appropriate to build a following on Instagram or Facebook, depending on the age of your demographic.

3. If you're serious about building an online profile and creating valuable relationships as part of this, it makes sense to go on a course or work with a social media expert to Power Up your virtual brand. The list of social media platforms is growing every day and many evolve regularly and so it pays to stay abreast of the latest developments.

Here are some tips on building relationships virtually, whether via social media, instant messaging or email:

1. Never say anything online that you wouldn't say to someone face to face: remember it lives forever.

2. Be accurate: it's easy to overlook your grammar when your tapping on your smartphone, but many people will judge you for sloppy writing, especially in a professional context.

3. Be careful with punctuation: CAPITAL LETTERS LOOK LIKE YOU'RE SHOUTING. And emojis or kisses could be misinterpreted, look childish and may undermine your credibility.

4. Don't be offended by short messages: often the most senior people in an organisation or people more used to verbal communication don't 'waste' time on pleasantries. The best policy is to match their style.

5. Set your own boundaries around the amount of time you spend on social media, including how quickly you respond to people's posts and your levels of engagement. If you never comment on other people's content, don't expect them to comment on yours. But don't overdo it, especially if your professional audience is online. If you're constantly posting, sharing and commenting, people may wonder whether you ever do any work!

Givers, takers and matchers

As well as developing your conversational ability, it pays to think about the kind of individuals you encounter, both in terms of how they operate within relationships and how you might want to. Organisational psychologist, Adam Grant, groups people in the following categories: givers, takers and matchers.

■ **Givers** are always doing favours for others, devoting vast amounts of time to mentoring and sharing their knowledge and putting others first, to the detriment of themselves. Takers, of course, love them! But you don't want to be taken advantage of, so avoid being too much of a giver.

■ **Takers** are out for themselves and, in a dog-eat-dog world, always put themselves first. Don't be a taker, who's only out for what you can get – always asking for favours and not giving back. But equally, don't be too much of a giver.

■ **Matchers** are an equal balance of give and take – 'I'll do something for you if you do something for me.'

If you're not sure which type you are, have a think about five people in your network and consider how you support one another. Are you usually the one helping others out or are you usually asking for favours? Most people are matchers, but don't obsess over getting something in return for a favour.

Authentic relationships aren't about giving to get, but about paying it forward. University of Michigan sociologist, Wayne Baker, developed the Reciprocity Ring, which shows how when a group is assembled with the goal of giving, it creates an environment of being generous and supporting others without expecting anything in return. So rather than helping others being a transactional thing – 'you scratch my back and I'll scratch yours' – he suggests it's about believing that you will get the support you need when the time comes. And you will.

Forming authentic relationships means believing that if you are generous with your time and help, the universe will respond and you will ultimately benefit – but be strategic about how you do it. It takes a minute to recommend a book or introduce a new contact to someone. In this way, you're proactively giving, not just responding to what you're asked, and certainly not bleeding yourself dry by giving too much of your time and energy. Stick with little nudges to help people, without vast cost to yourself. You'll soon find that people will want to reciprocate in kind and you'll have an avalanche of help and advice coming back to you. That's how successful people become successful – by leveraging their relationships.

You should also become a connector – a force for good within the system, putting people in touch with one another, always looking out for ways that you can enhance opportunities for people or make things better or bigger for them. Justin Collinge, founder of Leadability, a training company specialising in turning managers into leaders is a fantastic example of this. I was introduced to him by Chloe, the lady with the red shoes I mentioned at the start of this chapter. He, in turn, introduced me to Reetu Kansal, Senior Project Manager at the University of London, who invited me to speak at a Chartered Management Institute event last year and went on to recommend me as the keynote speaker for the University's leadership conference. Just one example of how connections lead to connections.

There are many ways you can connect people, ranging from introducing people who you intuitively know will get on, to recommending people to be considered for roles within your organisation, to introducing people with a shared common interest, but the best way is by simply asking people about their goals and thinking about what you can to do help them. The more you know about what they want to achieve, the more you will be able to help them and the deeper your connection to them will grow.

The important thing to remember is that you are not alone; everyone has moments of self-doubt, everyone is working on their own challenges and confidence issues. Opening up to the people around you is what will make your power strong rather than skin deep. Don't be afraid to reach out, but avoid only doing so in times of need as that would make you a taker, and people soon get fed up with those.

Following up

So you've made a great connection with someone. What next? Make sure you maintain relationships once you've made a new contact by sending a follow up email and following through on anything you've said you'd do for them, like making an introduction or forwarding them a contact's details. Offer to meet up if they seem equally keen, but don't pressurise them if they don't.

It also pays to be aware of generational differences. Older generations may prefer relationships to be centred around human connections, not having relied on technology since the year dot, whereas connecting on social media will be more expected and accepted by younger contacts (and many older ones, of course).

Be aware that your online presence will impact on these relationships, so make sure your LinkedIn, Twitter, Facebook and Instagram profiles are consistent and reflect your personal brand in the best possible way. Although some people have separate social media accounts for professional and personal content, it's worth bearing in mind that people may look at both and so the safest approach is to be careful posting overly-personal content and avoid contentious political opinions, unless it is relevant to your professional standing.

★ Step 6: Maintaining relationships over time

With our busy lives and hectic jobs, staying connected can be the hardest thing. When someone leaves an organisation or moves to a different city, we can soon forget to stay in touch. It pays to make a mental note – or even a written one – of the people who enrich your life and make the effort to stay in touch. Social media is an obvious route to achieve this, as it's quick, easy and immediate. We can stay up to date with our friends, associates and contacts' work lives by regularly checking their updates, so we know when they have a big engagement, a new job, a birthday or a new blog post and can respond appropriately.

Long-distance connections can work fine if we put the effort in. Making the effort to attend events so we get the chance to catch up with our contacts is always worthwhile, because this is how we stay up to date with industry 'intelligence' – hearing about the latest innovations, opportunities and openings. But it's more than that.

Choosing to be around people who lift you up, who make you laugh and give you their attention, even just for ten minutes, can help you stay engaged and excited, even on the dullest of days.

The easiest way to maintain long-term relationships is by having a system, whether that's for your professional or personal relationships. An effective way of maintaining and deepening professional relationships is by scheduling informal get-togethers where the agenda is simply to catch up rather than going into work mode. You can also organise your own gatherings or invite people to events that you know they'll be interested in. As mentioned earlier, it's helpful to keep a record of who you've met and when, in the same way as an organisation would have a Customer Relationship Management System as a way of tracking and managing interactions with prospects.

To maintain personal relationships, some of my most organised friends have a planner with birthdays, anniversaries and other significant events marked up, and keep a stack of greeting cards available so that they're never late. Others book their get-togethers a year in advance or meet up on the same date every month.

These techniques may seem laborious, but they often save time and angst in the long run, particularly if you forget a significant event and then have to over-compensate to make up for it. That said, the 'need' to maintain relationships over time can become another stick for a perfectionist to beat themselves up with, and it's worth remembering that friends, relations and business acquaintances who value you will do so even after a lapse in time. Often, it is the quality of contact, rather than the quantity, that's most appreciated.

Relationship-killers and how to move on

Although long-term relationships can be hugely beneficial and energising, there are many factors that can get in the way. Imbalance, where one of you is consistently not putting the same effort in as the other, can kill a relationship. Unless there's a good reason for this, it's usually an indication that it's time to move on and, of course, this doesn't mean that you won't be able to pick up where you left off years later.

What to do when a relationship ends

There will be times when a relationship is severely tested and it will be down to you to decide whether you want to maintain it, or not. If the relationship is worth saving, be brave and say how you feel and you may end up with a more honest, richer relationship than if you had avoided saying anything.

Equally, there are times when a relationship has naturally run its course. Perhaps one of you moves away – either geographically or in their thinking – and you no longer have those easy conversations that once cemented your bond. We are all continually evolving and sometimes, mentors, colleagues or leaders who we once valued highly for their expertise or wisdom no longer have as much to teach us. Or you may find that you end up having a disagreement or difference of opinion that you cannot move beyond.

There is no need to view these circumstances negatively as long as we can put to one side the powerful need to be liked, which many of us suffer from and can even drive us to maintain relationships that don't serve us. Sometimes we need to move on and appreciate that in doing so, we will be making space for new relationships to evolve, which will bring a whole new richness and power our progress to the next level and beyond.

RELATIONSHIPS CONCLUSION

What's important is to have people in your life who accept you for who you are, who you can be truly honest with, who will listen to you, and have your back unconditionally and vice versa. You don't have to have known someone your whole life to have that. Sometimes, you'll meet them and just have a natural affinity. Your 'spidey sense' tells you they're buddy material, they're 'one of us' and you instantly relax. It's important to have that belief; it's hugely empowering to feel someone is genuinely on your side. And being like that is a decision – not a matter of chance.

If we maintain our relationships, we know where to go when we need help. Women tend to be better at doing this than men – reaching out to friends and colleagues who may know just the right person for the advice you need, or give you support and reassurance through a difficult time. Our ability to develop meaningful relationships through the briefest of chats and to stay connected with the people who are memorable to us means that we are never short of a helping hand when it's needed.

Authenticity is key to relationships. Own who you are and what you're about; don't pretend to be something you're not. Be the best version of yourself and give people the chance to understand and value the truly powerful you.

IN SUMMARY

★ Relationships are formed through an ability to build and prioritise bonds with people around you.

★ Taking the time to build strong and wide-reaching networks at work means you'll find it easier to access practical support and advice when you need it. Making time for relationships outside work is essential for balance and support.

★ To create the most valuable relationships, it helps to understand the different categories of people you encounter so that you can prioritise time with the people who are most likely to support you in achieving your goals.

★ Planning your networking strategy is about mapping your current and ideal connections, targeting relevant organisations, developing a system to track your connections and making sure you nurture your priority relationships.

★ Learning to enjoy the whole networking process is about reframing it as an opportunity to have real, authentic conversations with a variety of people you wouldn't otherwise have met.

Chapter 9

ASSERTIVENESS

"I am woman, hear me roar."

–HELEN REDDY

THE POWER OF ASSERTIVENESS

Knowing how to be assertive is the secret to powerful communication and the key to getting what we want and deserve. Assertiveness is being prepared to stick your neck out, speak the unspeakable and walk knowingly into conflict. It's using your mind, body and voice to command the spotlight and confidently stand up for what you believe. It's about getting comfortable with the whole spectrum of emotions and knowing how to channel them for

"

ASSERTIVE
BEHAVIOUR IS
HONEST, DIRECT,
CLEAR, EXPRESSIVE,
SELF-ENHANCING,
PERSISTENT AND
RESPECTFUL.

the common good. Harnessing palatable emotions like love, kindness and compassion, as well as consciously unleashing the more challenging ones like anger, rage and passion.

Assertive behaviour is honest, direct, clear, expressive, self-enhancing, persistent and respectful. It's not about shouting loudly, being overbearing, bossy or pushy (a common misconception) – it's about knowing where the line is and calling out anyone who crosses it.

When we're assertive, we fulfil our inner promise and live fully in the world.

Assertiveness in action

Don't be shocked, but I haven't always been as assertive as I would like to have been. Once I was the only woman at a networking lunch and as we all sat down and introduced ourselves, one man said, "I run a business called The Right-hand Man". Cue: all the 'jokes' from fellow networkers about what they did with their left hand, the veiled hints at masturbation. And I just sat there thinking "Not cool", staring into space, pretending it wasn't happening.

It was mortifying. The minute the plates were cleared, I almost ran out of there. I was in such a hurry to leave that I left my coat behind. The whole experience made me feel dirty: when you don't react to something like that a little bit of you dies inside. I now realise I'd done my own sex a disservice by staying silent. But I hadn't wanted to make it uncomfortable for everyone by 'making a fuss' and calling something out that others would perceive as harmless banter.

This is a classic example of how being passive when we really should be assertive makes us feel bad, like we aren't doing ourselves justice. If that were to happen now I wouldn't make a massive deal out of it, but instead say something pointed like "Anyway, shall we move on?" making it crystal clear that I didn't want to hear comments like that again.

It's important to be assertive when we need to be. Because 'nice' doesn't get us respected, doesn't get us equal pay, and certainly doesn't get us to the top of our game. Assertiveness isn't beyond our reach.

We can do this. And we want to do this. We love stories of women who find their voice and stand up for themselves. It's hard to forget the air-punch moment in *Pretty Woman* when Julia Roberts returns to the designer store where she'd been made to feel like scum. Loaded down with designer shopping bags and dressed up to the nines, she is treated quite differently – and as she reminds the snobby sales assistant of her previous refusal to serve her, she says, "Big mistake: huge." We all want to be as feisty and outspoken as Julia on that day (without having to resort to the oldest profession in the world to get there).

How does assertiveness relate to Power Up?

Sitting at the heart of the Power Continuum mentioned in Chapter 1, assertiveness is the key to making our wants, needs and views heard. Although some people may think that being powerful is solely about being assertive, I have deliberately put it at the end of this book and positioned it as the final source of power in the Power Up Model© because it is only fully realised when exerted in combination with the other sources.

Many assertiveness courses will teach you to use power poses and power words to express yourself. This will take you so far, but it lacks substance. Assertiveness, when expressed in isolation, is a house of cards that can easily be knocked down by a stronger being. To be truly assertive, you need fire in your belly. You need a spark for your potential to be unleashed.

True assertiveness is powered by purpose, the driving force which sits at the heart of the Power Up Model©. It's fuelled by *Knowledge* – the intelligence and evidence that sit behind what you say – and sparked by *Intuition* – that voice inside that tells you when it's time to act and speak your truth. Assertiveness is strengthened through your *Resilience* – the courage and resolve that keeps you strong in the face of adversity and bolstered by your *Relationships*. To express yourself assertively, you need to know what you want and have the tools to express it.

Why do we need it?

This book has explored countless reasons why women feel powerless at various points of their lives and careers. Times when we have dearly wanted to communicate our needs and wants and have our value appreciated, but felt incapable of doing so. You wouldn't be reading this book if you hadn't experienced those times. And I wouldn't be writing this book if I hadn't experienced them either.

Just in the past week, I've heard women at different ages and stages of life share concrete examples of why assertive communication is so important.

- Marissa, who recently found out her male colleague had been earning 15 per cent more than her over the past three years, in a company that purports to champion diversity and inclusion.

- Bethany, who was invited to express her views about a networking event, only to have them thrown back in her face because the male organiser didn't like what she was saying about the lack of diversity.

- And the group of schoolgirls I've been working with recently who had been on the receiving end of sexual harassment which has become so normalised they feel unsafe calling it out.

Experiences like this make women angry, and they have the right to be. And yet, rather than using assertiveness to express themselves, they bottle it up, or show it in ways that undermine them, rather than furthering their cause. Unused to or incapable of dealing with this boiling upsurge of emotion, they lose control, scream and shout. Or worse still, a mixture of both. If you've experienced these feelings yourself, you're not alone.

So why do we find it so hard to be assertive? The answer is complicated. Women are hard-wired to avoid saying 'no'. We hate being 'difficult' and want everything to run smoothly with no raised voices or uncomfortable silences. It's a self-preservation thing, wanting to make everyone comfortable to the detriment of ourselves. We're conditioned to put everyone else first, be nice, not make a fuss. We over-nurture and over-compensate. Which means we lose out in the end.

The truth is, our failure to stand up and be counted is not serving us. And assertiveness provides a way out. A pressure valve. A needle to lance the boil. The key to calmly, rationally, passionately and truthfully expressing our views.

What gets in the way?

Although we all know that we want to be heard, there are times when we're more worried about the consequences of speaking up than what it will feel like if we're not assertive.

We justifiably find it more difficult to stand up for ourselves when we feel in danger. A friend was travelling home by train the other day. This is her text, verbatim: "Can we reschedule our call? I had a really horrible experience with a conductor and I'm still feeling emotional and upset about his aggressive, rude and threatening treatment. I have reported him, but am a mess." In the face of such treatment, how can we be assertive?

Let's look at some of the obstacles to assertiveness, because understanding what's stopping us is part of the secret to finding a way through.

■ **Old-fashioned beliefs**: we've all heard the phrase 'little girls should be seen and not heard'. This old-fashioned belief still exists, whether consciously or not. It is perpetuated through unthinking acts, such as the teachers at my friend's school who ignored parents' requests to introduce female authors to the curriculum, particularly significant since they had just started accepting girls to what was once an all-boys school. What message was that sending to the children about women's equal place in society?

■ **Aversion to being put on the spot**: it is rare for adults to put children on the spot and truly pay attention to the answer, so being put on the spot as adults can feel like being a rabbit caught in headlights. As a result, there can be mental resistance even when we know we need to speak up.

■ **Not wanting to cause a scene**: thoughts like "I don't want to make a fuss" hold us back. A good example of our reticence is making sure we're paid the same as our male colleagues, which feels like a dirty thing to do – even though it's not and inside we're seething about it. We're just not comfortable asking for what we want and simply don't know how. Women often feel like they have to edit themselves in some way or control themselves, often fuelled by a fear of the repercussions. If someone sitting next to you on a packed train is having a shouty conversation on their phone, do you speak up and ask them to keep it down? Or do you scuttle away and find somewhere quieter to sit? I bet I know the answer.

■ **Lack of tools**: we've been taught to be polite. Over polite. And as women we don't have the tools to be assertive – we don't know how. Sometimes when trying to behave assertively we end up having such an overly-emotional reaction that we get back in our box and never do it again. We're just not used to it.

WHAT IS ASSERTIVENESS?

The dictionary definition of assertiveness is 'a form of behaviour characterised by a confident declaration or affirmation of a statement, without the need for apologising, over-explaining or justifying'. As you'll see from this chapter, I believe it's so much more than that!

If you look at an assertive woman, you'll see she's standing strong, unbowed, her posture straight, her gestures precise and definitive. If you listen to her speaking, her voice is clear and unwavering, the volume not too loud or too soft, the words accurately conveying her needs, thoughts and wants.

Being assertive means respecting and valuing yourself, while respecting others' needs and feelings. It means setting your limits in terms of time, energy, privacy and money. It's about setting boundaries for yourself and others. It doesn't mean disregarding other people's limits, freezing with anxiety in the face of someone else's assertiveness or expecting people to know magically what you want or how you feel. It's calling out inappropriate behaviour, talking about the elephant in the room and surfacing conversations that people would rather keep under wraps.

Examples of assertiveness include my friend Mel, a really attractive girl, who's always being 'hit on' by guys. When this happens, instead of smiling or going along with it, she says, "Leave me alone, I'm not interested, I'm talking to my friend." None of them challenge her. It shocks them so much that they do what they're told.

Another example: I always travel in the quiet carriage when I go by train and one day at 5am, there was a really noisy family next to me. Rather than trying to ignore them I said, "Do you realise you're in the quiet carriage and everyone in here is either trying to sleep or work? Can you go and sit somewhere else?" They didn't move but they quietened down. In the past I would have just sat there and seethed, scared of retaliation. With assertiveness, I was able to express a boundary that, for me, had been crossed and politely ask for what I wanted.

To understand how assertiveness comes across, it's helpful to explore what it isn't. As mentioned in Chapter 1, assertiveness sits on a Power Continuum, with passivity at one end, aggression at the other and passive aggression in between. All four types of communication are linked to our response to a perceived threat and can be displayed either verbally or non-verbally.

A useful step in becoming more assertive is to consider where you are in relation to these four types of communication, how that has come about and what you want to do about it. Take a look at the table below and consider how you behave in various situations, noting any difference between your behaviour when you're relaxed or under threat in some way. If you find yourself stepping into passive or aggressive behaviour in certain situations, consider how you can change your verbal and non-verbal communication style in order to move into a more assertive position.

Some examples of aggressive, passive and assertive behaviour are provided in the tables below, as well as how they show up verbally and non-verbally.

Aggressive Behaviour	Passive Behaviour	Assertive Behaviour
Verbal communication style		
Heavy emphasis on 'I' statements: "My way is right"	Long, rambling sentences	Brief, to the point, factual statements
Opinions stated as facts	Frequent apologies and justifications	Questions to check what others want/feel
Threatening questions, instructions or threats	Hesitant phrases and fillers	Constructive criticism without blame
"You should/ought" advice	Lack of conviction	Explanations and suggestions (not advice)
Allocating blame, sarcasm and put downs	Non-committal	Empathy

Aggressive Behaviour	Passive Behaviour	Assertive Behaviour
Non-Verbal communication style		
Dominating eye contact	Poor eye contact	Steady eye contact
Leaning forward, hands on hips, finger-pointing	Slumped posture	Open posture
Strident voice	Nervous mannerisms	No nervous mannerisms
Sarcastic tone	Hesitant voice/ throat clearing	Clear, fluent voice

Where does assertiveness come from?

Having compared the examples of passive, aggressive and assertive communication above, it's clear that assertiveness comes from the ability to be strong and communicate your needs and wants clearly. It's also about overriding some of society's negative perceptions of an assertive woman, which is easier said than done. Many women struggle with the perception of female assertiveness and don't want to be branded negatively because who really wants to be called a bitch behind their back?

In my experience, this is a challenge that most women face. In a conversation between Michelle Obama and actress Yara Shahidi for the Let Girls Learn initiative[38], Shahidi said, "So many of us are haunted by the voices of other people who tell us what we can't do," remembering a time when a teacher told her she was being "too fierce" and "too aggressive". Michelle Obama agreed: "That's a word that's been used for me often, too". And yet, "What I realised is it's OK to take up space without the fear of being too loud or too aggressive... That just means I'm owning my space even more."

This indicates that assertiveness also comes from the 'don't give a damn' gene, where you're more concerned about doing the right thing or getting what you want than making everyone else feel OK, which is not always comfortable to be around. This is the difference between respect and like-ability. It's not that assertive people are deliberately making it difficult or awkward for others; it's that for them, there's a bigger agenda at play.

Of course, what some see as owning one's space can some-times come across as something quite different. According to a controversial study published in the journal *Development and Learning in Organisations*[39], 70 per cent of female exec-utives feel they have been bullied by women in their office and that this has stunted their professional progression.

Labelled 'Queen Bee Syndrome' (and also discussed in the *Relationships* chapter), this kind of behaviour arises when women treat their female colleagues in a demeaning manner, either by undermining them or using their social stature to manipulate others into thinking less of them. The study, which was undertaken by Cecilia Harvey, COO of Quant Network and founder and chair of global technology platform Tech Women Today, describes Queen Bee Syndrome as the "biggest hindrance to women advancing in the workplace".

While QBS no doubt exists and is a very real problem, there are grey areas too. The woman whose colleagues think is acting like a Queen Bee may herself think she's just being assertive. Colleagues may find they're unwittingly putting themselves in a passive position in the face of such strong behaviour.

What's clear is that assertiveness is something that remains a struggle for women – whether you're delivering it or receiving it and so it makes sense to proactively develop it for yourself, so that you can use it whenever you need to.

HOW CAN YOU DEVELOP IT?

To tap into your assertiveness, you need to understand who you are and what you want. Assertiveness will then become a life position for you, a superpower that's forever at your fingertips, as opposed to a technique you need to 'try out' in situations when you feel like you 'need' to be more assertive.

The following guidance and tips have all been road tested by women on their route to assertiveness and are proven to work. I know they'll make a big difference to you too.

Start with a clear mind

To be assertive, you need a clear mind. If your views are fuzzy, you will come across as wishy-washy and it will be easier for people to take advantage of you. And if you don't take yourself seriously, how can you expect other people to?

With clarity, you will feel more confident about expressing yourself and happy to reveal your authentic self to others. You will have a more positive view of your own place in society, be open to other people's perspectives and welcome them in, even if you disagree.

Clarity comes through understanding your purpose, identity, values and beliefs, as explored in Chapter 1. These will act as foundation stones that will keep you strong when under pressure, steel your resolve when the going gets tough and lend power to your voice when you want to be heard.

Being assertive with others

Unfortunately, no woman is an island, and the challenge comes when you have to interact with other people, none of whom will share the same purpose, identity, values and beliefs as you do and all of whom will be equally as wedded to their own ideals as you are to yours!

Although no one and nothing can *make* you feel anything, the more you know about which people and situations trigger feelings of being threatened, the more you'll be able to remain in the assertive position and the more powerful you'll feel.

EXERCISE 1:
GETTING IN TUNE WITH YOUR ASSERTIVENESS BAROMETER

Key to being assertive is understanding how you typically respond to different people, what stops you from being assertive and how you can stay on track. This exercise is about getting in tune with your own assertiveness barometer.

1 Start by noting down situations where you find it easy to be assertive and people you find it easy to be assertive with. For example, your weekly team update, deciding where to go on an evening out with friends, and leading a planning meeting with colleagues at the same level or below you.

2. Now write down the situations when you find it difficult to be assertive and who you find it difficult to be assertive with. For example, being invited to share

your unformed opinion to a large group of people, knowing you're the least experienced person in the room, being yourself around people in authority, those who dominate discussions, those you don't trust or individuals who remind you of people you've had challenges with in the past.

3. Consider when you're more likely to flip from assertiveness to passivity, aggression, or passive aggression, and why that may be. Look for any similarities, themes, and patterns of behaviour which you find challenging, identify personality traits in other people that trigger you and consider why this might be the case. Maybe it's men in a position of authority speaking to you in a way that takes you straight back to the classroom or a complaining female colleague who reminds you of an irritating aunt. Knowledge is power and the more you know about when you feel strong and assertive and by contrast, when you feel weak, the more you can do about it.

4. Now think about how you're most likely to respond when feeling threatened – either advertently or inadvertently. This might include:

   ▪ Feeling like you've got to over-explain, justify, second-guess or react to what you think the other person thinks about you, even though you don't know for sure that they are thinking that way.

   ▪ Putting unnecessary pressure on yourself to make everything perfect; overthinking every detail, adding and embellishing indefinitely; spending a disproportionate amount of time on a task, or not sharing your thoughts with anyone until you have a perfectly crafted set of words.

- Feeling like you've got to edit yourself in some way, rein yourself in or suppress your thoughts, feelings and emotions; compromising your own needs and wants and basically gagging yourself.

- Losing all empathy for others; becoming uncaring, unfeeling, distracted, self-absorbed.

- Having an overwhelming desire to swear, shout, dominate the discussion, put people 'in their place'; doing or saying something alarming or shocking; belittling others or become arrogant.

- Feeling like all you want to do is run away or hide; shrinking into yourself when asked your opinion; being self-effacing, apologising for no reason or wanting to disappear altogether.

Understanding your brain's response to a threat

In all the situations described above, you are in fight or flight mode. When triggered, your mind may be telling you to exert 'power over' (where you use aggression to dominate) or that you need to run away because you're powerless (where passivity kicks in).

Although we'd all like to think that we can be as assertive as Beyoncé on her sassiest form every day of the week, there will be times when all we want to do is curl up under the duvet and other times when we lose the plot and end up doing or saying something we later regret. We're going to explore an example of being triggered to show you what happens to the brain and the steps you can take to work with your emotions when you're triggered, to ensure you act assertively instead.

Imagine someone has criticised you for a piece of work you've put your heart and soul into – and in front of a roomful of colleagues. You believe this person has always had it in for you, they probably resent or feel threatened by you, and by the same token, you have very little time for them.

Their detailed verbal attack has incensed you at a number of levels:

- Partly because you believe their feedback is largely unfounded.

- Partly because you have been publicly derided.

- Partly because, underneath it all, you suspect that their criticism, however poorly worded, may have a grain of truth in it and you're worried that the audience will think less of you as a result (even though you won't be admitting that to yourself at the time).

This powerful cocktail of feelings unleashes an immense and uncontrollable response – your heart beats faster, your throat constricts, your face goes red, and you may start to sweat or shake. You have by this point lost all control of your senses and are looking for an outlet, a place to vent all these feelings of rage, insecurity and hurt that are threatening to engulf you.

When the meeting is over, you explode in a variety of ways, firstly swearing about them loudly in front of a group of colleagues, then confronting them directly about their inappropriate treatment and finally, when they express no remorse, bursting into hot, mortifying and uncontrollable tears of anger and frustration.

A few days later, when the indignation has somewhat simmered down, you are still hurt and angered by what happened, but also feel some remorse about the magnitude of your response, which you realise now was disproportionate to the comments that triggered it in the first place. You wish you could have kept your cool and not wasted so much energy on the whole sorry episode.

Sound familiar at all? We've all had experiences like this, which often stay with us far longer than is healthy and stop us from moving towards where we want to go because we're too busy dwelling on what's happened. So what happens in these situations and, more importantly, what can we do about it?

What can happen when we're triggered in this way is what Daniel Goleman calls the 'amygdala hijack'. Our amygdala is one of the oldest parts of the brain and responsible for our emotions, memory and survival instincts, which sounds the alarm when we feel like we're in danger. Whereas in caveman times our amygdala would have alerted us to an attack by a sabre-toothed tiger, these days it can be alerted when we are criticised, feel stressed or threatened.

Daniel Goleman coined the term based on the work of neuroscientist Joseph LeDoux, which demonstrated that, under normal circumstances, our thinking brain (or neocortex) is in the driving seat, but when we feel under threat, the amygdala hijack occurs and our 'emotional brain' takes over.

In this state, we've essentially lost control – with the modern age response to that sabre-toothed tiger being mounting anxiety or even bursting into tears or flying into a rage. During an extreme response, we will revert to one of the states on the Assertiveness Continuum: either aggressiveness (fight), passivity (flight) or somewhere in between. Remember when Donald Trump grabbed Theresa May's hand and continued holding it as he led her down the path alongside the White House colonnade, and she just looked awkward and let him? That's freezing. It's a weird 'power over' thing where you don't want to make a fuss and so don't act.

Knowing about the amygdala hijack allows you to prevent it by remaining aware of your emotions during potentially triggering events. For example, before delivering a presentation in front of an audience you suspect will be hostile, think carefully about how their words and actions might stimulate an extreme reaction in you. Recognising this will enable you to plan your response in advance or even take action to prevent them from being critical in the first place.

What to do when you've been triggered

Although you can't control which emotions arrive and when, you can control how you respond to them, giving you greater choices, behaviours and ways of relating to others. To help you do this, I have created the **CLEAR©** model, five steps to communicating assertively, starting with managing your mindset (**C**alm, **L**evel Up, **E**ngage) and ending with managing your behaviour (**A**ct, **R**eact).

This system has been tried and tested and enabled many women I've worked with to take control and confidently express their views when under pressure. We're going to explore each step in detail. Just knowing that you have a model available at your fingertips, which you can turn to whenever you've been triggered will be enough to move yourself into a more empowered position. And if the trigger is too powerful to ignore, it will definitely give you the tools to do yourself justice.

Using CLEAR for Assertive Communication

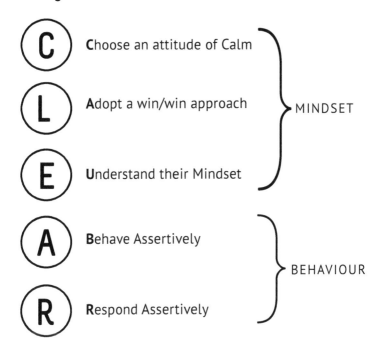

C Choose an attitude of Calm

L Adopt a win/win approach

E Understand their Mindset

} MINDSET

A Behave Assertively

R Respond Assertively

} BEHAVIOUR

★ Step 1: Calm

The first step to remaining assertive is to choose an attitude of **Calm.** This might feel like an impossible task when you've been provoked and everything in your mind and body is telling you to run away or stand and fight.

Ideally, what you want to do is to avoid getting irate in the first place because this will avoid an over-reaction that you will later regret. Understanding which situations and people trigger us is half the battle. The other half is understanding what is happening in our brains, so that we can manage our response and remain cool, calm and collected – and be more able to act assertively. Here are seven techniques that have been proven to bring about a state of calm, however much you've been provoked.

■ **Breathe:** slow down by taking a series of deep breaths. This will counter your body's natural response when stressed or angry, which will be to take quick, shallow breaths which will reinforce your fight or flight response. Research shows that it only takes a few deep (diaphragmatic) breaths to dramatically change our physiology and, in turn, calm our mental state[40]. As you breathe in and out, imagine the oxygen flushing away all your negative emotions, opening up your mind and bringing power to you. You can also use the 6-second rule. Waiting for just six seconds will be sufficient time for the cortisol and adrenalin that cause an amygdala hijack to take place to dissipate.

■ **Relax your body:** when you're anxious or angry, it can feel like every muscle in your body is tense – and they probably are! Practising progressive muscle relaxation will help you calm down and centre yourself and you can do this either standing or sitting. Start at your toes and slowly move up, telling yourself to release each part of your body until you get to your head. Pay particular attention to your posture. Imagine you're an angel rearranging your wings: sit up tall and bring your shoulder blades together and down, which, in turn, will allow you to drop your shoulders.

- **Notice:** tune into your emotions and feelings. Don't try to negate or suppress how you're feeling – for example, by saying "I'M NOT CROSS" – you have a right to feel whatever emotion you're feeling, so give it the space to be felt in your own head. Label the feeling – "I'm feeling livid right now" or "I'm feeling trapped by this conversation". Think about why you've been triggered and notice how your brain might be going into 'worst-case scenario' mode, exaggerating, dramatizing or catastrophising the 'attack'.

- **Take control:** now you can start to bring in rational thought, re-engaging your neocortex or 'thinking brain'. Ask yourself whether what you're thinking is true, what would be the worst outcome or, even more powerfully, the best outcome for everyone concerned, for example: "What I'd like to do right now is 'put down' my anger and find a resolution." This will remind you that all your thoughts are transitory and within your control, drawing attention away from your negative emotions and refocusing you in the direction of empowered choice and resolution.

- **Pay attention:** while you're mentally interviewing yourself in this way, bring your attention to your surroundings. Notice the people around you, their expressions and body language. Assess the temperature in the room and how hot or cold you're feeling. When we lose control of our senses, we often go up into our own heads, spinning off into a world of indignation, hurt, impatience or fear, which can amplify what's actually going

405

on so that we 'stop' seeing, hearing and feeling reality. To counter this, imagine yourself rising above the situation, looking down on yourself and the people around you, detaching yourself from the intensity, whilst at the same time remaining fully present to what is going on. If you feel like you are going to cry, move your eyes: look up, count the ceiling tiles, notice the light fixtures. Some research has actually shown that blinking may help stop the flow of tears[41].

■ **Change the scenery:** sometimes the best response to an extreme situation is to remove yourself from it. Look in a different direction, visualise yourself in a different place and if you need to, walk away.

■ **Train your brain:** to remain calm when faced with unplanned or unwanted situations you can deliberately put yourself in high-adrenaline or controlled risk situations, so that you become aware of the potential for the fight or flight response to kick in and choose to take a different path instead. Examples might include extreme sports or time trials or doing something you find scary, like karaoke, speaking in front of a large audience, volunteering to lead a breakout session at an event or spending time with volatile animals.

Over time, it will be possible to change the way your brain responds to emotional triggers, thereby preventing the amygdala hijack.

★ Step 2: Level Up

Once you've mastered the art of Calm, the next step is to **Level Up.** This is about reminding yourself that you have an equal right as the other person to be heard and have your needs met. Levelling up is also about realising that just because someone is good at something, that doesn't put you in a 'less good' position by default.

Developing a win-win mindset isn't about giving in to someone's demands or overpowering them, it's about using your emotional intelligence (as discussed in Chapter 1) to 'do assertive' in a way that works for you. As speaker and author of *A Mind At Home With Itself*, Byron Katie said: 'Life happens for you, it doesn't happen to you' but this is only the case if you can make challenges manageable and act accordingly. If you are tuned in to other people's inner worlds, you will be more able to manage your relationships and communicate more assertively.

In psychiatrist Thomas A. Harris' ground-breaking 1960s self-help book, *I'm OK, You're OK*, he explains that a person's psychological state changes in response to different situations, with four 'life positions' that each of us may take, as illustrated in the grid below. These are: I'm Not OK, You're OK; I'm Not OK, You're Not OK; I'm OK, You're Not OK and I'm OK, You're OK.

I'M OKAY

AGGRESSIVENESS	ASSERTIVENESS
I win/you lose	I win/you win
Forceful	Confident
Hostile	Realistic
Blaming anyone but themselves	Taking responsibility
Ignoring others' rights	Recognising others' rights

YOU'RE NOT OKAY ⋯⋯⋯⋯⋯⋯⋯⋯⋯⋯⋯⋯⋯⋯⋯⋯⋯⋯⋯⋯ YOU'RE OKAY

DESTRUCTIVNESS	PASSIVITY
I lose/you lose	I lose/you win
Dismissive	Avoiding
Manipulative	Submissive
Denies others' rights	Surrenders own rights
Apathetic	Runs away

I'M NOT OKAY

As you can see from the grid, negative traits like aggressiveness, destructiveness and passivity come out either when you're OK and the other person isn't, or when you believe they're OK and you're not. When there is imbalance we feel under threat, or we become threatening.

Getting into an assertive state of mind, or levelling up, is about being OK with who you are, but also treating and viewing the other person with respect. When you see others as equals you do not feel the need to be passive or aggressive.

We need to get better at viewing other people as our equals, as people with strengths but also their own flaws. They're no better than us and our opinions matter just as much as theirs.

"

WE NEED TO GET BETTER AT VIEWING OTHER PEOPLE AS OUR EQUALS, AS PEOPLE WITH STRENGTHS BUT ALSO THEIR OWN FLAWS.

EXERCISE 2: ADOPTING A WIN/WIN APPROACH

In order to adopt a win/win mindset, it's helpful to understand those situations where you haven't felt OK and where you saw the other person in relation to the four positions on the I'm OK/You're OK quadrant. From there you can think about how you can get yourself into a more assertive mindset by changing your thinking and influencing theirs through the techniques in this book.

1. Think of a time when you've felt like your assertiveness has been compromised. Explore which of the positions on the grid (above) you 'went to' and why.

2. Now think about which position the other person adopted and why.

3. Finally, challenge yourself to think about what might be a win/win outcome for you both and how you could make that happen through how you choose to think, speak and act.

    For example, one of your colleagues has been selected for a role you wanted for yourself. You have gone into the I lose/you win quadrant because you feel sorry for yourself and your colleague has gone into I lose/you lose because they now feel guilty. The I win/you win outcome might be that she agrees to share some of her responsibilities with you so that you can progress in your role, and you agree to support her with the tasks you're familiar with. To do this, you would need to initiate a meeting with her to discuss this.

★ Step 3: Engage

Once you've developed the ability to Level Up, the next step is knowing how to **Engage.** You may be approaching the situation with a zen-like Calm, but the other person may not be. So how do you handle someone who's playing some kind of mind-game, whether intentionally or not? And how do you stop their behaviour from triggering an unhelpful response in you?

The only way that you can effectively Engage is by switching on to what's actually happening for the other person, as opposed to becoming completely absorbed in what's going on for you, and then adapting your behaviour accordingly.

So you might be livid that your brand new mobile phone has stopped working and that the person you finally speak to after twenty minutes on hold can't find your account details... And although their apathetic attitude is threatening to trigger a major meltdown in you (amygdala hijack here we come!) you know, deep down, that it isn't their fault and that by losing your rag you will be pushing yourself further away from reaching any kind of resolution.

The secret here is to firstly acknowledge that they are a human being just like you, with their own hopes, dreams, challenges and aspirations. So the person you're talking to about your faulty phone may seem apathetic but there is a whole host of reasons why that might be the case: she may have just come off the phone from a customer who belittled her, she may not have had training on the new system, she may have just received some bad news, it may be her first day...

Rather than going into 'power-over' mode, adopt a 'We're all in this together' attitude – note the 'We' rather than the 'I'. Put yourself in their shoes and imagine how frustrating it must be to deal with irate customers all day, especially when the system lets you down.

Demonstrating that you can see the situation from their point of view will encourage them to do the same, so tell them you know how it feels when a new system is introduced but also explain that your ability to do your job is linked to your phone. Be careful not to go overboard when you express your frustrations. Personal attacks, inappropriate language and unfair threats will only put them on the defensive. Talking about how 'we' can resolve the situation will bring you closer together and you'll get much better results when you speak calmly and firmly.

My friend Roz always gets an upgrade in hotels. She says, "It's because I go in and use the word 'We' and make out we're all in this together, we know this is bad so how are we going to make it better? It disarms people so they don't put up a barrier – they collaborate. It's not blaming, it's 'Let's sort this out together'. In this way, we're not on either side of a brick wall but on the same side working out how to get over the other side."

★ Step 4: Act

Now that we've explored an assertive mindset (the Calm, Level Up and Engage of CLEAR©), let's move onto assertive behaviour (how we **Act** and **React** so that we do ourselves justice and get the best possible outcome for all).

Being assertive is not always easy. Sometimes it's easier to revert to one of the other communication styles. We have to learn to be assertive in the moment – not after the fact. When we do nothing but promise ourselves that we will try and be a bit more feisty next time around, we've already shown our relenting side, our self-doubt.

The tricky thing is getting assertiveness right. As I write, there's a great image doing the rounds on Facebook from the Minnesota Women's Consortium which shows two women at their desks. The first one asks: "What's the difference between being assertive and being aggressive?" The second one responds: "Your gender."

Acting assertively is achieving the Goldilocks 'just right' balance between being too weak and being too strong.

If we've been told repeatedly in childhood to pipe down and shut up, we grow up believing that what we have to say is of no value – or that no one will listen. This can get in the way of being assertive. If we Act from a weak position, we've given those voices from the past permission to censor our present opinions. It's time to ignore those voices – for good.

Equally, we must be careful not to step over the assertive line into aggression. Think bullying, monstrous Meryl Streep as Miranda Priestly, the long-time editor-in-chief of *Runway* magazine in *The Devil Wears Prada*. An extreme example, yes, but it's easy to go too far and tip into full-on mean when we're trying to show our assertive side. One woman I was coaching thought she was being assertive in her workplace but was subsequently accused of bullying – to her absolute horror.

The opposite extreme of situations where we run the risk of 'powering over' the other person are situations when we're in danger of allowing others to overpower us. As acknowledged earlier, we give away our power because we are conditioned to be nice and make everyone else's world as comfortable as it can be to the detriment of ourselves. We're hardwired not to say 'no' or stick our neck out for what we want; we hate being difficult, making a fuss. And we are used to – and sometimes even encouraged – to sacrifice our own needs and wants for others. Our nurturing nature can backfire as we put the whole world before ourselves.

As we step into our power, we need to learn how to stand up for ourselves, because if we don't, who will? Awkward situations are an inevitable part of all our lives.

There are plenty of times when it's NOT OK: when a supplier doesn't deliver on time, when a colleague disregards our point of view, when a team member repeatedly turns up late or when we're passed over for a promotion or pay rise without any real explanation. So we need to find a way to communicate our opinions and share our perspective in a way that does us justice. When we disagree with someone's point of view, we need to find a way to convey that without disliking or doubting ourselves afterwards, or going into a vortex of doom worrying about the implications.

Becoming assertive and feeling comfortable with it means making friends with the more difficult emotions. Sticking with 'nice' and 'likeable' keeps us passive. Knowing how to summon up all our emotions and channelling them appropriately makes us assertive and brings us respect.

Here are seven strategies that you can use to Act assertively and get the balance just right.

ACTING
ASSERTIVELY IS
ACHIEVING THE
GOLDILOCKS 'JUST
RIGHT' BALANCE
BETWEEN BEING
TOO WEAK AND
BEING TOO STRONG.

1. Channel your emotions

Face up to your emotions and in doing so, encourage others to do the same. Assertiveness is about being comfortable with the whole gamut of emotions: anger, jealousy, rage, stubbornness, negativity, as well as positive emotions like excitement, joy and satisfaction. Allowing ourselves to feel these, rather than suppressing or being scared of them means we can learn to control them in the moment and tailor our behaviour to the situation. As Serena Williams said in her Nike ad, women should "Dream Crazier" and reclaim their expression of emotion, whether it be anger, pride, joy, or anything in between.

Recently, a client shared a presentation with me that she was about to give to 500 sales managers. The latest finance figures weren't great, she said, "So I'll quickly flash up the slide showing where we're in the red, then we'll move onto the solution." But I said no. "Show them the slide and leave it up there. You need to be OK with the uncomfortableness that part of the blame lies on your audience's shoulders – just state it and be OK with it. That's professional and respectful and not trying to hide away from the facts. It's being assertive. And from there you work together to sort the situation out."

Rather than letting challenging emotions run away with us – for example, swearing at a rude colleague and in doing so bringing yourself down to their level – use the labelling technique where you express the emotion you're feeling. Speaker and marketing expert, Bryony Thomas, was impressed in a recent conversation in which she was angered by what a person was saying to her when they responded: "Okay, this conversation isn't going as I'd imagined, can we unpick a little how we got here?" A technique that worked really well.

2. Take the lead

Recently, I've been involved in two incidents where a man has taken it upon himself to take control: one following a car accident where the man took the initiative to direct the traffic and, interestingly, the women looked after the victims; the other in a busy supermarket car park where a man averted a heated argument by showing people where the remaining spaces were. Both assumed roles that were important and welcomed, but it was fascinating to observe how the genders took on their traditional roles. Assertiveness is an act of leadership, so give yourself permission to go for it, rather than waiting for someone else to step in or give you the green light. Research shows that we tend to say 'yes' or follow the person who states their position first, so take the initiative and state your opinions first and then invite others to do the same.

3. Don't overthink it

Because we women can be perfectionists, we often feel like we need to know everything about a subject before we can say anything. We end up rendering ourselves dumb as a result and this lets us down. Assertiveness is being OK with what you know and what you don't, and not allowing the latter to stop you stating the former. In these cases, I would encourage you to trust your powers of Knowledge and Intuition and speak.

Speaking up when things aren't right is never easy. But holding back just leaves you feeling bad about yourself. From bullying or sexist behaviour to poor service, if we feel we're not being treated right, we need to be prepared to say so. No finger-pointing or ranting – just a clear statement of the facts and their impact.

If you're clear on your wants and needs, proactively stating what you want to take place and your desired outcome should be straightforward. So don't listen to that voice in your head telling you to keep your thoughts to yourself, otherwise your brain will hone in on all the reasons why you shouldn't speak and prevent you from taking action. Tell yourself that you have a right to be in the room and that if you're sharing your intelligence, you're not making others look stupid or showing off, you're actually contributing to the world in your own way.

To trigger action, use a technique developed by American motivational speaker, Mel Robbins, called 54321. As she puts it, "When you feel yourself hesitate before doing something that you know you should do, count 5-4-3-2-1-GO and move towards action. There is a window that exists between the moment you have an instinct to change and your mind killing it. It's a five-second window. And it exists for everyone. If you do not take action on your instinct to change, you will stay stagnant."

4. Use your body

The way we take up space with our bodies says so much about our self-belief and our place in the world. With open body language, you can convey subliminal messages of confidence and ease; with closed body language you can shut people off, appearing at one extreme timid and at the other arrogant. If you watch animals in fight or flight, the lion will puff out its mane, the cobra rear up, the swan will extend its wings and the mouse will scurry away. Don't be the mouse.

To convey a strong position, occupy your rightful space. A great tip, where possible, is simply to stand up as this immediately builds psychological strength. Having a symmetrical posture will convey power and solidity; putting your weight on one hip, crossing your legs or slouching will give the impression of imbalance or sloppiness. So plant your feet on the floor and ground yourself, stand up to your full height and lengthen your spine.

If you're going into a meeting, think about where to position yourself in the room for maximum impact. If you have a choice, arrive early and sit at the head of the table, granting yourself a superior position and strong vantage point from which to see and be seen. Alternatively, choose a seat facing the door, so that you are the first to greet everyone as they walk in.

When seated, position yourself squarely on the chair. To counter people encroaching your space, avoid folding your arms and instead imagine a box laid out on the table in front of you and place your arms on either side of it.

Maintaining steady eye contact will convey confidence and strength; smiling will illustrate your willingness to level up and engage. Keeping your head straight will send out a message of conviction, whereas tilting it to one side will make you appear more approachable and inviting.

Also, think about how you position your hands. Folded arms will send out messages that you're either feeling defensive or confrontational (even though this might be the most comfortable position in the world for you), speaking with your palms up can look placatory and put you in a subordinate position, whereas palms down will convey decisiveness and control.

5. Use visual cues

From laptop to lab coat to power blazer, your clothes, accessories and makeup can convey a message, so make sure yours is the right one. Image consultant and author of *Look Like the Leader You Are*, Lizzie Edwards advises that if we want to convey authority we should wear darker, stronger colours, with a high contrast, for example, a white blouse and a navy jacket, whereas if we want to appear softer and more approachable choose a lighter colour with lower contrast. Angular patterns will convey more conviction than flowery ones, and for some, wearing heels or statement jewellery sends out a message that they mean business.

6. Use your voice

Your ability to communicate assertively will be greatly enhanced when you engage the power of your breath and voice. Our bodies are designed to make noise, with sound resonating from our lungs, vocal cords, chest, mouth, tongue, teeth and lips. For maximum assertiveness, we need to override the message that we have received since birth to "shush" and "be quiet" and explore the range and breadth of our vocal chords. This is not about shouting, which the most impactful communicators avoid. Just taking a breath and filling your lungs with air before you speak will give you the 'fuel' to put your point across and the capacity to increase your volume.

To keep the attention on you, make sure you maintain volume to the end of your sentences, rather than fading off. If your voice has a tendency to get shrill when you're nervous, practise speaking in a steady, melodic and resonant voice so you convey confidence. If you have an important point to make, make sure your voice goes down at the end of the sentence. A lowered voice says, "I'm not asking you, I am telling you," whereas a voice that goes up at the end turns every statement into a question.

Consider too the pace of your voice. Speak slowly and you'll sound confident in your message. Speak fast and you'll either appear nervous or sound like you don't value what you're saying. Take care to enunciate your words: mumbling, mispronouncing or cutting words short gives the impression of laziness and can result in the meaning getting lost. Conversely, pronouncing every syllable will make it much easier for you to project outwards, with the added bonus of building self-confidence with every word you speak.

7. Choose your words

Take care not to detract from your message with fillers such as 'sort of', 'you know what I mean' or 'I guess'; disqualifiers like, 'I'm not sure if this is right but...' or 'does that make sense?'; or verbal ticks like 'ummm', 'urrr' 'so' or 'like'. These often creep in when you're nervous, unclear or searching for the next thing to say, but can easily become a habit. They convey a lack of confidence and can be hugely distracting.

Assertiveness is very much about what you choose to say – and not say. If you have a tendency to precede every point with a negative preamble, like 'I'm not sure if this is a good idea, but...', do everything to kill this habit. Keep your points succinct and avoid over-explaining – less is more. Avoid lots of justifications and ifs, buts and shoulds, as these can minimise the effectiveness of your arguments. A surprisingly quick and effective solution is to prepare your thoughts in advance and decide to replace your verbal ticks with silence. For example: "This is important because... This is what I want... This is how I want it... This is the outcome I'm looking for..." Pausing will also give your audience time to process what you've said and is much easier on the ear than an endless monologue or diatribe.

"Nobody can make you feel inferior without your consent."

–ELEANOR ROOSEVELT

In 2015, Ellen Leanse, a former Google executive, wrote a LinkedIn blog about the word "just'" which she claimed women use far more than men. "It hit me that there was something about the word I didn't like. It was a 'permission' word – a warm-up to a request, an apology for interrupting, a shy knock on the door before asking: 'Can I get something I need from you?'"

Leanse asked her co-workers to ban the word from their communication and claimed a notable difference in how confident people felt within a few weeks.

You'll notice that the word finds its way into our spoken and written communication, especially when we feel slightly uncomfortable about making a request. So try your own experiment by editing out all those times when you use 'just' and see what difference it makes.

Stating "I believe that..." is very powerful when you're making an incisive point.

EXERCISE 3:
ACTING
ASSERTIVELY

The best way to become more assertive is through practice. The more you do it, the better you'll become.

1. Identify three scenarios coming up where you'd like to act more assertively – these can be small things like asking for a refund or big things like telling a family member that you don't want to discuss politics at the dinner table, or telling a colleague that you find their jokes offensive.

2. Now choose three of the techniques outlined above you wish to adopt in your chosen scenarios and practice them.

3. Repeat until you have applied a whole range of techniques and monitor their impact on your ability to act assertively. Good luck!

★ Step 5: React

The techniques described in the Act section will ensure you'll experience fewer occasions when your assertiveness is compromised, however, there will be times when people strongly provoke you, at which point you'll need to know how to **React.**

I'm sure you recognise those moments when someone does or says something that you really don't like, but rather than reacting, you freeze. How many times have you thought, "I wish I'd said/done xyz," after the moment has passed? It's far easier to react assertively in our own minds rather than for real. Often, it goes back to childhood, when some 'little-girls-should-be-seen-and-not-heard' adult shut us down. Other times, the pattern is set at the start of a career, when plucking up the courage to speak leads to you being talked over, ignored or disagreed with, only for the point to be made by someone else later on.

These experiences are powerful. They send a message at the deepest subconscious level that it's unsafe to put our head above the parapet. So when we're asked to share our opinion in a meeting, even an unthreatening one, we can find it safer to keep our mouths shut.

The trouble is, society has a problem with women who stand up for themselves and are prepared to sacrifice likeability for respect. Words like 'bossy' and 'pushy' are often used to describe opinionated, assertive women. In 2017 via her *Rewriting the Code* campaign, health and education campaigner, Sarah Brown, tackled the way women and girls get described, from classroom to boardroom. "Words are loaded with meaning," she said. "When a woman's described as 'bossy' and a 'bitch' when she's simply showing her own strengths and assertiveness and getting the job done, it compounds an existing problem."

Unfortunately, if you don't speak up for yourself or call out inappropriate treatment, you may as well be condoning it, so we need to have techniques to hand. If we didn't fear negative labels, like being called a 'bitch', expressing thoughts would become something we could all do comfortably.

Here are some strategies for Reacting assertively, however hard your buttons have been pushed.

1. Develop a thick skin

Sometimes we need to decide it's OK for people not to like us and to swim willingly into troubled waters. I used to think that conflict was a bad thing, to be avoided at all costs. The trouble is, when we do this, we are compromising our own thoughts, feelings, wants and needs and putting those of the other person first. And although we might simmer down on the outside, our resentment just bubbles under the surface waiting for an outlet.

The Thomas Kilmann conflict model describes five different responses to conflict, each of which can be appropriate, depending on the context, as long as you go in with an assertive 'I'm OK you're OK' mindset. They are Competing, Accommodating, Avoiding, Collaborating and Compromising. Each of us is capable of using all five modes, but we all tend to rely on one more than the others.

So your usual mindset when boarding a crowded train is Compete? What would be different if you were in

Accommodating? And your usual response to a colleague's tinny headphones is Avoid? How would the outcome be different if you approached them in Compromise? The key thing is to prepare, so if there's someone or a situation that you know is going to bring conflict, think about how can you hold your own and reach a mutual agreement in advance, so that you know what to do when the moment comes.

2. Speak your truth

Just because someone has an opposing view doesn't mean what you have to say is invalid. Stick with your beliefs and don't be deterred by people's apparent lack of interest, which you may be misreading anyway. You don't need to have everyone fervently nodding their heads in agreement with you – this might not be their style and they may be taking a moment to process what you've just said. Make your statements without apology, preamble or disclaimers that undermine your authority. If you get accused of being bossy or pushy (even in jest) calmly point out that it's a requirement of your job to have opinions and state them. These tips should avoid interruptions, but if you do find that someone is repeatedly cutting in or interjecting when you're speaking, either keep speaking, but increase your volume, pointedly continue with: "As I was saying..." or calmly look them in the eye and say: "I would appreciate it if you would kindly stop interrupting me when I'm speaking," which should do the trick!

For maximum assertiveness when backed into a corner, remember what I call the Power Pause: first think (but not too much or you'll overthink it!), then take a breath, then speak. If you just blurt your thoughts out without doing this, you'll risk rambling on and you won't have the same power.

Although it can be tempting to say things like, "Does that make sense?" when you're met with blank faces, that sounds like you're seeking approval. Instead say: "What are people's thoughts on this?" Try using the rule of three to make your statements concise: "There are three points I want to make. The first is X, the second is Y, and finally Z..." In this way, you're stopping people interrupting you while encouraging yourself to be brief.

3. Cut in

When you want to actively participate in a conversation or react to a point you disagree with, lean forward into the group space. If you are struggling to make yourself heard, don't just lob in a bomb. Instead, use the hand you write with to 'cut into' the conversation by positioning your fingers as though they were a knife and subtly 'chopping' into the space between you. This is effectively using your hand as a silencer, without the negative connotations of pointing or using your hand as a stop sign. Accompany your hand gesture with 'building phrases' such as, "That's a great point, David, and I'd like to add to it by saying..." Using the person's name acknowledges them personally and can take away the sting of being interrupted. Using "and" rather than "but" (even though you may not agree 100% with what's come before) is another useful technique for maintaining rapport while bringing your own perspective into the conversation.

4. Disagree

Assertiveness is often compromised when we have a clash of opinions or feel threatened in some way. Arguing occurs when two people consider each other's opinions to be invalid and wrong, while 'disagreeing' is when people uphold their own point of view but maintain respect for the other person's opinion (I'm OK you're OK).

To ensure arguments don't escalate into full-blown conflict, look the other person in the eye and speak in a calm, even tone rather than increasing or decreasing your volume. Use precise language, stating your views simply, rather than exaggerating or using absolute terms like 'never' and 'always'. Make sure you demonstrate respect for the other person and acknowledge that they have a right to their own point of view. Ultimately, this may mean that you need to 'agree to disagree'. Paradoxically, you may find that your relationship deepens as a result of having exchanged impassioned views and given one another space to be heard.

5. Use humour

A common piece of advice for diffusing tension is to inject humour as it's impossible to stay mad with someone when you're laughing along with them. When you share a laugh, you're engaging in a process that rebalances the nervous system and puts the brakes on defensive stress responses, like fight or flight[42].

Rather than simply clowning around, which will most likely compromise your power, look for unifying humour, e.g. the classically British: "Nice day!" when it's pouring with rain. This highlights what you might have in common and turns the 'you' versus 'me' into 'us'. Make sure that your self-deprecating remark doesn't compromise your impact and, by the same token, avoid making other people the butt of your joke as this is likely to backfire. For example, it's OK for you to gently poke fun at the Liverpudlian accent if you have one yourself, but not OK to do so if you speak with the Queen's English.

6. Dealing with extreme emotions

Assertiveness tips over into aggression when our emotions run away with us. So how can we be comfortable with the full range of emotions, even the ones perceived as ugly? Chloe Sullivan, conflict expert and founder of the War to Peace® programme, has created a process called MOCHA that helps you to recognise your full range of emotions and know when you, or someone else, is in danger of losing control. This is a tried and tested adaptation of the method used by the FBI hostage negotiations team and will help you manage any situation where you're on the receiving end of high emotion.

First of all, you'll need to discover what Chloe calls your 'Magic Weapon'. Discovering this will help you to handle any tricky situation you find yourself in, and it's essential when encountering high emotion, in order to keep your own amygdala hijack at bay. To create your Magic Weapon:

1. Think back to a time in your life when you felt magnificent or 'in the zone'.

2. Now allow your body and face to move so that they exhibit this magnificent feeling. Exaggerate your body posture and facial expression to increase the feeling. Stay here for a while and really enjoy this sensation.

3. Choose a memorable word, phrase or character that represents or reminds you of yourself here in this magnificent state.

4. Now relax your body posture.

5. Repeat steps 2, 3 and 4 until you simply need to think of your memorable word, phrase or character to access this state. Practice this regularly, so you know you have it.

Once you can access this Magic Weapon whenever you want to, it will be much easier for you to recognise that the high emotion you're on the receiving end of is their stuff and not to take it personally. This means you're best placed to remain uninvolved in the content and help the person to feel understood, so that they can move out of their immediate emotional crisis.

Now that you have your Magic Weapon, let's see how you can use it as part of the MOCHA process. Just thinking about these MOCHA steps during a highly emotional encounter will help to keep your thinking brain engaged and prevent you from being triggered into a non-assertive state. And what's brilliant about this process is that you only need to follow the steps exactly as they are laid out to be successfully assertive:

Magic Weapon: access your magic weapon the moment you are on the receiving end of high emotion (or in advance if you anticipate a tricky encounter).

Observe and share: "It seems to me you're feeling ANGRY" [make your best guess at the emotion you're seeing].

Check: "Is that right?" If they say no, ask them what they are feeling. And then repeat it back to them. "Oh, so you're feeling IRRITATED, is that right?"

How much?: "How IRRITATED are you?" This allows them to vent. If we sense there's a lot of emotion, we would say: "Tell me more." They will only be able to think of solutions once they've vented out their emotions.

Action: "What has to happen for that feeling of IRRITATION to feel better?" NB we are not asking what has to happen for you to feel better, but for the feeling to feel better. Then, finally, we would ask them: "What will you do to make that happen?"

So, when the heat is on, always remember to grab a MOCHA.

Four steps to reacting assertively

1. **Use empathy**: express your own feelings, e.g. use "I" statements and state your feelings positively and reflect back the other's feelings if appropriate, e.g. "It sounds like you feel disappointed about that." Acknowledge and respect the other person's point of view, e.g. "I understand/appreciate/realise that you need to finish this project by the end of the week, but I can't work late tonight."

2. **Describe behaviour**: address the specific behaviour you want changed, not the person, e.g. "I felt that the comment you made about the senior management away day should not have been made in front of admin staff." Specify the place and time of the behaviour that upset you. Avoid labels or "always" statements, e.g. "You are always out to get me". Describe the action and not the motive.

3. **Specify the change desired**: be clear about what you would like. Request a small change or one or two changes at a time. Ask yourself whether the other person can reasonably meet your requests. Specify what behaviour you will change to make the agreement.

4. **Identify a workable compromise**: aim for a win/win outcome – respecting yourself and others, e.g. "I can't work late tonight, but I can come in early tomorrow morning if that would help."

EXERCISE 4: REACTING ASSERTIVELY

1. Think of times when you've felt under attack and how you've responded – both in terms of what you did and didn't do. Consider whether you have a tendency for fight, flight or freeze.

2. Reflect on which is your 'go-to' conflict mode based on Thomas Kilman's model and when it would be more appropriate to choose a different style.

3. Then think about how you would ideally like to react and the other person's response to this: visualize it, imagine what's being said and how you feel. Be prepared for a variety of actions and reactions. The more you play out scenarios where you react appropriately, the more likely this will happen in real-life.

CASE STUDY

Melissa is a 29-year-old project manager. When she signed up for my Gravitas Masterclass, she had received some pretty harsh feedback that in order to be promoted, she needed to increase her personal impact and command greater respect amongst her peers. According to her, part of the reason for this was that she was relatively young compared to her colleagues and one of the few female managers in a male-dominated environment.

Her key objectives were learning how to make her point clearly during the departmental weekly catch-up meetings and standing her ground during challenging conversations. She also wanted to find a way to stop one of the senior male leaders from invading her personal space.

Based on her self-description when applying to attend the course, I was surprised to meet a strong, articulate woman who had clearly made her way successfully through life. A single mum, she had juggled full-time employment since returning from maternity leave and was clearly intent on forging a successful leadership career for herself.

During the morning of the masterclass, it became clear that Melissa had very little appreciation of just how good she was. Speaking about her role, she came across as strong, intelligent, driven and mature and yet, according to her, her biggest barrier was confidence.

And so my first task was to address her negative self-image. Through a series of exercises (covered in this book), she gained clarity on her role, identity and purpose as a leader. As she took on board the positive feedback from the other people in the group, I could see her confidence grow.

The next step was to work on her assertiveness skills. Although inwardly strong, Melissa's communication style did hold her back at times. She confessed that she cared a lot about how other people thought of her and sometimes her willingness to please people got in the way of her drive to get things done. This showed up in her voice and body language, both of which came across as being quite soft and compliant.

Through practising a series of simple techniques, she began to realise that speaking in a clear voice and standing tall weren't seen as being pushy or aggressive. Her lightbulb moment came when she realised her team actually wanted her to be that way and appreciated it when she embodied her leadership role.

Since the Masterclass, Melissa has reported feeling much more confident. She now feels more in control of relationships rather than having people trying to control her. And, miraculously, she no longer has to deal with that male colleague getting too close.

Melissa's secret was to get crystal clear on her role and step into the shoes of a leader. Through applying the assertive skills in this chapter, she directly influenced how people behaved around her, so much so that challenging conversations and space invasion became a thing of the past.

ASSERTIVENESS CONCLUSION

Once we find our assertiveness mojo, it feels good and will invariably bring a positive outcome. Like my friend Jane stating her coaching fee to a new client without feeling the need to explain or justify, where in the past she would have struggled to do so, or my client Roisin talking about how she met her wife in front of a large group of predominantly male salespeople when previously she would have kept her sexuality hidden. Once you've acknowledged your worth and stated it loud and proud, there's no going back.

Yes, it can be tough. No, it's not easy to step out of your comfort zone. But the good news is, if you want to do this, you can. So I encourage you to put any bad experiences in the past, be brave, challenge yourself. Because the world is a poorer place if you stay silent.

Try these techniques – all of which I use, all the time. I guarantee that in time, you will notice the difference. We all have a voice that deserves to be heard.

IN SUMMARY

★ Assertiveness is the ability to make our wants, needs and views met, using our mind, body and voice to confidently stand up for what we believe in.

★ Assertive behaviour is honest, direct, clear, expressive, self-enhancing, persistent and respectful. It's not about shouting loudly, being overbearing or pushy (a common misconception) – it's about knowing where the line is and calling out anyone who crosses it.

★ To tap into your assertiveness, you need to understand who you are and what you want. With clarity, you will feel more confident about expressing yourself and have a more positive view of your own place in society.

★ Although no one and nothing can *make* you feel anything, the more you know about which people and situations trigger feelings of being threatened, the more you'll be able to remain in an assertive position and the more powerful you'll feel.

★ The CLEAR© model encompasses five tried and tested steps to communicating assertively, based on managing your mindset and behaviour:

- **Calm** = choose an attitude of calm

- **Level Up** = adopt a win/win mindset

- **Engage** = understand their mindset

- **Act** = behave assertively

- **React** = respond assertively

CONCLUSION

Congratulations on reaching the end of this book! I trust that you've found the guidance, techniques, models and exercises valuable, and hope that they are already making a difference in all areas of your life.

It seems fitting at the end of this adventure to go back to where we started, the title of this book: *Power Up: The Smart Woman's Guide to Unleashing Her Potential*, and my aspiration for you in the future. Words are powerful, they have the ability to build and destroy. They influence how we experience the world. And so it's important to choose them wisely. So why exactly did I choose each of these words? And what is my final message to you?

Let's start with the word 'Smart'. From the moment I started writing this book, I knew it was for smart women like you. Women who had already accomplished a great deal and had the self-awareness to acknowledge it for themselves. This wasn't going to be an instruction manual for women who needed 'help', it was to be a guide, a catalyst to convert the amazing qualities you already hold within into something more. Your route map to success.

And how about the word 'Woman'? In 1968, the legendary Tammy Wynette sang "Sometimes it's hard to be a woman" during a turbulent year of riots and uprising. In Tammy's song, it was all about "Giving all your love to just one man". I'd like to think that these days we have more than romance on our minds. As noted at the beginning of this book, fifty years on, there are still many, many hardships uniquely associated with being a woman in the Western world, let alone in underprivileged parts of the globe where women are still second-class citizens. That said, I'm heartened to see that with movements like #MeToo, women are using their collective power to effect positive change. And that can only continue to gain momentum if we work together.

In the process of writing this book, I've had the privilege to meet hundreds of wonderful women who've exemplified the six sources of power represented in the Power Up Model©, and to reflect on how women of all generations can continue to harness their strength. And the future appears to be very bright indeed. This week, I had the privilege to work with a group of teenage girls on a campaign to end modern sexual harassment, supported by a team of experts from a global PR company. These days it's not just about wolf whistles or a hand placed somewhere you don't want it. It's sexting, rumour-spreading, requests for nudes. These were smart, articulate young women, but this is a taboo subject. Their brief included not only coming up with the concept, but also presenting their ideas to the whole company. For many, this was their first time speaking in front of a large audience.

I needn't have worried. These girls are strong. And as they stood there talking about how harassment of any kind is not OK, bravely and authentically articulating their views, I saw true power in action. They nailed it. And as they stood there, representing the next generation of working women, I saw potential unleashed.

My hope is that as women, we acknowledge the precious qualities held by our sisters, mothers, daughters, friends and colleagues. Recognise the unique power we hold within and celebrate what it is to be a woman in society today.

The word 'unleash' carries a powerful energy. It implies an upsurge, a release, a break from what held you back towards what will set you free. My aim with the cover design of this book was to represent the experience of smashing through. As you think of the forces that have conspired to hold you back, I want you to connect with all the energy you hold within: your sense of self, your purpose, your love, anger and passion. Embrace all of it, channel it, smash through those barriers and set yourself free.

When I was younger, I used to think things would get easier the older I got. And I'm still waiting! One of the messages that has come through loud and clear with all the women I've interviewed for this book has been that there will always be times when our resilience is challenged. Setbacks, wobbles, doubts and fears. These experiences are extremely powerful and force us to ask: "Dare I?", "Could I?", "What will people think if I do?"

There have been many times in my life when people have said "No" to the dreams I've ambitiously shared. Times when I've thought that something was "too hard", "too much" or "too big". Times when I've thought it would be far easier to give it all up for an easier life. I'm sure you've thought something similar too. And in the end, each time someone has said "No", that has been the impetus I've needed to just do it. If I think back on all those big goals, nine times out of ten, I've accomplished them. And those I haven't, I've forgotten about anyway. When it comes to you unleashing your potential, I want you to know that everything is possible if you want it enough. Everything is achievable if you put the work in.

And so, when it comes to the word 'Potential', with each accomplishment you achieve, please take the time to acknowledge your success. Although each achievement might feel like a small step, collectively they will be a giant leap for womankind. Potential unleashed manifests itself in many ways. It doesn't always need to be a big bang explosion. It can be a steady, quiet surge. And when your power dips, you can take courage from the fact that you will find the strength to Power Up again. You are powerful not because of what you've done. You're powerful because of who you are and the potential you hold within you.

My aim is that this book will spark a revolution. Encourage us to think more broadly. Because now is a time of massive change. The words 'diversity' and 'inclusion' are no longer HR speak but part of everyday conversation: in the boardroom, in meeting rooms, around kitchen tables, on the street. My aim is that men and women learn to Power Up together and access the full spectrum of power in all its magnificent forms.

Because we are all in this together. We are better together. We all need to step up and support one another to achieve our goals.

My final hope is that all women recognise the amazing strength they have within them and find ways to unleash it.

You have the right, you are worth it. Let's do this. Together.

445

ACKNOWLEDGEMENTS

Writing a second book is like childbirth. You never remember how hard it is until it's too late!

At the inception of *Power Up*, I gave myself the challenge to complete it in a year. This would not have been possible without the encouragement of a 'power posse' of people who I would like to thank for their inspiration and encouragement.

First and foremost, to my dear friend and journalist, Marina Gask, whose Daily Telegraph article on 'The Smart Woman's Guide to Being Heard at Work' inspired the title of this book and whose strategic insight has helped to ensure it blends sound, practical guidance with a touch of sparkle.

To my editor, Leila Green from Known Publishing, whose eye for detail and empathy for the reader have challenged me to dig deeper and bring more of my voice into the mix.

To Aarti Parmar, who immediately understood the concept of 'smashing your own glass ceiling' and created the cover of this book. To Yolande de Vries, branding photographer extraordinaire, for the fabulous Notting Hill photoshoot. And to Lika Kvirikashvili, whose illustrations beautifully capture smart women everywhere.

To my writing buddy, Jackie Barrie, for your heartening reassurance, and to all the smart women – and men – who've shared their expertise and experiences with me: Dr Lynda Shaw, Darshana Ubl, Sarah Matthew, Claire Norwood, Natalie Haverstock, Sian Richardson, Jackie Handy, Jess Baker, Chloe O'Sullivan, Melody Kane, Anne Timpany,

Zoe Healy, Ellie Deeks, Benn Abdy Collins, Peter McCaffery, Angela Owen, Lisa Conway Hughes, Emma Stroud, Alan Stevens, Bryony Thomas, Julie Creffield, Jo Tocher and so many more.

To my clients, colleagues and all the women I've coached who encouraged me to write this book.

To my mother, Paulette, for your ongoing strength and vitality. To my father, Jeremy, for your wisdom and wit, you will always be in my heart.

To my daughters, Mia and Zoë, for the free hugs and silliness. And last, but by no means least, to my husband, Steve, for making me laugh, keeping it real, for the steady stream of tea/wine at appropriate times of the day and for inspiring me to find the inner strength and to power up, again and again, to get this book over the line.

Thank you from the bottom of my heart.

ABOUT THE AUTHOR

Antoinette Dale Henderson is an award-winning speaker, executive coach and founder of the Gravitas Programme, a leadership development course which has accelerated the career of thousands of managers, leaders and business owners and enabled them to communicate with confidence and credibility.

With over 25 years' experience in leadership communications, she works globally, delivering strategically-driven, results-orientated masterclasses that make a powerful difference to executives, boards and top teams.

As a Fellow of the Professional Speaking Association and TEDx speaker, she's regularly invited to deliver keynotes and speak on panels about gravitas, leadership and promoting the cause of women in business and is a regular speaker for VISTAGE, the global organisation for MDs, CEOs and leaders.

Her first book, *Leading with Gravitas* has been extensively featured in the mainstream media including Forbes, the Daily Telegraph, Marie Claire, Red, HR Magazine and Management Today.

Before setting up her company in 2007, she held senior positions at many of the world's top PR consultancies.

She's Chair of the Board of Trustees for BelEve, a charity that inspires and empowers girls aged 8 to 18 to become leaders of their world and lives in London with her husband and two daughters.

Would you like to continue your Power Up journey?

Are you inspired to take your career to the next level?

visit

www.womenpowerupbook.com

Connect with Antoinette

To keep up to date with all the latest news on Antoinette's blogs, events and more, sign up to her official e-mail newsletter at **www.womenpowerupbook.com**

www.facebook.com/thegravitascoach

Twitter @AntoinetteZomi

Instagram @AntoinetteDaleHenderson

www.linkedin.com/in/antoinettedalehenderson/

If you've enjoyed this book, there's a variety of ways you can work with Antoinette to accelerate your potential.

Sign up for the next FREE Power Hour webinar

Power Hour webinars are your opportunity to connect with Antoinette on screen and get your burning questions answered, live.

Come along to the next Power Up event

These seminars, held in London, will give you the tools, techniques and impetus to Power Up your career confidence.

Book onto a Gravitas course

Taking part in a Masterclass with Antoinette is life-changing. You'll come away with complete clarity on your personal brand and the confidence to express yourself powerfully, whatever your audience.

Invite Antoinette to speak

As an experienced keynote speaker and panellist, Antoinette will create a memorable and transformational experience for your audience, whether that's delivering a keynote at your next leadership conference or speaking at your next event.

Want to get taken more seriously as a leader?

Wondering how to stand out from the competition?

Ready for promotion but don't know how to make it?

**Gravitas is the #1 skill for business success.
People with gravitas lead better, manage better, present
better and network better.
The great news is, it can be learnt.**

Packed with practical tools, exercises and case studies, the
book has been developed based on global research into
what works for today's leaders.

Order your copy on Amazon

ENDNOTES

1. www.gov.uk/government/news/ftse-350-urged-to-keep-up-the-pace-to-meet-women-on-boards-target

2. 2018ReportonequalitybetweenwomenandmenintheEU.pdf

3. www.govinfo.gov/content/pkg/PLAW-106publ26/html/PLAW-106publ26.htm

4. French, J., & Raven, B. H. (1959). The bases of social power. In D. Cartwright (Ed.), Studies in social power 410 Philip M. Podsakoff and Chester A. Schriesheim (pp. 150-167). Ann Arbor, MI: Institute for Social Research.

5. Nye, Joseph. Bound to Lead: The Changing Nature of American Power (London: Basic Books, 1990).

6. www.pewresearch.org/fact-tank/2017/03/08/women-leaders-around-the-world/

7. www.forbes.com/sites/carolinehoward/2017/11/01/women-who-rule-the-world-the-25-most-powerful-female-political-leaders-2017/

8. The Guide to UK Company Giving 2017/18. Directory of Social Change.

9. Women in Business, Beyond Policy to Progress. Grant Thornton. 2018.

10. Shiliang Tang, Xinyi Zhang, Jenna Cryan, Miriam J. Metzger, Haitao Zheng, and Ben Y. Zhao. 2017. Gender Bias in the Job Market: A Longitudinal Analysis. Proc. ACM Hum.-Comput. Interact. 1, 2, Article 99 (November 2017), 19 pages. https://doi.org/10.1145/3134734.

11. Sheryl Sandberg, Lean In: Women, Work, and the Will to Lead.

12. TEDx Covent Garden Women, October 2016.

13. www.independent.co.uk/life-style/women/pay-rise-men-women-cv-library-lee-biggins-gender-pay-gap-a8880956.html

14. www.qz.com/799245/the-challenges-women-face-in-corporate-america-are-curbing-their-ambitions/

15. www.pregnantthenscrewed.com

16. blogs.lse.ac.uk/businessreview/2019/01/14/gender-inequality-at-work-and-at-home-a-double-whammy-for-women/

17. All the Workplace is a Stage. Online report by RADA in Business.

18. Speaker sex and perceived apportionment of talk. A. Cutler and D. R Scott. Applied Psycholinguistics 11 (1990), 253-272.

19. www.hbr.org/2014/08/why-women-dont-apply-for-jobs-unless-theyre-100-qualified

20. Immunity to Change. Robert Kegan and Lisa Laskow Lahey. Harvard Business Review Press (2009).

21. Brown, B. (2010), The Gifts of Imperfection: Letting Go of Who You Think You're Supposed to Be and Embrace Who You Are. Centre City: MN, Hazelden.

22. www.psychologytoday.com/us/blog/the-athletes-way/201504/alpha-brain-waves-boost-creativity-and-reduce-depression

23. www.science.unctv.org/content/reportersblog/choices

24. www.ncbi.nlm.nih.gov/books/NBK10822/

25. www.warwick.ac.uk/newsandevents/pressreleases/girls_feel_they/

26. www.youtube.com/watch?v=tNqSzUdYazw

27. www.psychologytoday.com/za/blog/the-science-success/201101/the-trouble-bright-girls

28. www.nbcnews.com/health/health-news/not-smart-enough-men-overestimate-intelligence-science-class-n862801?cid=sm_npd_nn_tw_ma

29. www.telegraph.co.uk/news/newstopics/howaboutthat/11745186/Brummie-accents-worse-than-staying-silent-study-shows.html

30. www.niu.edu/facdev/_pdf/guide/learning/howard_gardner_theory_multiple_intelligences.pdf

31. www.livescience.com/38059-magnetism.html

32. www.seths.blog/2009/12/define-brand/

33. www.psychologicalscience.org/observer/how-many-seconds-to-a-first-impression

34. Khomami, Nadia (October 20, 2017). "#MeToo: how a hashtag became a rallying cry against sexual harassment". The Guardian. Archived from the original on November 21, 2017.

35. Francine D. Blau and Jed DeVaro (2007). "New Evidence on Gender Differences in Promotion Rates: An Empirical Analysis of a Sample of New Hires". Cornell University ILR School. p. 16. Archived from the original on 2011-07-18. Retrieved 26 May 2010.

36. Bad Feminist: Essays, by Roxane Gay, published by Constable & Robinson. 2014.

37. www.the-vital-edge.com/building-relationships/

38. www.nbcnews.com/news/us-news/first-lady-michelle-obama-champions-education-day-girl-n664066

39. Cecila Harvey, (2018) "When queen bees attack women stop advancing: recognising and addressing female bullying in the workplace", Development and Learning in Organizations: An International Journal, Vol. 32 Issue: 5, pp.1-4.

40. www.psychologytoday.com/gb/blog/the-athletes-way/201705/diaphragmatic-breathing-exercises-and-your-vagus-nerve

41. www.ncbi.nlm.nih.gov/pubmed/11166137

42. www.helpguide.org/articles/mental-health/laughter-is-the-best-medicine.htm/